The Ulster Literary Theatre and the Northern Revival

To be forgotten for a hundred years and then suddenly rediscovered – that is fame.

Joseph Campbell

The Ulster Literary Theatre and the Northern Revival

Eugene McNulty

CORK UNIVERSITY PRESS

First published in 2008 by
Cork University Press
Youngline Industrial Estate
Pouladuff Road, Togher
Cork, Ireland

British Library Cataloguing in Publication Data
A CIP catalogue record for this book is available from the British Library.

ISBN 978-185918-427-1

Typesetting by Red Barn Publishing, Skeagh, Skibbereen, Co. Cork
Printed by ColourBooks Ltd., Baldoyle, Dublin

www.corkuniversitypress.com

Contents

Preface and Acknowledgements

Writing about Northern Irish culture and identity is a curious business. At times this is a place that seems filled with gaps and silences that refuse to be sounded, while at others 'the North' can feel, a bit like Synge's 'West' perhaps, like a space over-populated with people seeking to interpret it, a place that is over-full with possible meaning. In the end even the seemingly straightforward can turn out to be anything but; the easy allure of basic fact and the apparently obvious soon collapses to leave an endless skein of possible tracks to be followed. Just what we mean by the North, and indeed *where* we mean by the North, turn out to be far from straightforward or uncontested issues. One starting point here has been the understanding that the various meanings attached to the North have had a significant role in Irish history long before partition or the late twentieth-century troubles. This book is about the idea of 'the North' and/or 'Ulster' in the years before the creation of Northern Ireland. There are, of course, clear dangers in any attempt to read 'northern Ireland' back through and past 'Northern Ireland', but this is a task that has always seemed somehow necessary if we are to fully understand the North as imagined space.

Fortunately I have had many guides to whom I had could look for guidance; the idea of the North was something that much occupied many of its writers in the decades when our modern conceptions of Ulster and Northern Ireland were being formed. My main interest has been the ways in which the North's nationalist writers responded to the competing claims of an Irish literary revival and a nascent movement towards Ulster separatism. In particular the group of men and women who gathered around the Ulster Literary Theatre have left a fascinating record of how cultural nationalists in Ulster addressed the imagined communities for whom, and about whom, they performed. It is to them primarily that I have looked for a performance of the various conceptual Norths in the years of Home Rule and its attendant 'Ulster question'. Writing books about the theatre is also a curious business, of course; there is many a paradox in trying to recover an event that by its very nature is mostly unrecoverable. In text we can at best hope to find traces of the bodies on stage, of the bodies in the audience, and of the bodies who never entered the auditorium in the first place. However, recovering such traces is perhaps even more important for those performances that did not find their way into the Irish literary canon; and indeed, as is often the case here, did not find their way into publication. So writing this book has meant a return to the archives, a return to find the source of the traces left by the history of revivalist drama in Ulster. In the end I have tried to bring together as many traces of the northern revival and the Ulster Literary Theatre as possible, but I can make no claims to a complete record. In the course of this research I have learned too that I cannot assume a widespread familiarity with the Ulster Literary Theatre's work, and so I have presented much more primary material in the course of the chapters than would normally be the case in a study of this nature. This is a book, then, which aims to present and reveal as much as to explain; by doing so I have hoped to open up as many new questions as I have answered. After all, traces of identity are always important.

There are many people that have helped bring this project to its final stage. Its first and most important reader was Lyn Innes. Without Lyn's support I doubt this book would ever have seen the light of day: I hope some day to be half the scholar she is. Thomas Docherty and Christopher Morash were also early readers whose encouragement and incisive commentary did much to boost this project towards its final form. I would also like to thank Tom Dunne and everyone at Cork University Press for their help and support throughout. The nature of this work has meant I have relied heavily on the dedication and help of many librarians and archivists along the way. All the staff (past and present) of the Linen Hall Library have been especially unstinting in their assistance and time; John Killen and Hugh Odling-Smee have answered my (seemingly unending) questions with patience and extraordinary knowledge, and it is to Ophelia Byrne that I will always be grateful for my first introduction to 'Gerald MacNamara'. The keepers of the F.J. Bigger collection at Belfast Central Library and the BBC Community Archives at Cultra were similarly rigorous in their help. As always, any errors or omissions are my own. My thinking has also been shaped in one way or another by the many extraordinary friends and colleagues I have been fortunate to work with at the universities of Kent and Portsmouth. In particular, Elodie and Paraic have been there all the way through, and I thank them for everything.

My oldest and most profound debts are to those people who have little to do with the world of work. The place called home and all the McNulty clan are never far from everything I do – especially its youngest members (James, Anna, Matthew and Ronan); maybe someday they will read this and not be too disappointed that there are no wizards or dragons. Most of all, though, this book is for my mother Philomena and in memory of my father Gene: with much love, for everything.

Introduction

> What do we mean by 'the North'? Until you get to the North Pole, 'North', being a direction, is relative. 'The North' is thought of as a place, but it's a place with shifting boundaries. It's also a state of mind. It can mean 'wilderness' or 'frontier'. But we know – or think we know – what sorts of things go on there.
>
> Margaret Atwood, *Strange Things: The Malevolent North in Canadian Literature*

> One's horizon is not only the sum of directions from which one has to be prepared for the appearance of undefined things; it is also the sum of the directions to which anticipation of possibilities and reaching out toward them are oriented.
>
> Hans Blumenberg, *Work on Myth*

In the final few months of 1904 a group of determined cultural nationalists were preparing to present audiences with some new plays of their very own. Here was the opportunity all involved had worked towards for many years, a theatrical space under their control, and one that could be used to reconnect its audience with a similarly independent sense of self. Looking back, the idea seems simple enough; given the prevailing political winds of the time, however, theirs was an ambitious plan. The aim was to provide a nationalist cultural arena for the group's home city and hinterland. Staging this new type of play would, they were sure, provide a focal point for the energies and debates of those sympathetic to the idea of a more independent Ireland. There was also the sense that, if successful, this venture could form an indispensable part of a larger project: Ireland's own 'National Theatre'. In line with the thinking of the time, this group of nationalists perceived the cultural realm as a place to re-invent and shape a newly empowered Irish nation. The theatre in this regard was not merely a place to reflect nationalist sympathies, it was, rather, a place fundamental to the articulation and performance of a different kind of Ireland. While much was still to be decided, those involved were sure of their central tenets: this would be a place for Ireland to speak of itself to itself; the plays presented here would explore those elements of 'Irishness' that had remained largely unrepresented. It would be a space, in other words, untainted by the stereotypes, clichés and patronising representations of those who sought out 'Ireland' from beyond it as a refuge for their own desires, needs and fears. This would be a theatre that would not only present new ideas of Ireland and Irish identity but also provide a forum through which further new ideas and discussions could be generated.

A familiar tale it may be, but this is not the story of the preparations in Dublin for the opening of the Abbey Theatre. The city providing the backdrop for this project is Belfast, and the company in question is the Ulster Literary Theatre (ULT). However, the similarities between the two projects are more than simple coincidence or the result of some quirk of fate. The drive to open a nationalist theatre in Belfast was motivated by many of the same imperatives and much of the same thinking that had pushed Yeats et al. forward in their determination to change the cultural scene in Dublin. The Ulster Literary Theatre was formed by a group of Belfast's most engaged cultural activists as a means of representing the nationalist cause in the northern city, and in Ulster more generally. For some time many of Ireland's leading intellectual lights had been throwing their energies behind cultural 'revival' in a bid to reconfigure the debate on the 'Irish question'. Many in the North had sought to engage with this process and to ensure that the particular circumstances of Ulster were included in its rhetoric and imagery. Numbered amongst those who took this view were the Ulster Literary Theatre's founding figures, Bulmer Hobson and David Parkhill, both of whom had long been committed to cultural revival as a means of engendering political change. In establishing the Ulster Literary Theatre they saw an opportunity to stage the revival more fully in the North; it would also be a conduit, they hoped, for bringing the concerns and experiences of the North more fully into the thinking and practices of revivalist culture.

Despite contributing to the same project, the dynamic between the idea of revival in the North and its performance in other parts of Ireland was complicated from the beginning. This was not least because the development in 'Home Rule' politics towards the end of the nineteenth century had increasingly marked Ulster out as an exception to the Irish rule. Nevertheless, there is little doubt that the decision to establish a nationalist 'literary' theatre in Belfast was born out of many of the same frustrations that brought the Abbey into existence. In the preceding years Belfast's nationalists had also observed with growing dismay a cultural scene in their home town that left little or no room for the representation of (as they saw it) the real Ireland. As in Dublin, most of Belfast's theatres had become just one more regional stop for often second-rate touring productions. The Belfast-born poet and playwright James Cousins recalled the depressing fact, well established by the end of the nineteenth century, of London-based touring companies including Dublin and Belfast in their performance circuit:

> At the time of which I write, therefore (the late nineties), the materials for cultural sustenance especially in music and drama, came from or by way of England. The theatres of Dublin and Belfast came within the circuit of London companies and occasionally of eminent individual artists.[1]

The effect of this populist diet is recorded by the Belfast nationalist and future senator Joseph Connolly, who makes the case that: 'In those days, Belfast had little appetite for plays or drama that dealt with "subjects". I think the preference was for the matinee idol and musical comedy.'[2] Much like the Abbey's founders, it was this sense of an imported banality that many in the Ulster Literary Theatre sought to address. This was a banality, moreover, that they saw as not simply benign foolishness but actively damaging to the national sense of self. Both groups were certain that one of the prerequisites of a properly independent Irish identity was a culture that eschewed damaging 'stage Irishry' in favour of faithful narratives and imagery born out of a knowledge of the people and the land. The Abbey and the Ulster Literary Theatre were each engaged in providing such versions of Irishness for their audiences; both sought to perform a more authentic Ireland, seeking out the narratives, symbols and voices that their audiences would recognise as more faithfully their own.

Perhaps as a result of this revivalist search for grounded authenticity, there was an equally strong feeling in Belfast that the particular conditions of the North required a response attuned to this cultural landscape. The Ulster Literary Theatre's founders were only too aware that Belfast and its hinterland was a different kind of place from Dublin. They also knew that this difference was most radically expressed and contested by the politics that impacted on the audiences attending their productions. The decades either side of the turn of the twentieth century were marked by the development of a resistance to Home Rule in Ulster that was of a different order to that experienced in the rest of the country. These developments were revealed in cultural as well as political tensions in Belfast. From the very beginning, the cultural peculiarities of Belfast not only provided the context for the Ulster Literary Theatre's birth, they also provided the group with some of its main aims and objectives. Many at the heart of the Ulster Literary Theatre saw it as a forum for realigning the cultural life of the North in order to break down some of the political divisions that had grown stronger in the years of Home Rule. In this regard the 'new Irish drama' was an obvious choice for enacting cultural resistance and change; after all, the theatre was (and is) the most directly communal mode of cultural expression. A night at the theatre involves all kinds of performances and identifications, and not simply on the stage. The theatre scene in Belfast at this time provided evidence aplenty of the relationship between cultural performance and political identification.

In addition, for example, to the imported London stage shows, Belfast's theatre scene included a politicised phenomenon almost certainly unique (in the ferocity of its expression at least) to the northern city. St John Ervine recalls in his memoirs how he was a regular theatre-goer from an early age, for he had accompanied his aunt to whatever the Belfast theatres had to offer in the latter part of the nineteenth century, a diet that included mostly English classics or music-hall fare. He remembers quite clearly, however, that their theatre visits did not include anything with a more Irish feel; he is equally clear on the reasons why:

> I could never prevail upon her to take me to see Irish plays, such as *Arrah-na-pogue* and *The Shaughraun*, for although she had seen them herself, and had repeated the plot of *The Shaughraun* to me so many times that I knew it by heart, she was fearful lest there might be a row in the gallery between the Papist and Orange corner-boys who congregated there on 'Irish' nights to make a demonstration of their religious beliefs: one side cheering the British authorities, while the other side pelted them with orange-peel and objurgations (*sic*).[3]

On such 'Irish nights' a trip to the theatre in Belfast became an opportunity to express sectarian division and 'play out' political conflict; as the plays progressed, Belfast's communal divisions were reflected in the conflicting reaction to various historical figures on stage. The Ulster Literary Theatre took as one of its central goals the combating of this cultural bigotry; in its place its members hoped to discover in the theatre unifying codes for a society defined by boundaries of one sort or another (class, religious, political). Such hopes led Arthur Griffith to describe the new Belfast theatre company as an 'artistic and liberalising movement'.[4] However, while the group may have been as clear in its aims as such praise suggests, the best way to their fulfilment was a good deal more complex.

Established officially as the Ulster Literary Theatre in 1904, the company had actually been around since 1902, when Bulmer Hobson and David Parkhill initially decided to found the 'Ulster Branch of the Irish Literary Theatre'. At this stage the two Belfast men envisaged a Belfast branch to the literary theatre established earlier by Yeats, Gregory et al. But in the end this bid for 'sister-branch' status was rejected by the controlling interests of what would become the Abbey Theatre, leaving the Belfast nationalists no option but to go it alone. This early history would haunt much that the group subsequently achieved, and in the years ahead the Ulster Literary Theatre would continue to have a complex and ambiguous relationship with the Dublin company that had inspired its formation. In particular the feelings of rejection and exclusion would provide an unresolved source of tension and motivation. This is a story of more than theatrical rivalry, however; the relationship between revivalists in the two cities speaks to and of the broader political climate within which they performed. As Christopher Murray puts it:

> The theatre in the North is, historically, a mirror image of the political relationship between North and South. When the ULT was founded in 1902 it was with the ambition of establishing in Belfast a Northern version of Yeats's Irish Literary Theatre in Dublin. It was at once a form of imitation and a gesture of independence.[5]

The history of the Ulster Literary Theatre, then, stands in for a broader set of relations; it has much to tell us about revival in the years when the 'Ulster question' was being posed just as strongly as the 'Irish question'. It is the nature of these dynamics between politics and culture, and between north and south in the years of Home Rule, which will largely concern us here. The politics of 'imitation' and what exactly was meant by 'independence' – as conceived by those revivalists in Belfast – will need further scrutiny. We will, for example, have occasion to look again at Murray's suggestion that the 'ULT was founded in 1902', for this manages to negate a crucial period in the theatre's development. The fact that it was the 'Ulster Branch of the Irish Literary Theatre' that was first formed in 1902 is important. Even if this first incarnation was more or less identical in make-up (in terms of personnel) to the future Ulster Literary Theatre, the philosophy informing the latter was quite different. The transformation that occurred between 1902 and 1904, and not just in terms of the group's nomenclature, reveals much about the politics of culture in those years. More generally, the performative and philosophical histories of the Ulster Literary Theatre allow us to approach this period from a sometimes overlooked direction; or at least, in terms of the performance of revival, a direction that is not always anticipated. The resulting change in the critical horizon 'to which anticipation of possibilities and reaching out toward them are oriented' in turn allows us to reread the revival in some important ways. This study explores cultural nationalism in Ulster and is primarily concerned with the birth and development of a specifically 'northern revival'. It sets out to trace the ways in which nationalist writers in Ulster produced a form of revival purposefully attuned to the needs and circumstances of their part of the island. Not simply a history of the Ulster Literary Theatre, this book is about the contexts that produced a version of revival particular to the North. Beginning with its 'pre-history' and the motivations that informed its birth, the chapters that follow seek to recuperate the Ulster Literary Theatre and its work as products of Ulster's own version of cultural nationalism.

These interests also go some way to explaining the timeframe that marks out this exploration of 'Ulster nationalism' (a term that encapsulates the rather perilous nature of rethinking this period). Ireland's moment of revival is usually thought of as occupying that 'crease in time' between Parnell's death (1891) and the Easter Rising of 1916; it is during this period (as Yeats argues forcefully below) that the cultural realm appeared to have the greatest potential for influencing and shaping the wider debates on political and national identities. Looking back, it is clear that this crease in time was of a slightly shorter duration, and of a different order, in Ulster. Those living in the North did not have to wait until 1916 to witness the shift towards direct-action forms of nationalist engagement; as Pádraic Pearse (taking his lead from Eoin MacNeill) would famously note, 'the North began' some time earlier. The reaction in Ulster to the potentially successful third Home Rule bill of 1912, most notably the militarisation of Ulster unionist opposition in the form of the Ulster Volunteer Force (the UVF, established January 1913), meant that the window of opportunity for culture to act as national bell-wether was already closing in the North. Or, at least, the relationship between cultural invention and political action was of a different order in Ulster after 1912. The idea that the cultural realm could maintain a leading position in national renewal became increasingly difficult to sustain in Ulster earlier than was the case in the rest of the island. The focus of this book is thus the years that led up to Ulster's defining year of 1912; it is during these years that the issues of bringing cultural revival to the North had most purchase on broader events and problematics within a society gripped by fluidic processes of definition, resistance and invention.

The Ulster Literary Theatre would survive in one form or another, via a name change to the 'Ulster Theatre' in 1915, until 1934, but by then its ability for radical performance was somewhat diminished. However, recuperating the northern revival and the subsequent developments of the Ulster Literary Theatre is about more than the recovery of some neglected minor footnote in the history of Irish nationalism's cultural expression. Although rarely thought of in these terms, those iconic years of Yeatsian myth and Syngeian folk were also years in which Belfast's nationalists made a significant and often radical contribution to the performance of cultural revival. Looking back at the reviews and editorials that greeted the Ulster Literary Theatre's efforts, it is clear that many considered it to be one of Ireland's most noteworthy companies. The Belfast group was also notably productive. As Ophelia Byrne has noted: 'with at least one new play being produced each season, the ULT repertoire grew over the years until, by 1934, it had premiered some forty-seven one-act and full-length works both written and produced by the company'.[6] (A full list of all known Ulster Literary Theatre productions is included in the Appendix.) The responses to many of the earlier performances make it clear that the Ulster Literary Theatre was thought to be actively shaping the future canon of an Irish national drama. As it turned out, of course, that canon has been formed about the centrifugal forces of the Abbey's ultimately hegemonic powers, and the history of Belfast's revivalist theatre has largely dropped off most contemporary critical maps.[7] There is a sense in which the power and charisma of the Abbey's performance history has occluded other versions of revival from receiving their proper attention. More than ever, perhaps, the full complexity of revival's performance is in need of recovery; as Mary Trotter has pointed out, telling its full story has taken on a particular importance:

> To recover the diversity of ideologues and practices during the early years of the Irish dramatic movement is to discover new potencies within it, for these dramas were not merely nationalist assertions of a unified idea of Irish culture, but intranational debates about culture and identity being invented and enacted on Ireland's nationalist stages.[8]

It is high time that the Ulster Literary Theatre's northern nationalism was included in this recovered skein of cultural ideologies and associated practices; there is much still to be told about the complexity of Irish identity formed in the pressurised environs of revival. To fully reveal how national renaissances are formed we must not simply recover 'forgotten artists' but re-create 'the contentiousness of the times in which these authors wrote'.[9] A return to Belfast at the turn of the twentieth century may help us do just that.

Such a return is undertaken here with a very specific aim in mind: not simply to re-create those years of revival and their impact on nationalist thinking in Ulster, but from the point of view of those cultural nationalists in Ulster who had decided to make 'the North' the main subject of their work. What follows is not an attempt to revisit the revival as a whole, or indeed to solve its essential holistic 'truth'. Rather, this is a study of how the revival was received in Ulster, and how northern revivalist writers responded with a mode of expression attuned to, and produced by, the particularity of their experience and position. The point here is to explore the forces and pressures that brought about a uniquely northern version of revival and to examine the language, form and imagery through which such a position was articulated. With this in mind, and in order to fully set the scene for the arrival of the Ulster Literary Theatre, we begin by returning to the work of the 'Ardrigh circle', a group of nationalist activists who gathered at Francis Joseph Bigger's house, Ardrigh, using it as a place to meet, debate and organise. Out of these gatherings came some of the most important cultural projects to speak to a nationalist agenda in Belfast at the end of the nineteenth century. Most notably the 'Henry Joy McCracken Society' and its newspaper the *Northern Patriot,* along with the later *Shan Van Vocht,* were all instrumental in shaping and giving voice to the revival in Ulster. In the pages of these two nationalist newspapers we can trace the emergence of a singularly northern nationalist 'vocabulary' – in the sense of imagery, symbols and narratives representative of that particular position. Key to the success of these ventures were figures such as Alice Milligan, 'Ethna Carbery' and F.J. Bigger himself. It was this group of activists that did more than most to motivate Belfast and Ulster in the run-up to that most crucial of years for cultural nationalism, 1898. It is worth paying such close attention to Belfast's efforts to commemorate the United Irishmen, as it was these attempts that most fully defined the relationship of the North to the project of cultural revival. Most importantly in this regard, what we see throughout the activities in 1898, and in the years leading up to them, is the northern revival taking up a clearly 'doubled' position in relation to the larger project.

This position is most fruitfully thought of in terms of an inside/outside duality. On the one hand, Belfast's cultural nationalists sought to incorporate their project fully into the philosophy and methodology of revivalist practices. But they were also only too aware that their surrounding hinterland was the space that most powerfully resisted any perceived moves towards cultural or political independence from Britain. In this key period in the history of Home Rule agitation, it was Ulster that became the space most able and willing to conjure resistance and rejection. As a result, those involved in bringing the revival to the North knew that they – more than any of their contemporaries – had to perform a series of simultaneous multivalent dialogues. The work that resulted was marked by a form of double-voice, as northern nationalism stood, Janus-like, speaking to several quite different constituencies at once. Assuming a nationalist stance in Home Rule Ulster entailed taking up a clearly minority position, one which had to engage with the emergence of an Ulster-centric unionism in order to create a viable and valid position for its very existence. Added to this, the sense of an 'Ulster difference' that increasingly emerged in the wake of Home Rule as a political possibility meant that nationalism in the North had to resist and respond to a perception of Ulster as a 'lost cause' within some elements of Irish nationalism. The northern revival's process of self-validation engaged with, and was directed towards, both the unionist majority in Ulster and those revivalists from outside Ulster who were clearly unsure of the North. This problematic for revivalists in Ulster is perhaps best captured by the memory of one such writer, James Cousins, of meeting one of the key figures in revivalist letters, Douglas Hyde. On meeting Cousins in Dublin, Hyde sought to encourage the Belfast man with the words: 'I knew you had a southern soul in your northern body.'[10]

Increasingly, as the search to bring revival to Ulster gathered pace, the northern revival operated as an uncanny doppelganger. Ulster's cultural nationalism was simultaneously part of the revival while also operating at a slight distance, drawing on different resources of imagery, landscape and language. This duality would not only motivate the very idea of forming the Ulster Literary Theatre, it would also go on to shadow everything the Belfast group did in its early years of existence. Interestingly what was first perceived as a problem to be fought (Ulster's peripheral position within revival) became for the Ulster Literary Theatre an enabling source of creative potential. Operating at the perceived edges of nationalist endeavour, the writers associated with the Ulster Literary Theatre were able to draw on the logic of revival for particularly radical ends. Indeed, in the end the Ulster Literary Theatre may be read as having deconstructed the revival at the same time as contributing to it. This argument is explored here through the work of those playwrights that were key to the development of a specifically 'Ulster nationalist drama' – an idea replete with its own very obvious tensions and problems (of which the playwrights themselves were only too aware). Exploring the performance of a northern revival involves a return to the work of a number of playwrights who have fallen outside most formulations of the revivalist canon. Such work need to be reassessed and be credited with its proper contribution. With this in mind, writers such as Rutherford Mayne, 'Lewis Purcell', Joseph Campbell and 'Gerald MacNamara' provide examples of the northern revival's performance. Most of these figures have either been relegated to the position of 'minor writer' or occluded altogether from studies of the revival on stage. Re-placing their work in its full political and cultural context reveals the ways in which these writers not only challenged the hegemonic desires of the Abbey's hierarchy but also sought to perform a new 'horizon of expectation' for Irish nationalism. In their work we can discern a process of 'writing back', with many of their plays responding with powerful and eloquent incisiveness to what they perceived as the occlusions and tensions at the heart of the Abbey's attempts to stage revival.

As we will see, for example, in response to Yeats's very particular recuperation of mythic narrative on stage, writers like Joseph Campbell and Lewis Purcell (David Parkhill's pen-name) responded with supplementary and/or counter narratives designed to recover and emphasise the possibilities of a specifically northern mythology. Their plays attempted not simply to recuperate Ulster's mythology but also to highlight the 'northern origins' of many of the myths 'appropriated' by revivalist writers from outside Ulster. These strategies reveal the Ulster Literary Theatre engaged in an aptly doubled methodology: their mythic plays clearly attempted to 'northernise' the revival as well as to bring revival north. In response too to the fixation on images of the West's peasantry, canonically associated with Synge and Lady Gregory, Rutherford Mayne's contributions to the Ulster Literary Theatre addressed the lack of a northern dimension to this search for an Irish rural authenticity. Lewis Purcell would also contribute to this responsive gesture with work that was amongst the earliest to represent the political and cultural tensions within Ulster's rural communities. As Laura E. Lyons has noted: 'Their plays insist[ed] that the North of Ireland, no less than the celebrated West of the Abbey, represent[ed] a crucial domain of the Irish cultural imaginary.'[11] The Ulster Literary Theatre's northern perspective, in other words, enabled it to address some of the gaps and/or silences that its writers perceived in revival.

The final logic of this argument is in many ways revealed by the work of Gerald MacNamara (the pen-name of Harry Morrow). It was his work that most fully and most radically drew on the singular inside/outside position allocated to and assumed by the experience of revival in the North. The plays of Gerald MacNamara were the most remarkable productions of the Ulster Literary Theatre, and amongst the most sophisticated expressions of the northern revival. If any of the Ulster Literary Theatre's playwrights deserve more recognition it is Gerald MacNamara. MacNamara's work is truly extraordinary in its sophistication and intent: each of his plays demonstrates an ambition to destabilise and deconstruct the very fabric of representation that shaped the cultural and political life of the time – in Ulster and the rest of Ireland. It was MacNamara who embraced the latent potential of Ulster's version of revival to interrogate the various debates on the nature of Ireland and Irishness. Moreover, as well as being the Ulster Literary Theatre's most significant playwright, Gerald MacNamara's work may well be one of the most important 'missing elements' to our understanding of revivalist performance. Throughout his work there is evidence of a powerful will to deconstruct the strategies and occlusions informing Ireland's body politic in the years of Home Rule. Crucially, MacNamara's critique extended not just to the obvious targets – in terms of northern nationalism – of the Orange Order and an emergent Ulster unionism, but to the ways in which any form of 'nationalist' position was built upon layers of tension, paradox and inconsistency. In the work of Gerald MacNamara we find a space beginning to open up in the fabric of revival. It is a space, one could argue, that pre-empts the territory and concerns taken up more fully in the work of Ireland's post-revival writers. Key to this performative potential was MacNamara's mastery of parody and burlesque. Through these modes of performance MacNamara manages to create a kind of post-revival space within the very fabric of revival. Drawing on his uniquely northern nationalist perspective, MacNamara explored an intellectual territory that points towards a post-nationalist position. His work, perhaps more than any other from this period, points to the complexities of a northern nationalism attempting to find space within revival from which to speak of the reinvention of Ulster as well as the reinvention of Ireland. It is work, moreover, which confirms beyond any doubt the achievements of the Ulster Literary Theatre and their value for rethinking this formative period in the twin histories of Ireland and Northern Ireland.

Chapter One

The North in Search of Revival

The war, people said, had revived their interest in poetry.
Virginia Woolf, *To the Lighthouse*

Boundary Situations and the Idea of the North

In recent years there has been a renewed interest in reconnecting the performance of revival with its political contexts.[1] The need 'to counteract the long-standing assumption that Irish theatre exists outside politics' has provided the impetus behind at least two of these notable recent interventions.[2] As a result it has become ever more clear that Ireland's theatrical stages could not have been, and were not, insulated from the various political *mises-en-scène* into which their audiences re-emerged as they left the auditoriums. While sharing this recent critical focus and motivating drive, this study also attempts something different in terms of the politics of performance with which the northern revival and Ulster Literary Theatre had to negotiate. As suggested above, this book is shaped by an attention to the revival's reception in Ulster and the northern viewpoint which this generates. A major consequence of this perspective is the need to re-examine the kinds of political discourses that shaped the performance of revival in Belfast and Ulster more generally. The politics of Home Rule Ulster and its relationship to revival has been much under-studied. In his recent book, *Revival: The Abbey Theatre, Sinn Féin, the Gaelic League and the Co-operative Movement,* for example, P.J. Mathews has made the point that the Abbey Theatre and Sinn Féin have histories that are mutually significant:

> Despite the contemporaneous evolution of two of the most important institutions in modern Irish history, there has been no scholarly attempt to map or analyse their comparative geneses.[3]

The history of the revival is also contemporary with the development of an 'Ulster-centric' unionism in the years of Home Rule. In line with Mathews's argument, we may add that this historical coincidence is also rarely explored in our critical engagements with these years that 'invented Ireland'. These are also the years, after all, that gave birth to our modern conceptions of 'the North', 'Ulster' and, finally, Northern Ireland. The revival in Ulster was shaped by a place occupied by multiple political signifiers, each of which strove to contest and control its 'true' meaning. Those involved in bringing revival to the North had to negotiate with all of these processes of signification; how they went about this task will occupy us throughout what follows.

If this study privileges a different kind of political focus, it is also engaged with a very particular kind of cultural analysis. The chapters that follow explore the various forms, narratives, imagery and voices that northern cultural nationalists drew on to represent the nature of their position within the idea of revival. Informing this series of staged debates is the understanding that a major element of any cultural-nationalist project is the (re)discovery of narratives and/or spaces that may be deemed exceptional, exclusive, or indeed, 'sacred'. Such a suggestion is not intended to return the revival to the hazy extra-political mysticism from which we are attempting to recover it; rather, the focus here is on the manner in which cultural-nationalism's exceptional/exclusive narratives are shaped by its profane political needs. The idea of 'the sacred' here does not suggest some form of divine revelation; it is, rather, concerned with those narratives which are presented as standing apart, as revealing something integral and essential to those doing the telling. Any community in search of self-definition may be seen as searching out narratives that it deems to be exclusive to itself; narratives, in other words, that explain the nature of the community to its members. One possible pathway to thinking about the nature of this relationship between profane need and exceptional/sacred narrative is provided by what Paul Ricoeur (following on from Karl Jaspers) terms 'boundary situations'.[4] For Ricoeur, these are moments of crisis, 'such as war, suffering, guilt, death etc. in which the individual or community experiences a fundamental existential crisis'. Ricoeur goes on to argue that at 'such moments the whole community is put into question'; and if in extreme cases it feels itself to be 'threatened with destruction from without or from within' such a community 'is compelled to return to the very roots of its identity' – what he posits as the 'mytho-poetic' core of its existence.[5] While Ricoeur was clearly more concerned with the apocalyptic implications of extreme events (holocaust, genocide, world war), there is also a sense in which this thinking is applicable to a nationalism in search of not only modes of resistance to imposed external structures, but narratives of communal bonding and self-definition.

Such a return to the putative 'roots of identity' (or mytho-poetic core) certainly casts a useful light on the work of many of the revival's key writers. We need only think of the 'sacred' temporality of Yeatsian myth, or those spaces implicitly deemed exceptional in Synge's appropriation of a western peasantry. A central contention of what follows is that those engaged with the revival in Ulster were experiencing a qualitatively different boundary situation to those cultural nationalists at work in the rest of Ireland. This study is concerned, then, with the politics of narrating the nation, but in terms of those permutations other than the hegemonic, those voices and narratives that were – either at the time or since – relegated to the periphery or to the status of 'minor'. The northern revival by necessity had to search out different models of exception and/or exclusivity; its writers had to construct different pathways to the roots of identity that gave sustenance and meaning to the nationalist community in Home Rule Ulster. The narratives of the northern revival reveal the fears, needs and desires of those nationalists in Ulster who saw their position as increasingly under threat. The stories they told demonstrate the processes of self-knowledge that informed the drive to bring revival to the North. By paying close attention to the kinds of 'sacred' or exclusive models proposed by any such nationalist discourse, in other words, we may read, in reverse as it were, the nature of the profane needs and desires out of which such models emerged.

The Politics of a 'Northern Revival'

> Earlier I asked the question: What makes a Poet out of a boy? – and tried to answer it. Now I broach another: What are the determinant causes that bring about a National Revival? As well might I try to explain the origins of the legend of the Sleepers of Aileach Neid. Whatever they are, the Poet senses and appraises them; the Soldier by force of arms consolidates them into shape; the Statesman builds a superstructure on the foundation thus laid.
>
> Joseph Campbell, *Northern Autobiography*[6]

In terms not only of the 'invention' of modern (Northern) Ireland but also of Ireland's engagement with modernity, the decades either side of the turn of the twentieth century represent an important boundary moment. It is to this period that we can trace the origins of a renewed engagement with Irish culture and, more specifically, the cultural expression of just what it meant to be Irish. This process of revival sought to rethink or reinvent the very idea of Ireland and its place in the world (Union and empire primarily), and Campbell locates it as the progenitor of the more directly political innovations in Ireland's history. For Campbell the nation's sense of self as it searches out revival (read independence and/or postcolonial moment) is first picked up on, and then given expressive form, by those who shape its cultural life. Having given this search a form, language and vision, he suggests, it is up to others (for him these include the soldiers and politicians) to enact its logical conclusions. While this is a somewhat oversimplified model of national resistance and the nature of the postcolonial moment, it does seem apt that Campbell should link the activities of the poet, the soldier and the politician, as he had played the first two of these roles in his own lifetime. Indeed Campbell is now mostly remembered as a minor revivalist poet who fought on the side of the anti-Treaty republicans during the Civil War.[7] Long before the militarisation of Irish life, however, he was a major figure in the Ulster Literary Theatre, as both a playwright and an actor. As such he was a key player in the performance of a northern revival and its articulation of the needs of those nationalists in Ulster who wished to play their part in 'National Revival'.

This now often overlooked connection throws an interesting light on Campbell's insistence on the links between cultural invention and political motivation. It would appear that those operating out of the revival's northern wing were in little doubt that their activities had strong political ramifications and consequences. The politics of the North, it seems, left no room for any other conclusion; the Ulster that was gripped by Home Rule was not a place where the political realm could easily be escaped. Campbell's northern perspective on the links between culture and politics casts a new light on W.B. Yeats's more famous statement of cause and effect:

> The modern literature of Ireland, and indeed all that stir of thought which prepared for the Anglo-Irish war, began when Parnell fell from power in 1891. A disillusioned and embittered Ireland turned from parliamentary politics; an event was conceived; and the race began, as I think, to be troubled by that event's long gestation.[8]

For Yeats, culture was only able to achieve such social primacy because of a dysfunctional politics. It is this reading that informs Declan Kiberd's assertion that in the wake of Parnell the 'way was open for a literary movement to fill the political vacuum'.[9] While this does not contradict Campbell's sense of culture and/or politics, it is certainly a more distanced reading of their relationship. This is a fundamental dynamic and how we read it defines much of our thinking about Ireland's search for independence at the beginning of the twentieth century. It is of note, then, that Yeats's version of a culture that withdrew from political engagement has recently come under increasing pressure. At the level of basic historical narrative, Yeats's vision of a people turning away from a defunct politics towards culture as their primary engagement with issues of identity and nationality has been revealed to be in need of further interrogation. While an increasingly large section of the populace did indeed become more interested in cultural signifiers of a unique Irish identity, they would always have read these signs in terms generated in exchange with wider political contexts. More importantly, perhaps, the claim that revivalist cultural production worked at a remove from political consideration and influence has become increasingly difficult to sustain.

This more intimate relationship between culture and politics in many ways returns us to Joseph Campbell's reading of the latter as a natural extension of the former. Given this, it is all the more curious that this drive to re-engage the cultural and political dimensions of revival has consistently managed to occlude the Ulster dimension to this dialectic. There has been a general lack of engagement with the North's role in revival, and there is a related uneasiness regarding the links between the history of revival and the contemporary history of Ulster separatism. In this sense our approach to the emergence of dual nationhood often repeats a very specific reading of Yeats's culture–politics schism. When we talk of 'Ireland' we turn to the revival as a site of cultural exploration: we find there a discourse with the potential for national reinvention, a significant moment in the development of modernism and even a model for other emergent post-colonial struggles. When we talk of 'Northern Ireland', we look to Home Rule, violence and *real politic* for our models of understanding. While Ireland set about a process of cultural self-invention, such a model seems to suggest that the North remained solidly in the grip of political machination. Such a reading actually manages to replicate a certain dismissal of the North from within the ranks of the revival itself. Ulster was often cited as a cultural wasteland lost to the vulgarity of industrialisation and a work ethic inimical to the proper articulation of 'national culture'. Just as Yeats's model of a post-Parnell culture/politics schism has been revised, this rendering of the North is in need of revision too. The relationship between the North and revival is much more complex than this: culture and politics were in constant exchange (as they always are), and the 'idea' of the North/Ulster and of Ireland were in a constant dialectic of adaptation, reflection and process. The North played its part in revival, and the experiences of those writers who sought to map revival onto Ulster record much about this period's cultural politics. A more considered recuperation of the revival's northern dimension will help reveal the full complexities involved in the twin inventions of 'Ulster' and 'Ireland'. The revival had something to say about the former as well as the latter; to fully understand such a claim, we must return to the political and cultural contexts that emerged in the North of Ireland in the final decades of the nineteenth century. These contexts reveal specific moments of crisis in Ulster during the Home Rule debate; they also reveal the ways in which the North's nationalists responded to them.

Alternative Ulster? Some Notes on the Idea of a Province

While the ontology of culture's politicisation stands outside simple numerical representation, a brief survey of electoral patterns in the final decades of the nineteenth century reveals the emergence of a new form of Ulster politics, and with it, just as importantly, of a new idea of Ulster as imagined space. It is the emergence of these potentially conflicting discourses that is fundamental to an understanding of the position of cultural nationalists in the North at this time.[10] As early as the 1874 election an Ulster 'difference' in respect to Home Rule was evident. The result of this ballot in Ulster was to return two pro-Home Rule members to Westminster; in this same election Leinster returned twenty-six 'Home Rulers', Munster returned twenty-one and Connaught ten.[11] By the time of the 1885 election, Home Rulers in the North had gathered a degree of momentum that took unionists in Ulster by surprise. The results of this election returned eighteen Home Rule members from Ulster, along with seventeen members that were openly hostile to the Home Rule cause. This result has to be read in light of the broader situation revealed by this vote: the rest of Ireland was completely represented by Home Rule Members of Parliament (except for the two seats allocated to Trinity College in Dublin). All the same, this surprising result, when combined with Gladstone's conversion to the idea of Home Rule, jolted the North (and, in particular, its large unionist/conservative constituency) into the beginnings of a political reorganisation.

This period is crucial in the development of what we would now recognise as an Ulster unionist political formation; more generally, it is vital to the development of a very particular identity politics in the northern province. In reaction to the twin pressures of Home Rule success in the recent elections and the gathering enthusiasm of Westminster liberalism for a settlement of the 'Irish Question', unionist politics in the North reacted with moves of inward consolidation and outward resistance. Thus the penultimate decade of the nineteenth century witnessed a realignment of broadly conservative/unionist politics in Ulster. The effect, as Patrick Buckland puts it, was striking:

> Until then politically conscious Protestants were divided into conservatives, liberals and Orangemen, and were more concerned with outbidding one another than with forming a united front against home rulers. The advance of the home rule movement in the 1870s and 1880s forced its opponents in Ulster to sink their differences in a new Ulster unionist movement.[12]

The consequences of this political reconstitution are no less striking. By the time of the 1892 election the anti-Home Rule groupings in the North had started the process of imagining (and proposing) Ulster as a more coherent, focused political entity. The results of this election reversed the previous pattern and returned once again a majority of unionist members from the province. While brute numbers can often mislead, it is clear that these electoral results represent an underlying shift in the 'representation' of the northern province. This period sees the development of a unionism specifically of and for Ulster. The emergence of this Ulster-centric unionism is confirmed by the establishment of organisations such as the Ulster Loyal Anti-Repeal Union (founded 8 January 1886) and the Ulster Defence Union (March 1893). We should, however, be clear – none of this is to suggest that Ulster Protestants (the political/religious alignment was only reinforced by these elections) had turned away from the idea of 'Irish unionism'. Instead, at this stage at least, there was an acknowledgement that the battle for the retention of Union could most strongly be fought from Ulster. Nevertheless, looking back, these moves certainly reveal the beginning of a process that evolved in tandem with the Home Rule debate, a process that resulted in – certainly by the time of the Parliament Act of 1911 – a focus on the retention of Ulster as a special case (space) within the constitutional debate.

This chapter opened with the suggestion that the final decade of the nineteenth century is usually read as a crucial boundary situation (or moment of crisis) in the development of the modern nation. It is of course more accurate to say that these years witnessed the development of several simultaneous boundary situations. These election results provide not simply a numerical graph of the Home Rule issue in Ulster, more fundamentally they trace the emergence of a radical boundary situation for unionists in the North. What is perhaps sometimes overlooked is that, just as was the case for Irish nationalism, unionist politics did not operate at a hermetic remove from cultural expression. As well as political reorganisation, the 'advance of the home rule movement' also necessitated a return to and recovery of the mytho-poetic core of unionist identity. While this was true for Irish unionism more generally, it is certainly the case that the specific demographics of Ulster meant that the process arrived at a critical mass with greater momentum in the North. As a result, these decades saw the development of a newly politicised language and cultural expression; this was a discourse that sought to realign the signification of 'Ulster' as a discrete case within the Union and thus highlight its need for special attention. As early as 1886, Randolph Churchill, following a massive meeting of the Ulster Loyalist Anti-Repeal Union in Belfast's Ulster Hall, provided Ulster unionism with one of its iconic mission statements: 'Ulster will fight, and Ulster will be right'. While as a rallying cry Churchill was calling on Ulster to fight for all of unionist Ireland, the geo-politics of the phrase also plays with a shifting notion of Ulster as discrete powerhouse of ideological force. A letter written to a friend this same year reveals just how much emphasis Churchill placed on this need for an ideological base: 'I decided quite some time ago that if the G.O.M went for home rule, the orange card would be the one to play. Please God it may turn out the ace of trumps and not the two.'[13]

Churchill, astute politician that he was, had quite correctly read the reinvigoration of the Orange Order as an important factor in the resistance to Home Rule. It was not lost on him, or many other contemporary figures, that this re-energisation had taken place primarily in the North, the place where the Order was born and remained most active. The Orange Order would become (and remain) central to the articulation of an Ulster unionist identity, and its importance provides us with an almost perfect example of Ricoeur's reading of a communal moment of danger. In reaction to a perceived threat of destruction (alteration or repeal of the Union), northern unionism was 'compelled to return to the very roots of its identity'.[14] At the heart of the re-emergence of the Orange Order as a vital political force is the recovery and reprivileging of narratives and mythic models that spoke with renewed vigour to the contemporary needs of a community under pressure. This process of communal redefinition would gather pace in the decades that followed, and would be driven ever more urgently by the need to represent Ulster as political 'other' within the Home Rule debate. This is a complex process that drew on innumerable narratives and operated on several levels of scale, but it also fairly evident that at the heart of its mytho-poetic core Ulster unionism privileged two foundational events: the Battle of the Boyne and the Siege of Derry. These two iconic moments would become essential sites of ideological meaning and tension throughout the decades of Home Rule campaigning.

Of the two, it is the Siege of Derry which provided the most resonant image of cultural resistance for a nascent 'Ulster unionist' identity. Indeed, as Ian McBride has noted, the mythology born out of the seventeenth-century Siege of Derry has been a sustaining one for Ulster Protestants throughout the subsequent history of Northern Ireland. The reasons behind this powerful afterlife are, as McBride relates, easy enough to discern and decode:

> The basic themes of the siege myth – defiance, solidarity, sacrifice, deliverance – are obvious enough. The story serves to reinforce the social cohesion and political resolve of Ulster Protestants by recalling the unchanging threat to their faith and liberties posed by the Catholic majority in Ireland; 'No Surrender', the watchword of the defenders of Derry, has become the arch-slogan of loyalism.[15]

The still-apparent power of this historical reclamation for modern-day Ulster loyalism is clear. The city of Derry is situated within post-partition Northern Ireland, whereas the site of the Boyne battle has been geographically 'stranded' by the very act of partition that created Northern Ireland. The officially bounded space of the Northern Irish state finds a usefully coherent echo in the bounded space described by Derry's city walls, the very walls that refused to yield to James's forces. Thus the story of Derry's protection by the city's Protestant 'Apprentice Boys' amenably foreshadows a modern-day Ulster loyalism intent on defending the imagined community of Northern Ireland.

The implications of this historical reclamation were no less powerful for those who sought to resist any weakening in the Union at the end of the nineteenth century. In 1893, for example, the Revd Phillip Dwyer republished George Walker's pamphlets on the siege (in a collected edition that included many of his other speeches, sermons and letters).[16] The collection also 'included an attack on Home Rule under the heading, "moral to be drawn from the Siege of Derry", which called for Protestant unity to resist the growing power of the Roman Catholic Church in the United Kingdom'.[17] The Revd Dwyer's reformulation of the historical siege in terms of the contemporary Home Rule issue is just one example of the discursive shifts performed by unionism during this period. As with any emergent nationalism, the nascent discourse of an Ulster-centric unionism repeatedly refocused historical frames of reference, shifting the historical logic of distant events onto the idea of Ulster as a separate political space. In these years, in other words, Ulster became the place where the siege would recur and where a defence would have to be re-enacted. The return to such moments provided Ulster unionism with the narratives that explained its own existence; in the years ahead they would become powerfully energising models of communal self-definition. The very definite emphasis on place within such coded narratives also, of course, described the boundaries of this community's 'home-place'. The subsequent history of the North has ensured a form of hegemony for this form of narrative-mapping; it has, most obviously, provided the pre-history of the new Northern Ireland state. But this period in Ulster was much more contested than this would suggest; other forms of northern identity were engaged in mapping 'the North' in different ways throughout this period. The emergence of a distinct Ulster unionism undoubtedly did, however, provide the context within which those Ulster men and women with nationalist sympathies had to operate. Ulster unionism's boundary situation, in other words, helped define northern nationalism's moment of crisis. This can be seen most clearly in the cultural-nationalist endeavours in Ulster during the period of Home Rule uncertainty.

Alice Milligan, Ardrigh and the search for a 'northern Revival'

The political situation in Ulster may have radically altered the form that cultural-nationalist discourse took, but it certainly did not mean that the revival was excluded from the North. Not only did Ulster engage with the revival project, there was a distinctly northern version of revivalist practice. This northern wing of revival is marked by the search for a counter-narrative to that of the emergent Ulster-centric unionism. In response to unionist reformulations of Ulster's 'meaning', northern nationalist writers articulated their own counter-position. The end result was a conflict of representation, as unionism and nationalism each sought to privilege their moment of crisis. In these years Ulster became an imagined space layered with overlapping and conflicting narratives all searching for ownership of its true representation. This dialectic meant that Ulster's cultural nationalists constantly had to engage with a set of complex negotiations. While attempting to work within the revival's cultural modes, northern nationalist writers were further required to negotiate not merely their minority status in Ulster, but also their perceived dislocation from the mainstream of the revival's activities. The problematic of how to accommodate Ulster within revival was thus played out within a series of interconnected processes.

Firstly, the articulation of a northern revivalist voice required a negotiating strategy within the communal structures of the North. Northern nationalists were, in this sense, required to justify (or at least explain) the validity of their position. Just as importantly, however, any northern cultural-nationalist position necessitated a dialogue with the condition of displacement allocated to Ulster by many of the revival's practices of non-engagement and silence. The nature of this problematic has led some modern-day critical practice to propose a certain 'impossibility of identity' inherent in the performance of revival in Ulster. John Wilson Foster, for example, has suggested that writing a revivalist Ulster was not really achievable; or, at least, that the act of writing such an Ulster was only possible through a process of reinvention that implicitly undermined the nature of the act:

> Ulster writers, such as Bullock, went to England (or if they stayed at home, like [Forrest] Reid, wrote for English readers) or, like Ethna Carbery (née Anna Isobel Johnston), Alice Milligan, Seosamh MacCathmaoil (né Joseph Campbell), AE (né George Russell), and Moira O'Neill (née Nesta Higginson), they joined the romantic nationalist movement, in the process Gaelicizing or otherwise altering their identities. This they had to do, for the Protestant North, with its incorrigible nonconformism, industrialism, and political unionism, was not to be a part of the cultural revival.[18]

Foster's assessment, however, is too straightforward. The form of cultural and historical representations deployed by Ulster revivalists at this time suggests a process much more complex than the curious negation of identity (or even bad faith) proposed here. Interestingly Foster also rehearses exactly the perception of the North that its revivalists had taken as their *raison d'être* to resist.

Foster does, however, provide us with an important route to decoding the impasse proposed by his argument. Alice Milligan (1866–1953), rather than the curiously undermined figure presented by Foster, was in fact a key figure (perhaps *the* key figure) in northern cultural nationalism throughout the 1890s. As a result, she is also one of the central characters in the pre-history of the Ulster Literary Theatre. Indeed, the relationship is even more direct than this: Milligan profoundly inspired those involved in setting up a nationalist theatre for Ulster. Perhaps even more importantly, Alice Milligan's work established many of the imaginative frames of reference within which the Ulster Literary Theatre would later operate. For these reasons alone Milligan's work is worth examining closely in its own right; it is of even more interest to us here, however, as on closer inspection it perfectly counters Foster's thesis on the impossibility of an 'authentic' northern Revival. Rather usefully in this regard, it was exactly her northern origins that Milligan was to draw on throughout the 1890s as a site of potential within the revival project. As we will see, Milligan continually drew on her northern Protestantism as precisely the rationale for her engagement with revival, rather than something to be negated and/or transmuted, as Foster would have it.

In place of that negated image we may now read this northern Protestant as the figure who (perhaps more than anyone else during the 1890s) sought not only to engage the North with revival, but also to locate the North firmly within the revivalist re-imagining of Ireland. Milligan's work represents one of the very earliest attempts by a northern nationalist writer to construct a position that accommodated both the North's specificity and its potential within the wider revivalist project. In response to the re-presentation of Ulster's meaning by the northern unionist community, Milligan's work offered a very different dialectic of place and history. Her whole project was largely based on the belief that a fuller understanding of Ulster's history would ensure that the *whole* of the North would come to realise the wisdom of a nationalist position. The 'Protestant North', for example, is situated in her work as the birth place of, amongst others, Cúchulain, many of the last Gaelic rebels – most notably the O'Neills – and modern Irish nationalism (the emergence of which she reads through the United Irishmen). Thus for Milligan Ulster's history firmly locates it as the most crucial of places in any Irish nationalist project: its history provided the very reasons for its inclusion and not a rationale for the separate settlement proposed by Ulster unionists in response to the gathering momentum of Home Rule.

To fully understand her work, we must place Milligan's writings within the kind of doubled position outlined above. Her acts of historical reclamation and mythic recuperation were undertaken in response to both the revival (as viewed from the North) and Ulster unionism. The reclamation of Ulster as the site of development for Irish nationalism, for example, clearly operates in conversation with the revival as a demonstration of Ulster's 'natural' place within the movement. It also operates in a relationship with Ulster unionism, with the vision of a Protestant-led Irish nationalism (as in the United Irishmen) demonstrating the unifying potential that a broad-church nationalism could exert in Ulster. All of this is not to suggest a simplistic binary opposition between the 'real' Alice Milligan and the one proposed by Foster. With even the briefest exploration of her work, one can detect a certain slippage in Milligan's position, but it is of an order more complex than simple negation or alteration. What we see is a slippage that in fact becomes an integral element in the building of a specifically northern version of revival. Milligan's drive to present Ulster's historically defined, and therefore natural, inclusion in the nationalist schema opens up a counter-space; it is in this space that we can detect the perception of exclusion from which Milligan works. She would have had no need to insist on inclusivity, in other words, if the nature of that inclusion was not in question. There is no doubt that this kind of slippage does complicate the project of revival in Ulster. Milligan's search to write Ulster in the 1890s functioned along a fluid inside/outside line. It is this dialectic that informed much of the North's continued engagement with revival in the years after Milligan's most productive years, the conclusion of which we will see most radically in the work of the Ulster Literary Theatre.

John Wilson Foster has not been the only critic to underestimate the importance of Milligan to revival. FSL Lyons also dismissed Milligan and her closest collaborator, Ethna Carbery, as 'secondary figures . . . who subordinated their art to political purposes'.[19] It is in place of these ideas of Milligan as a peripheral figure that we may now reposition Milligan as key in representing the North to the revival and the revival to the North. A radical journalist and poet, Milligan was also a significant early playwright in the revivalist mode; in 1900 the first of her trilogy of myth-based plays, *The Last Feast of the Fianna,* was one of the earliest productions of the Irish Literary Theatre.[20] In these years too she devoted much energy to the production of nationalist *tableaux vivants* at various festivals throughout the country. Milligan and Ethna Carbery were also founding members of Maude Gonne's *Inghinidhe na hÉireann.*[21] It is in the context of these energetic contributions that an article published by Susan Mitchell in 1919 recalls Milligan as one of the foundational figures of nationalist drama in Ireland, and a significant progenitor of the Abbey Theatre:[22]

> In almost every one of the national and intellectual activities in Ireland now known to everybody – the Gaelic Revival, the dramatic movement, the literary renaissance – this indefatigable Irish girl was at the start of them. She was lecturing for the Gaelic League all over Ireland, she was writing plays and staging them . . . and she was the most successful producer of plays before the Abbey Theatre started on its triumphant way.[23]

While Mitchell's overview presents Milligan as a roving revivalist figure with an influence 'all over Ireland', however, most other assessments cannot escape closely binding Milligan's work to the dynamics of Ulster and Ireland – and the co-invention of these two ideas. Thomas MacDonagh, writing in 1914 (in the best-known summary of Milligan's contribution), makes the case for Milligan as the 'most Irish of living poets, and therefore the best' in the following terms:

> I have no time to spare in a time of war when my country is preparing for her own part, I have no difficulty of choice because my ears can listen with joy only for the song of a poet who sings for Ireland . . . It is meet that this Irish national poet should be a woman. It is meet that she, like so many of the leaders of Irish Volunteers, should be of North-East Ulster. Alice Milligan, Ulster Protestant, Gaelic Leaguer, Fenian, friend of all Ireland, lover of Gaelic Catholic as of her own kith, strong in faith and in hope and in charity, clear of eye and of voice, single-minded, high, inspired and inspiring, humorous and solemn, taking praise and encouragement and blame and rebuff as they come, without thought of herself, with thought always of Ireland's cause – Alice Milligan is the most Irish of living Irish poets, and therefore the best.[24]

MacDonagh's highlighting of a key nationalist voice from within the north's Protestant community is inextricably linked to the situation of the Great War, Ulster Volunteers and the final solution of Home Rule. Interestingly his intuitive case for Milligan as the best of Irish poets manages to index many of the key dynamics proposed by Milligan's work. The North is represented here, as it is throughout Milligan's writing, as the 'home' of modern Irish nationalism: 'It is meet that she, like so many of the leaders of Irish Volunteers, should be of North-East Ulster.' In such moments we can see that sense of slippage emerging, even in the assessment of Milligan's work by a fellow nationalist and poet. MacDonagh's privileging of Ulster implicitly reveals the difference between representation and political reality – his summation seeks to resist the perception of an emerging state of alterity: the act of centring cannot escape the problems of periphery. Importantly, however, this is not simply true of MacDonagh's assessment of Milligan's importance: combating this very problem was one of the driving engines motivating her energetic and wide-ranging cultural output throughout the 1890s.[25]

Alice Milligan was born into a prosperous Protestant family in Omagh, Co. Tyrone, in 1866. Her primary education, which was undertaken in Omagh, was followed by a move to Belfast's Methodist College. She would later move to Dublin (in 1888), where she stayed for three years and befriended the likes of Michael Davitt and O'Donovan Rossa. It was in these years that Milligan began to devote much of her time to writing poetry and short sketches with a broadly nationalist message. She sent work to many of the Dublin papers, including the *Weekly Independent,* for which she would later write a regular column. Around this time she also collaborated on a writing project with her father: *Glimpses of Erin* was published in 1888 and was an early tourist guide to the 'natural beauties' of Ireland.[26] In the course of her secondary education the Milligans had moved their family home to Belfast, and it was here that Alice returned in 1891. A further family move in 1893 would help shape much of her future work and life; it was in this year that the Milligans settled at the Cave Hill end of the Antrim Road. This move was to prove particularly successful for Alice, as it granted her easier access to the small coterie of cultural nationalists that often gathered at this end of town. The fulcrum of Milligan's new social, intellectual and cultural life was Francis Joseph Bigger's house, 'Ardrigh', which was situated close to the Milligan's new family home. Bigger was a wealthy Belfast solicitor who operated as an energetic cultural philanthropist throughout the revival period. He was an ardent naturist, antiquarian and archaeologist, and his home became the meeting place for a small but dedicated coterie of Belfast-based nationalists. As Eamon Phoenix writes: 'During the decade and a half before the 1916 Rising, Bigger's home was a power-house of Irish music, cultural renaissance and revolutionary politics.'[27] His house contained a massive library of texts connected with Ireland's history and culture, and many of the city's writers used it as an open resource for their own work, prompting some to refer to Ardrigh as 'a miniature university of Irish ethos' and Bigger as 'the personification of the reawakening of Irish culture and tradition in Ulster'.[28]

It was at Ardrigh that Milligan became friends with the likes of Roger Casement, James Connolly, Joseph and John Campbell, and, of course, F.J. Bigger himself.[29] It was here too that Milligan formed her closest friendship, with Anna Johnston, the daughter of the old Belfast Fenian leader, Robert Johnston. Anna Johnston (or 'Ethna Carbery', her better known pen-name) and Alice Milligan became not only great friends but collaborators, working closely in the following decade on numerous projects, from the production of plays to the running of their own nationalist journal. The network of friendships and contacts born out of the environs of Ardrigh, moreover, would prove to be one of the most significant elements of cultural-nationalist life in Belfast in the years to come. Most importantly (for this study at least), it would provide an organisational fulcrum for the establishment of the Ulster Literary Theatre. Alice Milligan would, for example, introduce the young Bulmer Hobson to the Ardrigh grouping (she was a friend of the Hobson family), a move that would bring Hobson into contact with such influential figures as the Campbell brothers and F.J. Bigger. Indeed, Ardrigh's influence was pretty central to the Belfast nationalists' sense of themselves as a coherent grouping. Some form of organisational locus was, after all, crucial when confronted with the strengthening hegemonic presence of Ulster unionism.

During these early years Milligan was to become one of the most energetic and productive figures connected with the new cultural movements of the 1890s. She was one of the earliest Belfast members of the Gaelic League, for whom she toured Ireland giving lectures on subjects such as Irish history, literature and folklore.[30] During this time she also wrote extensively as a poet and playwright and published her first novel (*A Royal Democrat,* 1890). Readers of practically all the nationalist papers of the time would at some point or other have come across a stridently nationalist piece of poetry or short story above the name Alice Milligan or Iris Olkyrn (her sometime pen-name). She also contributed many poems and short sketches to the two Belfast-based nationalist papers she helped edit, the *Northern Patriot* and *Shan Van Vocht.* Involvement with such activities increased Milligan's belief that the North needed to establish a framework for getting its own voice heard within the emerging cultural projects. It was with just this in mind that in 1895 F.J. Bigger provided the financial backing to establish the Henry Joy McCracken Literary Society, an organisation designed to promote the ideals of the United Irishmen (such as McCracken) as a model for contemporary unity in the north of Ireland. The society organised lectures, evenings of traditional song and readings of nationalist verse around Belfast and its hinterland.

Later in this same year, and again backed by Bigger, the group began the publication of the McCracken Literary Society's own journal: the first number of the *Northern Patriot* appeared in October 1895. Alice Milligan was appointed Editor and Ethna Carbery as General Manager. An argument concerning editorial policy, however, resulted in Milligan and Carbery only overseeing the production of the first three numbers. The nature of this argument is hard to pin down, but it seems to have revolved around the form of nationalism to be promulgated by the *Northern Patriot.* Despite this, Milligan and Carbery remained as a journalistic team and in January of 1896, the month after their third issue of the *Northern Patriot,* they produced the first number of their own nationalist journal, *Shan Van Vocht.*[31] As with the *Northern Patriot,* the main focus of Milligan and Carbery's new project was to promote knowledge concerning the United Irishmen. Indeed, as discussed more fully in the next chapter, much of the content of *Shan Van Vocht* was taken up with motivating the North in the lead-up to the centenary year of 1898. Despite chronic financial problems, Milligan and Carbery kept the monthly *Shan Van Vocht* in print for three years before succumbing to a lack of funds and the arrival of Arthur Griffith's *United Irishman* (a paper that was in turn a forerunner of *Sinn Féin*). After the final number of *Shan Van Vocht,* Milligan and Carbery gave their list of subscribers to Griffith, many of whom became subscribers to his paper.

Moving back to the beginning of this process, we can see the ways in which Milligan first articulated her view of how Ulster should engage with revival. Her appointment as Editor of the *Northern Patriot* in 1895 provided Milligan with an early opportunity to promulgate her specific vision of nationhood, and the North's role in its achievement, to a reasonably large co-ordinated audience. Beginning publication two years after the failure of the second Home Rule bill, the *Northern Patriot* strove to provide a space for the North's voice to be heard in the emerging cultural-nationalist project. Confronting this very issue head-on, Milligan's editorial for the first number begins with a clear setting out of the problems confronting northern nationalism. It is an editorial that frames northern nationalism as a minority discourse twice over:

> We have no national paper within the borders of all Ulster, to speak for us to the rest of Ireland; and in the Dublin press we have no claim to more than a brief notice of anything we attempt.
>
> This, indeed, is the reason of the existence of our little paper, which may be regarded as the voice of a body of staunch and energetic nationalists, speaking out boldly to remind their brethren in the other provinces that here, in the darkest part of the land, surrounded by an overwhelming majority of opponents, few in number, but strong in faith and determination, they are still fighting their corner and keeping the green flag flying. (October 1895)

The defiant stance of nationalist solidarity adopted in the declaration that northern nationalists were 'still fighting their corner and keeping the green flag flying' is tempered by the acknowledgement that nationalists in the North needed to 'remind their brethren in the other provinces' of their existence. This sense of Ulster as the site of greatest challenge for a nationalist discourse is confirmed by Milligan's description of the North as 'the darkest part of the land', where nationalism was 'surrounded by an overwhelming majority of opponents'. It was this context that informed the decision to form the Henry Joy McCracken Literary Society. Milligan spoke on behalf of all those involved when, in this same editorial, she presented the society as an intellectual forum enabling and supporting links between the nationalist communities in the north and south of the country:

> We purpose at every opportunity to enlist the services of good Nationalists from several parts of the country to deliver sound and instructive addresses to our members. By this means the North will be put in touch with the other provinces, and a bond of love and union will cement all in pushing forward the good cause that has braved increasing persecution for seven centuries.

Milligan's is a doubled reading of northern nationalism, one that will become ever more familiar in the years ahead. The nationalist North is here the place under most pressure, a place in need almost of a life-line from the rest of nationalist Ireland. Yet at the same time the North is also a place of enormous potential, a place that will provide the final and holding linchpin in 'pushing forward the good cause' of Irish nationalism. The main job for Ulster's revivalists, Milligan suggests, is to unlock this latter potential in an effort to correct the former state of affairs. The editorial for the third number of the *Northern Patriot* provides an example of this cultural thinking in action. In this piece Milligan explicitly sets out to counter the normative reading of the North as a particular kind of politicised space. In place of the North as the part of Ireland most fully colonised by the processes of empire and union, Milligan insists on a place more correctly read as the keeper of a lost nationalist lineage:

> A Christmas greeting to Ireland round and round out of the North; and, added to this, a heartfelt hope that in the years to come our brother patriots of the other three provinces will drop a tone of distinction which they too frequently adopt, and cease to speak of the North as if it were an alien-colonised district of Ireland, which is being gradually absorbed into union with the nation proper. This tone is pardonable if our Irish brethren are following the example of English political orators, and mean by the North its largest city and the towns and districts surrounding and most in touch with it. But, Irish friends, believe me, this assertion of Ulster's colonialism is exaggerated vastly. Belfast is not all Ulster, nor even representative of that province. There is a Native North, as thoroughly Celtic as any part of our island. (December 1895)

As would often be the case in the years to come, the case for this 'native North' is made via that moment at the turn of the sixteenth and seventeenth centuries when the final power of Gaelic Ireland rested in Ulster. The history of the O'Neill clan (and in particular its iconic leader Hugh) in the lead-up to Gaelic Ireland's final defeat at Kinsale (1601) provided Milligan with a representative history of and for Ulster nationalism. Her insistence on the importance of this moment has to be read in the context of Ulster unionism's similar insistence on the Siege of Derry as the primary imaginative kernel of modern Ulster identity; for Milligan, the return to Ulster's mytho-poetic core meant something very different indeed. Drawing on a counter-history, Milligan sets out to replace the image of Ulster as an anti-Home Rule stronghold with a vision of northern proto-nationalism:

> In the pages of our paper this month we awaken the memory of a Christmas-tide, when one of our northern heroes came for cheer and shelter to a Leinster chieftain when hard pressed by his enemies: let us at the same time remind our friends of the remotest south of another Christmas which the tribes of Munster and Ulster celebrated together, when before the battle of Kinsale, O'Neill and O'Donnell encamped Belgooly in Kinelea, and observed as the old chronicler relates, 'The feast of the Nativity of the Saviour Jesus, feasting and rejoicing together in delight and gladness of soul, as if they were in their own great royal castles, though then they were very far from them'.

This renarration of a classic historical moment of danger also takes the form of a call for pan-Irish co-operation. The effect of Milligan's historical narrative is to propose an intellectual and cultural frame for the resolution of contemporary northern nationalism's doubled boundary situation. The evolving Home Rule north/south axis is resolved in the recourse to a site of (pan-Irish) nationalist co-operation; the notion of Ulster as essentially unionist is also redirected to encompass a vision of Ulster as the one-time controlling centre of counter-imperial resistance.

As it turned out, this was to be the last editorial written by Milligan for the *Northern Patriot;* by January 1896 Milligan and Carbery were publishing their own independent nationalist journal, *Shan Van Vocht.* Free from any interference, Milligan continued her radical stance in the pages of *Shan Van Vocht,* with much in the new journal representing a natural extension of the intellectual ground tilled by her earlier editorial work. Time and again Milligan would return to some of her most treasured cultural tropes: the role of the North in the emerging cultural-nationalist movements, and the recuperation of historical (and mythic) narratives as models for internal Ulster unity. In this regard the nature of Milligan's position necessitated that much of her work was often a more or less oblique examination of the problematics of its own production. One of the most powerful examples of this self-reflexivity is provided by Milligan's particular version of that central revivalist totem, Cúchulain.

Cúchulain and the Revival: An Ulster Hero?

From the earliest moments of the Irish Literary renaissance, the figure of Cúchulain was appropriated by a wide variety of writers. Cúchulain's attraction for the revivalists is nicely sketched out by Declan Kiberd, who suggests that this mythic hero enabled cultural nationalists to counter a colonial discourse of Ireland that emphasised Irish femininity, dependence and cowardice with responding images of bravery, strength, masculinity, historical independence and self-sacrifice.[32] Standish O'Grady's *History of Ireland: Heroic Period* (1878–80) 'had made the exploits of Cúchulain available in English to a national readership'[33] and Cúchulain would remain a central totem in nationalism's proposed altered (alternative) history of Ireland. In the decades that followed, Cúchulain would become a crucial figure in not just the articulation of cultural nationalism, but in the motivations of direct-action nationalists. In this regard Alice Milligan drew on a source that would also energise the imagination of W.B. Yeats, Lady Gregory and Pádraic Pearse, to name but a few. However, one could argue that Cúchulain was all the more important for those who sought to bring revival to the North; after all Cúchulain, in his original incarnation, was of course very definitely rooted in an Ulster terrain. It was this specificity of the Cúchulain story that was incorporated into Milligan's work, and its recuperation functioned as a key part of her drive to establish imaginative links between northern nationalism and the rest of Ireland. Cúchulain became for her not simply a model of Ireland's heroic (pre-colonial) period, but also a representational bridge connecting the nationalist cause in Ulster with the rest of the island.

In this sense Milligan's 'Ulster nationalist' version of Cúchulain was driven by, but also complicated by, the original narratives involving this mythic character. In this regard too *any* cultural-nationalist reclamation of Cúchulain was always going to be made more complex by the very nature of the mythic cycle in which his deeds are recorded. The central story of the *Táin Bó Cuailnge* involves a moment of tension defined by a north/south axis. In the *Táin* Cúchulain, rather than a hero of all Ireland, is quite explicitly a northern hero defending Ulster from an invading force sent by the southern Queen Maev.[34] John Wilson Foster, for example, rightly states that Cúchulain 'from the manuscripts reads like an Ulster rather than Irish culture hero, defending Ulster as he does against the men of Ireland'.[35] He goes on to suggest that the revival sought to write over this fundamental dynamic in its transformation of Cúchulain into an all-Irish cultural hero:

> The north–south distinction is there in the Táin, as well as the east–west distinction, even though the revivalists sought in their exploitation of the story and the cycle of which it is the centrepiece to 'southernize' the saga (and much else besides in Irish culture) as they sought to 'westernize' it (and much else besides). The mutual suspicion and dislike in the Táin between the Ulstermen and the men of Ireland is an odd thing to read in the light of the partitioning of Ulster from the rest of Ireland something over a millennium later.[36]

In this context, Alice Milligan's version of the Cúchulain myth provides an alternative space within which to interrogate the function of Cúchulain in the revival project. Milligan's Cúchulain records a clear duality in terms of northern nationalism's relationship to the rest of Ireland. At many points Milligan's very Ulster Cúchulain is obviously intended to respond to, and resist, the 'southernisation' of the northern myth. But this emphasis on his Ulster-centrism is further couched within a performance of Cúchulain that expresses the North's natural and essential position within the cultural-nationalist project. Milligan's Cúchulain, in other words, became a synecdoche for Ulster and its importance not only to the revival but to the nation that the revival sought to bring about.

The first number of the *Northern Patriot,* for example, includes a short story by Milligan (under her pseudonym Iris Olkyrn) entitled 'The Dark Rose of Rathmullan'. The story returns Milligan to one of the 'roots' of identity that informed much of her work. The place is west Ulster (in this case Donegal) and the time is the seventeenth century. As with the Christmas editorial above, in this story Milligan establishes an Ulster nationalist genealogy in terms of the O'Neill clan; in this instance it is centred on Hugh Roe O'Neill as a young boy. The story's tactic is to connect the deeds of myth with those of Irish proto-nationalism, and thus create a seamless narrative; and so Milligan presents Hugh Roe O'Neill in a way that establishes a clear line of descent between him and the stories of Cúchulain's deeds. What makes the tale so interesting is that it also appears to comment on the appropriation of Cúchulain by revivalist writers. The story begins in classic nationalist form with the image of Hugh Roe O'Neill as a young boy already committed to the cause of Ireland; we first discover him in the act of placing a garland of flowers on his mother's head:

> 'Now art thou crowned, my mother', he said 'like the Lady Elizabeth that is queen over England, and is fain to be queen of Ireland and our Donegal too; but that shall never be'.[37]

The reframing of Elizabeth's sovereignty establishes the importance of place: loyalty to Ireland is couched in the more localised terms of north-west Ulster. This idea of an Ulster strongly resistant to any version of colonialism resonates throughout the story's subsequent replaying (and re-placing) of Cúchulain's deeds. Hugh's mother (Ineen) tells him how his determination to defend his place reminds her of Cúchulain. Cúchulain's story is thus embedded within Milligan's tale of sixteenth-century Ulster and its resistance to early imperialism:

> 'Yes' said Ineen 'he came back to fight the battles of his country', and she told how, by his single arm battling at a ford on Ulla's border he repelled the whole army of Connacht led by Queen Maeve, and saved the North from alien yoke.

Ineen's version of Cúchulain's story, framed by her role as mother of a northern rebel, clearly seeks to reclaim the northern origin of the mythic cycle. The emphasis on 'Ulla's border' (i.e. Ulster) and Cúchulain's deeds as saving 'the North from alien yoke' affirms the importance of the tale as an originating moment of proto-nationalism in the North. Milligan in this way establishes a clear lineage between the future rebel O'Neill and a distinctly 'Ulsterised' mythology; the story is also revealed to have contemporary relevance, as Milligan implicitly introduces the revivalist image of Cúchulain as a figure of Irish sacrifice. The young Hugh tells his mother that he would follow a leader from the north or the south of the country, and even if he does hope for a *northern* reincarnation of Cúchulain the battle to be fought is about Ireland, as well as his own Donegal:

> 'Surely' said the boy, 'against the Saxons and in defence of Ireland and our holy faith I would serve any chief whatever, even were he to come of the Southern race that hath ever hated us; could they send us a king like their great Brian to lead us to another slaughter of foreigners such was made at Clontarf; but dearly I hope that it will not be from Munster, but from our own northern land that God will send a chief to lead; and to God I shall pray night and day, that it may be in my lifetime the great war of deliverance shall be fought; but whatever come, I warrant you, though peace should be in every quarter of Ireland, there shall be grim war and slaughter of the English in Donegal, when I am a man.'

The reincarnated Cúchulain is here inscribed as a specifically Home-Rule-era northern hero, who is willing to fight for all Ireland but who also knows that Ulster must be included in a complete vision of national resistance. The story thus accommodates both Cúchulain as northern hero and as revivalist totem, and as such eloquently demonstrates the kind of representational duality that Milligan was engaged with: the narrative allows her to write Ulster into the heart of revival, while also resisting an Ulster unionist discourse of northern separatism.

The energising potential of Cúchulain's 'northern-ness' was also a central presence in much of Milligan's poetry during this period. The long poem 'The Harper of the Only God' is one of Milligan's major achievements of the 1890s (first published in *Shan Van Vocht,* December 1896). It is a poem that would later establish the thematic core of Milligan's collection *Hero Lays,* which was published in 1908 and described by Thomas MacDonagh as 'the best book of national poems by a single author'.[38] 'The Harper of the Only God' tells of a meeting between a messenger from God and Cúchulain, and throughout Milligan nuances Cúchulain as an Irish Christ-like figure who is called back by God after he has carried out his duties. The poem begins with the messenger (disguised as a harper, but later revealed as Death) appearing to Cúchulain to summon him to appear before one who is 'greater than Ulandh's King'. Thinking the messenger is from some other royal house, Cúchulain proclaims his eternal loyalty to the defence of Ulster, a task he will not abandon:

> Bard, bring homeward this answer then,
> Thou hast seen me, the Hound of the Ulstermen;
> Kings are my cattle, hosts my hunting-prey,
> Uladh I guard until my dying day.[39]

In the end Cúchulain's loyal resistance forces the visitor to reveal his true identity: 'Death men call me; when I draw near / The lips of the mighty are blanched with fear'. Death has, in fact, finally come to take Cúchulain away from the mortal world: 'To my Lord's presence I bid thee come', and coaxes Cúchulain by reassuring him that his *physical* guardianship of Ulster is at an end: 'The days of thy watching are forever o'er'. From this point onward the poem is concerned with the nature of Cúchulain's deeds as a form of nascent nationalism sanctioned by a divine presence and encouragement. Cúchulain, now convinced of his fate, asks what tribute he should bring to his God, but is assured that none is needed:

> Then smiled the harper, 'O son of Suailtim,
> Thy great deeds for Erin were service to Him;
> And in drops of thy heart's blood on Uladh's sod
> Thou shalt count thy tribute to the only God'.

The verse's slippage is crucial: the actions of Cúchulain that entailed his 'heart's blood on Uladh's sod' are translated into 'great deeds for Erin' in the service of God. It is here that the complexity of Milligan's Cúchulain is revealed: as with her fellow revivalists, Cúchulain's defence of Ulster gets reread as the defence of Ireland, but what this northern nationalist poet privileges just as strongly is Ireland's need of an Ulster hero. The final verse goes on to make this link even more clearly, with a form of translation similar to that seen in the short story of Hugh Roe O'Neill. The description of Cúchulain's Christ-like death presents the myth as a multivalent narrative, revealing more than one sacred body. At one level Milligan highlights the 'northern-ness' of Cúchulain's body, but she also seeks to embed this body into the transformed revivalist Cúchulain:

> Next day at sunset, erect, alone,
> Cuchulain died by a standing stone –
> Died, but fell not, with sword in hand,
> And his face to the foes of the Northern land.

The 'foes of the Northern land' in this expression of 1890s northern nationalism may now be read as doubled. The originating mythic cycle posits these foes as the armies of Connaught; Milligan's recuperation of this narrative, however, presents them as those who sought to remove Ulster from an Irish 'nationalist history'. Milligan's Cúchulain articulates the Ulster origins of a revival totem and, hence, the necessary inclusion of the North in any narrative which Irish nationalism was in the process of creating.

Looking more closely at Milligan's work, then, reveals something very different from the straightforward process of self-negation proposed above. Rather it was her Ulster origins that Milligan interrogated most fully in her work. Pádraic Colum, after visiting Milligan in Tyrone, commented with a sense of wonder that this northern Protestant woman could write 'as if there was nothing between her and Gaelic Ulster – no plantation, no John Knox, no industrial Belfast'.[40] Colum, like Foster, in some ways misread Milligan; there was something between her and Ulster's past, and that something was the revival. Milligan attempted to write a revivalised Ulster, but she also in the process managed to remind the revival that Ulster must be central to its methods and aims. Her reclamation of Ulster mythology was not simply a rewriting of Cúchulain, it was also a rewriting of the 'revivalised' Cúchulain. This complex process of negotiation and recuperation would haunt almost everything Alice Milligan did. In particular, that doubled process of invention and resistance can be seen most powerfully in action in that vital year for northern nationalism, 1898. As we will see in the next chapter, it was in this year that Milligan achieved her most radical cultural reclamation, countering an ever-strengthening Ulster-centric unionist discourse with a re-imagined northern Protestantism, a Protestantism that is read by Milligan as the origin of Irish republicanism.

Chapter Two

Belfast in 1898: Echoes from the Tomb

What should we fear
Who never lost by dying?
What should we not as,

Gunsmiths, botanists, having
Taken the measure of
Life, death, we comb our
Bright souls for
Whatever the past holds?
Derek Mahon, 'Deaths'

What matters is myth, not in the sense of fiction, but in the sense of a construction of the past elaborated by a political community for its own ends.
Robert Gildea, *The Past in French History*

The United Irishmen's rebellion of 1798 bequeathed to modern Ireland one of its most powerful, resonant and enduring political events. As Kevin Whelan writes: 'The 1790s cast a long shadow, and the names of Tone, Russell, Fitzgerald, McCracken and Emmet were to reverberate down the echo-chambers of Irish history, enjoying a resonant afterlife in the two centuries following their physical defeat.'[1] Indeed, the United Irish movement of the 1790s has been, in line with Robert Gildea's terms, perpetually reclaimed as subsequent political communities have sought in its recovered image a resolution of crisis. In many ways this process goes to the heart of commemoration's social role. Edna Longley, thinking about just this social function, discerns a doubled quality in what we seek to commemorate. On the one hand commemoration 'is a means whereby communities renew their own *religio:* literally, what ties them together, the rope around the individual sticks'. But there is also the sense that commemorations 'are as selective as sympathies. They honour *our* dead, not your dead.' Such moments, as Longley suggests, go beyond simple acts of remembering: 'commemoration, communal *religio,* does not merely remember. It reinvents and reconstitutes according to present needs.'[2] In the place of remembering, then, commemoration often offers a process of 're-membering', of putting things back together in a different way, generating new sites of meaning and reception. This chapter explores just such an act of recuperation performed by Belfast's cultural nationalists in the 1890s. While 1898 is still some years before the founding of the Ulster Literary Theatre, it is this centenary year, and Belfast's attempts to mark it, which provided the impetus and direction for the group's engagement with nationalist drama.

The Society of United Irishmen was founded in Belfast in 1791, formalising, as Marianne Elliot parses it, an alliance between Protestant patriotism, Presbyterian radicalism and the middle-class leadership of the Catholic Committee.[3] The architects of this 'watershed in Irish history' – Theobald Wolfe Tone, Thomas Russell, William Drennan and Henry Joy McCracken – retain an uncanny haunting presence in the Irish imaginary.[4] Indeed the society's philosophical base and 'direct-action' tactics have marked it out as a foundational event for modern Irish nationalism and Republicanism. As Joep Leerssen puts it, 'the legacy of 1798 in Irish historical thought is highly similar to the legacy of 1789 to Continental thought'.[5] Vital to the United Irishmen's importance in Irish nationalism's self-image has been their insistence on 'unity' (displayed in the very naming of the society), unity in terms of 'Irishmen' joined in action and in control of their future. In place of ethnic and religious division, the United Irishmen proposed a pan-religious union of purpose, with the nation superimposing itself as a shared model of communal loyalty. Wolfe Tone in these very terms provided the society with its now iconic aim: to posit 'the common name of Irishman in the place of the denominations of Protestant, Catholic and Dissenter'.[6] Over the last two centuries it is this image that has been recalled in the service of various contemporary situations. In the 1840s, for example, R.R. Madden's *The United Irishmen: Their Lives and Times* provided a key source of inspiration for the Young Ireland movement. The idea of sacrifice in the nation's cause, articulated through the rhetoric and actions of the United Irishmen (and also Robert Emmett's subsequent rebellion of 1803), would also inform much of the rhetoric of Fenian leaders such as John O'Leary later in the century. Even in the midst of Northern Ireland's most recent boundary situation – the 'Peace Process' begun in the 1990s – the image of 1798 was recalled, as Irish Taoiseach Bertie Ahern expressed the hope that the process would 'fulfil some of the ideals of the United Irishmen'.[7]

It is no surprise, then, that the first centenary of the United Irishmen in 1898 proved to be an event charged with extraordinary political energy. In the political climate left in Parnell's wake the United Irishmen's rebellion was seized as a totemic event around which the Irish nationalist project could be rethought. Throughout the 1890s (and in particular, of course, the centenary year of 1898) the *idea* of 1798 was constantly appropriated and re-articulated, with shifting nuances, by any number of competing post-Parnell cultural/political formations. Peter Collins, for example, has traced the ways in which the Catholic Church felt compelled to get involved with commemoration, despite its virulent opposition to the actual events in 1798. By inserting itself into the continuing story of 1798, the Catholic hierarchy had hoped to retrospectively detach the United Irishmen from their original secular philosophy. While constitutional nationalists, initially wary of being associated with Republican direct-action tactics, also threw their energies behind commemorative events to avoid losing popular ground to their Republican opponents. As Collins puts it, such groupings, 'while hostile to the separatist, secular, revolutionary Republicanism of the United Irishmen, got involved in commemoration due to pragmatic political necessities of their own day'.[8] While the nature of many of these necessities has been much studied, less attention has been paid to the geo-politics of this narrative. In particular, the manner in which Ulster's nationalists had to negotiate a very specific position in the drive to 'remember '98' has been somewhat overlooked.[9] As with the revivalist Cúchulain, there is a strong sense that northern nationalists felt that Ulster's importance to the United Irishmen narrative was being sidelined by many who sought to claim the 'commemorative rights' to 1898.

It must be remembered that the centenary of 1898 arrived at a very particular moment in Irish politics. Most obviously, in the years following the fall of Parnell and the subsequent split in the Irish Parliamentary Party the very idea of Irish 'unity' was fragmented, at least at the level of constitutional politics. These years witnessed an increasingly bitter feud within parliamentary politics as various factions competed for legitimacy and control. As we have seen, Yeats also argued that the problematics of a divided Parliamentary Party provided an important driving force for the emergence of cultural revival. The difficulties in defining just what was meant by Irish political unity certainly opened up a space to be filled by a newly relevant cultural energy, even if the political did not disappear in quite the way Yeats has proposed. We should now add another related emerging problem: these years are marked by the rapid development of a more vigorous geo-political dimension to Irish political life. The various directions in which the Home Rule debate had evolved radically complicated any attempt to reconfigure a unity of purpose; all shades of political thought now had to negotiate the added tensions of an ever more powerful north/south political axis. The centenary year of 1898 thus became a totemic centre around which various competing visions of Irish unity could vie for representational control. As Selina Guinness puts it:

> The 1898 commemorations might be best described as a post-Parnellite attempt at a successful double exposure in politics: the first spectacle of the United Irishmen rebellion rewound so as to superimpose seamlessly the image of an Irish nation on top.[10]

Guinness's image captures nicely the form of historical ellipse performed in the reclamation of an eighteenth-century movement in the cause of various late nineteenth-century nationalist groupings. At moments of discursive resonance the operation functions seamlessly, as Guinness would have it, 'showing no sign of the process that has created it', but inevitably there are moments when 'the trace of an image from one narrative shows through', thus creating 'a dissonance in the final picture'.[11] As we will see, the process of commemoration in 1898 contained many such dissonances as the concept of unity was reclaimed and recast by various interested parties.

At one level the planning for the centenary year was envisaged by radical figures such as Maud Gonne, Alice Milligan, James Connolly et al. as a perfect cultural weapon with which to counter the celebrations for Queen Victoria's diamond jubilee in 1897. As such, the lead-up to 1898 was seen as an opportunity to demonstrate a united Irish anti-colonial front in opposition to imperial ritual. As early as April 1897 *Shan Van Vocht* began printing a monthly collection of '98 ballads, in the hope that they would prove 'suitable for recitation at meetings of Centenary Committees'. It was also in the year of Victoria's jubilee celebrations that, as Leon O'Broin reminds us, 'Maud Gonne, dragging Yeats after her, conspired with James Connolly to prevent the illuminations of shop fronts by cutting off the electricity supply. She led marches to where United Irishmen were interred and set crowds wild with her oratory.'[12] Most famously, the main anti-jubilee march in June 1897 (organised by the Irish Socialist Republican Party) combined tributes to the United Irishmen with the carrying of a coffin marked 'British Empire' at the head of the marchers. The decision to counter the images of the jubilee commemorations with those of the United Irishmen was a classic response to a cultural moment of crisis (many in Dublin had, after all, shown enthusiasm for Victoria's celebratory visit). If the 1897 celebration of monarchy had been intended as 'a copperfastening of constructive unionism and a consolidation of Ireland's place in the Empire', countering this with the image of the United Irishmen's sacrificial deaths was a move 'brilliantly orchestrated as a separatist riposte'.[13]

As already noted, the notion of 'unity' and 'union' would also become significant tropes in post-Parnell constitutional politics. The years after Parnell had been marked with rhetoric of political disunion and disharmony. On the surface at least, the centennial year of 1898 provided both wings of a divided constitutional party with an opportunity for *rapprochement*. However, this opportunity also gave rise to some of the most overt problematising of just how such Irish unity was to be brought about: the search for representational control of the United Irishmen's legacy actually disguised covert agendas and tensions. Public and private tensions surrounding the organising committees for the commemorations reflected this search for representational control. In almost every district of the country committees were established to organise local centennial commemorations, but the make-up of these committees often proved contentious. As Peter Collins has noted, 'radicals such as James Connolly, Maud Gonne and Alice Milligan felt strongly that the constitutionalists should be excluded on the grounds that they were opposed to the ideology, aims and methods of the United Irishmen'.[14] Despite such problems, by the end of 1898 the output of these various committees resulted in more than thirty major monuments[15] to the United Irishmen.[16] It was, as Gary Owens puts its, 'the most concentrated outpouring of commemorative statuary that Ireland has ever seen'.[17]

The Dublin Executive Committee was charged with organising the centennial commemorations in the capital. John O'Leary was its chairman and delegates were drawn from all the major provincial committees. The influence of Ardrigh's most energetic journalistic talents was confirmed when Alice Milligan and Anna Johnston (Ethna Carbery) were appointed as the North's representatives. Along with Maud Gonne, they would also be the only women on the committee.[18] This grouping planned and organised the main commemorative event that took place in Dublin on 15 August 1898; its focal point was a large march which made its way to the top of Grafton Street, the proposed site for a monument dedicated to Wolfe Tone. Once the march had reached this site a rally was held and on the platform, along with John O'Leary, stood John Redmond and John Dillon, the two rival centres of power in the Irish Parliamentary Party. Their presence on the same platform was intended to present the potential for unity embodied by Wolfe Tone and company. Indeed Redmond and Dillon had repeatedly expressed their dedication to the commemorative process in just such terms, of a post-Parnell reunification.[19] John Redmond, leader of the party's Parnellites, had clearly attempted to map the United Irishmen's position onto the Home Rule issue: 'Irishmen of all shades of Nationalist opinion, divided as they are into many sections upon the politics of that day, are uniting as one man to celebrate its centenary.'[20] While John Dillon had also grasped the vision of eighteenth-century unity as a way of re-presenting late nineteenth-century problems, writing that he hoped those nationalists who had been 'unhappily separated from each other for the past eight years would in the great centenary celebrations find a common platform, would stand together'.[21] While these steps towards *rapprochement* may well have played a significant part in bringing about the 'reunification' of the Parliamentary Party in 1900, the public utterances of '98 were still papering over some serious feuding between party factions. On the one hand, the two wings of the constitutional party sought to gain a controlling influence in the commemorative process, something that at times only managed to highlight the distance between the two sides. At the same time, there was a clear tension between the parliamentary politicians and other more radical figures, who sought to keep the commemoration process separate altogether from constitutional politics. The United Irishmen's ideals had, after all, they argued, very little to do with constitutional procedure. As early as April 1897 Alice Milligan had succeeded in getting local commemorative committees to adopt a resolution prohibiting official communication 'with any organisation engaged in disseminating party politics'. Milligan's aim had been to ensure that 'Irishmen shall lay aside all existing political distinctions and meet one another in a spirit of friendship and brotherhood to honour the men of the United Irishmen'.[22]

Milligan's plea for a non-partisan celebration of the United Irishmen's legacy may be read as a political move in itself, of course. More particularly it may be read as a response to the highly partisan politics of Belfast and Ulster, thus indexing one more contested site in the search for unity – the role of the North in the commemoration of the United Irishmen. From the very beginning it was clear that Ulster politics were going to play a role in the development of the centenary. Representatives of the Orange Order in the province were quick to articulate their alienation from this part of northern

Protestant history and to call for members to stay away from any involvement. Perhaps most ironically of all: 'Presbyterians in the north . . . were now to a great extent . . . hostile to the commemorations of the exploits of many of their ancestors'.[23] Joseph Campbell, for example, recalled how the topic of 1798 was a doubly tricky one in his Belfast home-place:

> At home, there was scant mention of '98. Father, narrowed in his loyalties by Parnellite nationalism, then in a slough of disintegration, knew nothing of it. Mother, come of 'blackmouth' blood on her father's side, knew of it by family tradition, but she shunned it as a familiar topic. She would praise rebels hanged a hundred years ago, but feared revival of their intransigence in this day and age.[24]

Recovering the nationalist heritage of Ulster's involvement in the United Irishmen's rebellion was, then, an especially delicate operation. It is of note, for example, that from the beginning of the Home Rule issue in the 1880s some in Ulster had 'drawn on United Irish imagery to illustrate to the British administration the strength of their anti home rule stance'.[25] Gillian McIntosh in her study of Ulster unionist culture (*The Force of Culture*) cites an editorial from the *Northern Whig* of 5 November 1888 that aptly demonstrates this tactical use of Ulster's 1798 heritage:

> The muskets of '98 have been beaten into ploughshares and the pikes into pruning hooks, and the cursed arts of civil war have been abandoned for the blessed industries of peace . . . But, sir, reverse all this – force a Dublin parliament on Ulstermen anew, and so re-establish a more ignorant and intolerant ascendancy, and it will soon be seen that the spirit of the sires yet lives in the sons, and that Ulstermen have still in them the stuff of rebels.

Nationalists in the North knew that the idea of the United Irishmen and their relevance to the contemporary search for cultural and political independence would need radical adjustment in Ulster. Other complications were also all too apparent, most importantly the North's attempts to organise for 1898 were not immune to the more general fall-out that resulted from the death of Parnell. Joseph Devlin, an anti-Parnellite member of the Belfast '98 Committee, sought to shift control of the commemorations away from the now Redmondite-dominated Dublin Executive Committee by emphasising Belfast's history as the intellectual home of the United Irishmen.[26] In the Dillonite paper, *Freeman's Journal*, Devlin wrote a piece suggesting that the northern city had 'the right to the foremost place in honouring the glorious struggle for liberty, because in this city was founded the Society of United

Irishmen' (15 October 1897). Indeed during a meeting of the Belfast Committee Devlin opposed the very idea of a Dublin Committee having a say in how Belfast chose to commemorate 1798,[27] suggesting that he was opposed to 'any gentleman from Dublin coming down to interfere and dictate in Belfast'.[28] It was Alice Milligan who reminded him that a man coming up to Belfast from Dublin was the very thing they were commemorating.[29] In the end Devlin succeeded in gaining control of Belfast's '98 Clubs, a result which prompted Milligan and other like-minded Republicans to leave the meeting in disgust.

Alice Milligan was from the beginning suspicious of Devlin and his motivations, not least because she had been and would remain an admirer of Parnell. Milligan sought in the commemoration of the United Irishmen a different cultural pathway to that proposed by the factional in-fighting of constitutional party politics; as with her involvement in Dublin's Committee, Milligan fought hard to keep the commemorative process in Belfast away from party politics. She had been quick to spot that the split Parliamentary Party was more concerned with an 'official' Home Rule version of 'United Irishmen', one which recast 1798 as a prototype for the constitutional negotiation of the Irish question. In contrast, and in line with her more radicalised nationalist position, Milligan emphasised the centenary as an opportunity for a complete refusal of imperial power; for this kind of nationalist thinking 1798 represented a unity in terms of extra-political action rather than constitutional negotiation. More specifically, Milligan read '98 as crucial to the proper articulation of Ulster's position in the nationalist project; throughout the lead-up to the centenary she would promote the United Irishmen as a model for *territorial* unity. Time and again Milligan recast 1798 as a historical model of political co-operation that bridged north and south. Throughout this period the memory of 1798 was called upon as a warning cry from the North to be included in the nationalist push for independence. The United Irishmen provided Milligan with the perfect rebuttal (and refutation) of an Ulster unionist discourse that was gathering strength at the end of the nineteenth century. The image of Ulster Protestant radicalism in the eighteenth century also provided Milligan with a site of cultural knowledge, one which enabled her to re-present her Ulster Protestantism as the very reason for her radical nationalism, rather than a reason for her exclusion from it.

The choice of nomenclature for the 'Henry Joy McCracken Literary Society' (established 1895) was, in these terms, a very deliberate act of northern commemoration. For the Ardrigh group McCracken represented exactly the image of 1798 that they wished to present.[30] Most important in this regard was the fact that McCracken was a solidly Belfast figure, born in the town in August 1767, and his family also had a long attachment to Belfast – his father was captain and part-owner of a ship that traded between Belfast and the West Indies, while his grandfather, Frances Joy, established the *Belfast News-Letter* in 1737. Henry Joy McCracken was also hanged in Belfast, providing a useful specificity to his martyrdom. The new Literary Society's purpose was to disseminate the sort of cultural knowledge that could aid a nationalist reawakening in Belfast. Its establishment has to be read, of course, in the context of a period that witnessed the formation of many such specifically cultural-nationalist organisations. Its *raison d'être* was, in this regard, very similar to that of the Gaelic League (1893), in that it aimed to culturally sidestep and thus sideline the normative political routes for resisting colonial rule in Ireland. This sense of nationalism as a cultural project is clear in the Belfast nationalists' insistence on forming a 'Literary Society'. Linking this society to the Belfast-born United Irishman Henry Joy McCracken, however, points to an even more specific set of intentions. This is something that can be seen quite clearly in Alice Milligan's description of its establishment:

> In the month of February of the present year a few men met to take counsel with one another, each conscious of the great need that existed for a national literary educational society in their midst. Having given the matter full consideration, a unanimous decision was arrived at, and as an outcome of their endeavours, the above National Society was established in Belfast on the 9th February, 1895.[31]

A number of telling points arise out of Milligan's very deliberate presentation of the society's foundation; indeed the establishment specifically of a 'Society' already suggests some fairly clear resonances. This meeting of minds in Belfast to address an issue of national need and/or danger suggests an oblique re-creation of the meeting of United Irishmen in 1795 that decided upon direct action. The typographical emphasis placed upon the Henry Joy Society as a 'National' society also highlights Belfast as involved in a pan-Irish movement. As such, Milligan implicitly rejects the idea of the group as a provincial set-up of marginal interest and value to the wider nationalist scene. This rejection is largely performed through paralleling the Literary Society with the Society of United Irishmen, emphasising both as Belfast-based collaborations with more expansive and inclusive geo-political implications. Milligan's description of the Society's *raison d'être* continues by suggesting that the 1898 commemorations were an opportunity to pass on knowledge of Ireland's heroes and martyrs to the younger generation.[32] Her piece concludes by emphasising that 'The Henry Joy McCracken Literary Society since its foundation has endeavoured to render such a service to the national cause in Ulster.'[33] This constant shift between Ulster and pan-Irish 'National' frames of reference searches for a coherent and harmonised unity of purpose. Even in such moments as these, however, this constant shift in framing also manages to problematise an underlying north/south dialectic. The sense that the nationalist North had to struggle for its inclusion within a nationalist history manages, despite itself, to create a certain kind of discursive 'instability'. The possible nuances of this instability are of particular interest for us here, as it is this problematic that largely informs the terms upon which the Ulster Literary Theatre would be founded some years later.

Milligan reinforces this sense of shifting referents as she informs her readership that one of the first engagements carried out by the new 'Henry Joy Society' had been to arrange the Belfast delegation that went to Dublin to join in the celebrations of Wolfe Tone's birthday:

> Wolfe Tone's birthday was celebrated, and on that occasion the north joined hands with the south in honouring the memory of the most powerful organiser of insurrection in Ireland since Rory O'Moore.

Milligan's description perfectly articulates the duality at work within northern nationalism's search for a workable vision of 'unity' at this time. The notion that the 'north joined hands with the south' articulates the United Irishmen as an imaginative space around which a north/south nationalist union could be formed. However, the articulation of an acknowledged gap (across which hands were joined) also reveals a certain slippage between the eighteenth- and nineteenth-century political landscapes. The article's politicised historiography is also evident in its framing of Wolfe Tone as 'the most powerful organiser of insurrection in Ireland since Rory O'Moore'. The reference is indicative of Milligan's drive to re-articulate the United Irishmen and their actions through an Ulster framework. O'Moore was a seventeenth-century rebel of Ulster origins (his family came from Armagh) who was instrumental in the insurrection of 1641. Reading Tone through O'Moore establishes an Ulster-centric (or at least Ulster-inclusive) lineage of Irish rebellion. Milligan's insistence on 1641 as a model of nationalist 'insurrection' also has to be read in the context of an

Ulster unionist discourse that was increasingly drawing on 1641 as an exemplary moment of Irish nationalist/Catholic betrayal. Milligan's alignment of her cause with that of the leaders of 1641 as well as 1798 reveals her need to refute 'Ulster Protestantism' as a synonym for 'Ulster unionism'. In many ways, of course, this was just one more in a long line of battles for historiographical hegemony over 1798. As early as 1801 the loyalist rejection of 1798 had begun with Sir Richard Musgrave's *Memoirs of the Various Rebellions.* The main purpose of this work had been 'to present the Irish Loyalist case to an English audience' and in so doing 'made the link between 1641, 1690 and 1798, portraying each as a successive phase in the Catholic campaign to overthrow Protestant hegemony in Ireland'.[34] Read in this context, Milligan's insistence on an Ulster-centric genealogy of modern Irish nationalism becomes a powerful call both for a nationalist inclusivity and a rejection of the Ulster unionist version of history.

We can see this again in the front cover of the *Northern Patriot*'s first number (October 1895), which is dominated by a signature poem that functioned as a form of manifesto for the paper. 'The Northern Patriot' is an example of textual mapping which is at once a cry for northern inclusion and a detailed mapping out of the (literal and metaphorical) space within which this inclusion may be read as natural and, indeed, essential. The poem's opening verses clearly set out to simultaneously 'describe' the North as the historical 'stronghold' of United Irishmen values, while also visualising the contemporary city of Belfast as essentially the same space that nurtured them in the 1790s.

> Here in the stronghold of the North,
> In brave M'Cracken's native town;
> We, who have known the patriot's worth,
> Would wake the news of his renown.
>
> The hill-top where his life was vowed,
> Stands fair against our northern sky,
> And daily do the heedless crowd
> Pass where unmarked his ashes lie.
> Up from the very street they tread,
> The martyr mounted to his fate,
> On steps that to the scaffold led,
> One summer eve of ninety-eight.

The description of the physical terrain of Belfast is matched by a constant shift in tense, from past to present and back again – 'The hill-top where his life was vowed / Stands fair against our northern sky'; 'Up from the very street they tread, / The martyr mounted to his fate'. The effect created is one of a temporal ellipse matched to physical stability. The Belfast streets walked by McCracken are the same as those occupied by its 1890s citizens; the Cave Hill (hill-top) upon which he vowed his life is the same that looks down upon the citizens of Belfast who read the *Northern Patriot.* The fact that the steps taken by McCracken here recounted were his last as he approached the gallows on which he was hanged for treason further inscribes these Belfast streets as a sacred space and 'keeper' of a sacred lineage of nationalist deaths. The highlighting of 'The hill-top where his life was vowed' also reinforces Cave Hill as the most important place within the United Irishmen's legacy, its articulation as sacred further adumbrating Belfast as vital to the process of nationalism's evolution.

The final two verses, indeed, openly speak of rediscovering in the past a model for contemporary actions. The final lines reveal the North as a still functioning nationalist space where the United Irishmen's ideals may still find a home:

> We speak from records of the past,
> Of all who fought, of all who fell;
> Of Ireland's martyrs, not the last–
> We have more cheering news to tell:
>
> For in this city, 'neath that peak,
> Where Ireland's sons in union met;
> Our aim shall be the hopes to speak
> Of Northern patriots toiling yet.

By now it is clear that the concept of 'union', in 'Where Ireland's sons in union met', is as much concerned with north/south geopolitics in the 1890s as it is with the religious and philosophical unity of late eighteenth-century Ireland. The specific image of 'Northern patriots toiling yet' links the nationalist project with a call for territorial inclusion. It also, of course, establishes those nationalists in the North as involved in the same (ongoing) project as the United Irishmen. This sense of a northern nationalism 'writing back' to and against the image of Ulster as a purely unionist space would recur in many of the *Northern Patriot*'s and, indeed, *Shan Van Vocht*'s pages. In the *Northern Patriot* of April 1896, for example, we find the poem 'The Northern Men', which resists the notion of Ulster as not fully committed to, or part of, the nationalist project:

And now, when Ascendancy closed its foul reign,
And the notes of the Angelus peal o'er the plain.
Shall we suffer disunion to raise its vile head
In the long-suffering land where our fore-fathers bled?
Oh, no, 'neath the old flag united we'll stand,
In a peaceful endeavour to lift up our land
To her long vacant place 'mid the nations again,
Nor look with distrust on the Northern Men.

The poem's rebuke – 'Shall we suffer disunion to raise its vile head / In the long-suffering land where our fore-fathers bled? – when read in terms of the clearly framed northern point of view, exemplifies the translation of meaning inherent in the remapped concept of 'unity'.

Northern nationalism's refutation of Ulster as a location of 'distrust' and, indeed, as the clearest point of nationalist schism is perhaps best seen in an article published by Alice Milligan in the 1895 Christmas edition of the Dublin newspaper, *Weekly Independent.* The article is entitled 'The North is Up!' and re-narrates the Belfast origins of the United Irishmen. Milligan's very deliberate title is telling in just these terms. In 1895 she had started writing a regular column for the *Weekly Independent* entitled 'Notes from the North'. Milligan's intention in the column was clear from the start: she felt her Dublin readership needed to be reminded of nationalist activities in the North. The title of the Christmas entry ('The North is Up!') perfectly announces Milligan's motives: it is at once a cry of burgeoning success (northern nationalism on the march), while also striking a note of chastisement – Milligan reminding her Dublin readership quite literally where they will find the nationalist North. Once again these dual issues of a strong northern nationalism matched with a call for territorial unity are resolved in a return to 1790s Belfast. The implications are clear: an acknowledgement of the historical importance of the North would have to lead to some reconsideration of its position in the contemporary political landscape. Milligan's retelling of the reputed day in 1795 when the United Irishmen resolved on direct action begins by highlighting the Belfast connections of many in the party.

> The Belfast men present were Robert Simms, a merchant of wealth and position; Samuel Neilson, editor of the 'Northern Star' paper; Henry Joy M'Cracken, a young linen merchant from Falls road.[35]

The meeting thus posited within a very specifically northern terrain is further described as a foundational moment of modern nationalism, with

Milligan arguing the case that: 'The nationalists of Ireland from generation to generation since historic '98 have been true to the principles of Wolfe Tone.' Nationalism is read through Tone, but Tone's deeds are firmly embedded within an Ulster frame of reference. In this way Milligan requires her Dublin readership to approach Wolfe Tone via Belfast and the North. Just as importantly, she further embeds her northern framework within a reading of the role of Protestantism in the nationalist cause:

> When Ireland is free that bond between Protestant and Catholic will be held as sacred. It has been sealed with the blood of the Protestant leaders and peasants who died heroically on scaffold and battle field in '98 side by side with their Catholic United Brethren. Since then the names of Emmet, Davis, Mitchel, Parnell are sureties for the fact that the cause of Ireland is no longer merely the Catholic cause; but is identified with the highest ideal of Nationhood, which implies liberty and justice for Irishmen of every creed and station.

The description performs a perfectly executed 'double-exposure'. The 'blood of the Protestant leaders and peasants who died heroically on scaffold and battle field in '98' places the Protestant community at the very heart of nationalism's development. This point is confirmed by a genealogy that highlights the leading hand taken by Protestant thinkers in the national cause: 'Emmet, Davis, Mitchel, Parnell'. It is a narrative that allows Milligan to resist a presentation of the Home Rule issue as a contest between Ulster Protestant unionism versus the rest of Ireland's Catholic nationalists.

Throughout the article Milligan seeks to recover an image of Belfast as a place historically vital to ideas of Irish unity and thus a properly inclusive Irish identity. In all of this Milligan was, of course, attempting to fix in history something that was in fact increasingly difficult to counter; her insistence upon a radical nationalist Belfast of the past served to highlight just how different the city was at the end of the nineteenth century. She describes, for example, how after the meeting was completed (one that committed the men to the actions that would culminate in 1798) the men left this now 'holy' place:

> They rose and went down to Belfast. The old fort on the mountain top with its pile of boulders was henceforth one of the most sacred spots on Irish soil. It was an altar of self-sacrifice; for of the men who took that solemn pledge three were to redeem it by death for Ireland's sake.

With Cave Hill thus presented, Milligan requires her Dublin readers to approach Belfast as a place integral to what any future nation holds to be sacred. It is an image that Milligan would continually return to; in her biography of Tone (published three years later) she writes again about Cave Hill in just such terms: 'In the eyes of all patriots it is sacred ground, to be looked on reverently as an altar.'[36]

Her Christmas article concludes, indeed, with a final description of the link between Henry Joy McCracken and Belfast that further develops this idea of sacrificial (and thus sacred) ground. The link provides one more radical expression of Belfast as a nexus for modern Irish nationalism's sense of identity, origin and territorial aims. It also draws on an image that has remained central to the expression of nationalism in the twentieth century: the cenotaph. Benedict Anderson has suggested that: 'No more arresting emblems of the modern culture of nationalism exist than cenotaphs and tombs of Unknown Soldiers.' He draws further on this idea, reframing the key paradox of modern nationalism in terms of a parallel paradox regarding the nature of the cenotaph: 'Yet void as these tombs are of identifiable mortal remains or immortal souls, they are nonetheless saturated with ghostly *national* imaginings.'[37] Anderson's case is that the cenotaph describes a national sacred space that is at once empty and yet overfull (saturated), which in turn identifies an anterior move made by a nationalism still in search of its actual nation. The physical reality of the cenotaph is pre-dated by a more abstract search for a sacred national space. It is here that Milligan's concluding remarks may find some resonance. In rounding off her discussion of McCracken's importance to Belfast and the United Irishmen, Milligan provides an image of a proto-cenotaph. Indeed her description attempts to present the entire city of Belfast as a cenotaph-like space for the imagined nation:

> In the town of Henry Joy McCracken's birth there is not a space of ground consecrated to his rest. There is no monument to his memory, nor any of the United Irishmen whose work commenced in Belfast. No such monument is needed whilst we have for ever before our eyes the majestic outlines of the hill sacred to the memory of a vow taken on its summit by three men who died for Ireland – Wolfe Tone, Thomas Russell, Henry Joy McCracken. The mountain is their monument. Look up at it in the evening when the white stars are coming out over its brow, and it lies outlined against the clear, cold northern heaven, like an effigy of some slain warrior carven in the darkest purple marble.
>
> Over the tombs of knights and kings in stately cathedrals of England and the Continent their effigies recline under pointed arch or golden dome.

> There is not among them all an image so great, and calm, and beautiful as this, and the roof over it is the ever-changing heaven with light of sun and stars, passing of clouds and mists, arching of rainbows, quivering of lightnings.

The whole of Belfast thus becomes sacred ground, the sort of place around which the future nation would have to be built. Milligan's image of an abstract cenotaph is a radical attempt to write the North into the very fabric of what Irish nationalism proposed itself to be.

In the years between 1895 and 1898, moreover, much of the cultural production of the Ardrigh group was dedicated to the commemoration process; the pages of the *Northern Patriot* and *Shan Van Vocht* were occupied with little else. F.J. Bigger's own project, the *Ulster Journal of Archaeology*, also gave much of its space over to various accounts of '98. It serialised extracts from books printed in Belfast around this time such as W.S. Smith's *Memories of '98,* and *Ulster Biographies – Relating Chiefly to the Rebellion of 1798* by W.T. Latimer. By the time of the centenary year itself, Alice Milligan was determined to take advantage of this interest in the late eighteenth century. Her editorial for the January 1898 number of *Shan Van Vocht* illustrates just how important the centennial commemorations of that year had become to the city's cultural nationalists:

> If the Centenary of '98 should pass by and leave us still engaged in internecine warfare, then we will have given proof that we are slaves indeed. It will have been in vain that the heroes of '98 offered themselves as a sacrifice on the alter of their country; it will have been in vain that others of our brethren suffered exile or imprisonment, and the bitter agony of a breaking heart, if we are blind to the necessity that should bring us together in the bonds of brotherly union to do honour to the memory of THE DEAD WHO DIED FOR IRELAND.[38]

The idea of 'brotherly union' has by now been radically transformed by a northern nationalist fear of exclusion (or, at least, of occlusion from power).

In 1898 Milligan also published her *Life of Theobald Wolfe Tone;* her introduction makes it clear that she was only too aware of how important the 'Ulster card' had become to the Home Rule issue. The idea of division has become for Milligan a multivalent signifier; it certainly indexes a pan-Ireland religious divide, but also points to the contemporary development of a north/south schism that was increasingly being deployed by those who sought to resist Home Rule:

> England has again and again cunningly tried to introduce the dividing lines of sectarianism, and to entangle Irish Nationalism on one side or the other. She

is doing so in this very year, but we have faith in the spirit of Young Ireland, which is turning its face towards the graves of '98. The memories which will be awakened will save us from falling a prey to England's insidious policy, well summed up in the *dictum* – 'Divide and Conquer'.[39]

In response to this emerging discourse of Ulster as historically 'other' deployed by Ulster unionism, Milligan proposes a radically different historical lineage. Milligan's biography of Wolfe Tone once again provides a historical narrative that overtly reads a nationalist lineage through Ulster:

> The penal code did not spare the staunch Presbyterians of Ulster. The very men who had fought on Derry Walls for civil and religious liberty found all too late that they had been fastening shackles to their own limbs. In the early part of the 18th century there was an exodus of the Presbyterians of Ulster to the land of promise beyond the Atlantic, and in the War of Independence, which transformed the America Colonies into a free Republic, these Irish exiles helped to avenge the wrongs of that Ulster Colony from which England's bigotry had driven them.
>
> The spirit of revolt awoke in the hearts of the Presbyterians who remained behind. In 1782 an Ulster Presbyterian Church was the scene of that armed gathering of the Volunteers, which dismayed England into recognising the independence of the Irish Parliament. They linked with the cause of Catholic Emancipation and Irish Independence the principles of complete religious toleration, and no Irish National movement has since that time retreated an inch from the lines marked down in '98.[40]

This introductory narrative is filled with moments of conflation, inversion and anachronism; all of which manage to locate the men of 1798 as essentially motivated by the same ideals as those that held on to Derry a hundred years previously. To be loyal to the memory of the Siege of Derry, Milligan here argues, is to be loyal to the memory of the United Irishmen, and hence to be loyal to Irish nationalism. The Siege of Derry thus reframed becomes a moment of proto-Irish nationalism. Milligan's historical logic provides a cyclical narrative that leaves no room for an Ulster unionist identity; in these terms Ulster unionism becomes an 'impossible' identity (or at least an 'illogical' one). To be Ulster Protestant, Milligan's argument runs, is to be an Irish nationalist.

1898 would in the end turn out to be an important turning point in the development of Ireland's nationalist cause in the early years of the twentieth century. Just two years later a report by Ireland's Inspector General (October 1900) would refer to:

> the very serious wave of sedition which has spread over the country, and which found expression openly in many cases in election speeches last month. This seditious feeling was originally inflamed by the '98 demonstrations two years ago; which, though they had no practical result at the time, undoubtedly revived the old feeling of animosity to England, and awakened anew the sentiment of Irish independent nationality.[41]

More specifically, 1898 marked a pivotal year in the development of northern nationalism's sense of self. It is the year that forced nationalists in the North to closely examine their relationship to the historical narrative and mythology that informed late nineteenth-century Irish nationalism. In the end 1898, and in particular the Ardrigh group's efforts at commemoration, was also to be the foundational experience that shaped the subsequent emergence of the Ulster Literary Theatre.

CHAPTER THREE

'Damn Yeats, We'll Write Our Own Plays!' The Beginnings of the Ulster Literary Theatre

History is not so much fact as performance.
Greg Dening

If the political effects of the activities in 1898 would take some time to percolate through to the realm of officialdom, the organisational energies that accompanied the commemorations provided a much more immediate impetus and cultural focus for many of those involved. Most notably, perhaps, the cultural momentum created by the centenary would carry through to the next year with the establishment of the Irish Literary Theatre. Indeed the move towards the possibilities held by drama and the theatre is wholly understandable in terms of the forces that had shaped the drive to 'remember '98'. Many of the events planned for the centennial, as well as those that came in its immediate aftermath, were driven by the desire to explore a key cultural force: identity as performance. Writing just a few years later in the first issue of *Samhain,* Yeats would sum up exactly this sense of a latent performative need:

> I may say . . . that we have turned a great deal of Irish imagination towards the stage. We could not have done this if our movement had not opened a way of expression for an impulse that was in the people themselves. The truth is that the Irish people are at that precise stage of their history when imagination, shaped by many stirring events, desires dramatic expression. (pp. 3–4)

Looking back at the tactics of commemoration with this Yeatsian eye, it is clear that many of the activities drew on the need to make nation a shared experience. Yeats's point was that the idea of nation as 'performable' space was crucial in any such proposed re-articulation of this sense of communality. Thus the centennial marches, the proliferation of statuary, the anti-jubilee rallies, as well as more oblique political gestures such as Maud Gonne's massive children's 'picnic in the park', all shared a sense of a spatial performance reinhabiting an Irish national territory.[1] Even the normally stand-offish Yeats had been drawn into what we might think of as 'street theatre'. As noted above, inspired and provoked by figures like John O'Leary and Maud Gonne, Yeats took part in the anti-jubilee march of June 1897. He was also, of course, a leading organiser of the main 1898 march through Dublin to lay the foundation stone for Tone's memorial. All of these activities are linked by a common purpose; as P.J. Mathews puts it: 'If the British authorities were beginning to use street theatre to harness popular sentiment, nationalists were quickly learning how to use such methods to oppose these manifestations.'[2]

So it is in the wake of 1898 that we see a number of important revivalist figures either consolidating their interest in the possibilities of theatre or, as in the case of Lady Gregory, discovering an interest in this mode of cultural activism. By this time, however, they were intent on resituating the potential of performance from the street stage to the more orthodox environs of the theatre itself. As is often remarked, it was Yeats's hope (as it had been Victor Hugo's) that, in the theatre, the mob would become a people. The theatre was to be the place, in other words, where the masses could be shaped into something more focused and 'definable' (and more controllable too of course). It was with just such thoughts in mind that in 1899 Lady Gregory, W.B. Yeats and Edward Martyn (joined a little later by George Moore) established the Irish Literary Theatre and began the search for 'a theatre of their own'. In the years ahead the nature of this search and the question of ownership would be highly contested issues. What is notable about this venture (in its first incarnation) is its generally co-operative and open character. New Irish plays made it to the stage during this period only because the group could draw on the co-operative spirit inherent to the idea of a shared amateur society. In the absence of a strict hierarchy, the Irish Literary Theatre's performances evolved by drawing on a wide pool of talent. This was a pool that included, for example, Alice Milligan's experience of staging nationalist sketches, as well as Maud Gonne's eye for the wider possibilities of a nationalist theatre. In the years to come, however, the nature of this co-operative society would change, in ways that would in effect end it as a viable possibility. In particular the issue of 'ownership' (read here as a conflict between élitism and a more inclusive democratic model) would inform much of the later interaction between the Dublin group and other regional projects such as the Ulster Literary Theatre. At the heart of these relations stood a number of very important questions: just what did a national theatre for Ireland mean, what form should it take and 'where' should it be? Related to these issues were the more expansively political questions: what kind of Ireland did such a theatre seek to represent, on whose terms should such an Ireland be presented and/or invented?

Rather usefully, the history of the divergent models for Ireland's 'national theatre' can be read pretty directly in the various stages of the Irish Literary Theatre's development and its subsequent reincarnations. While the Irish Literary Theatre would only last for a couple of years, from its embers arose the 'Irish National Theatre Society' in 1902, a company with a more expansive set of ambitions. Indeed the new nomenclature revealed the reformed company's ambitions quite clearly: here was a theatre proposing itself as the 'National' stage for the nation-in-waiting. With this move it was now clear that Dublin had a company with a quite startling horizon of ambition. However, this newly confident range of ambition, and the best way to attain its related goals, had already begun to reveal points of tension within the company's make-up. Many in the group, including one of the original founders, Edward Martyn, began to question the direction proposed by Yeats and Gregory – reading their motives as overly hegemonic and élitist. These tensions would come to a head when the company was reconfigured once again in 1905. This was a reorganisation that resulted in the 'National Theatre Society, Ltd.', the company more usually known by its home-place (since 1904), the Abbey. The move to limited company status effectively meant abandoning all pretensions of a co-operative amateur society, an ideal that had been close to the heart of many of the original participants in the venture.

This is now a well-known story; after all, the Abbey's formative history must be one of the best documented in the literary world and thus needs no extensive rehearsal here. That said, there is a strong case to be made that these developments had a number of repercussions that impacted, either directly or more obliquely, on the actions and opinions of those outside Dublin who also sought to use the theatre as a nationalist forum. For this reason, it is worth briefly paying closer attention to that final move towards limited company status by the company that had just taken up residence at the Abbey. The subtle alteration of the company's name, as well as the more significant technical modification in its administrative structure, revealed (and instantiated) a site of tension in terms of representation and control. It was a move that stood as a final rejection of a specific earlier conceptualisation of 'national theatre'. The transformation from an essentially co-operative (and democratic) theatre society, with much of the amateur spirit about it, into a more professional company was engineered largely by its leading figures, Yeats and Gregory, who became directors (and effective controllers) of the newly shaped enterprise.[3] Thus the power-brokers of Ireland's 'national theatre' moved away from a sense of this performative space as a collaborative and/or federalist project. Such a translation in the structures of representational control was clearly important; how we read its ultimate significance, however, depends largely on our interpretative strategies. Most straightforwardly, this move may be read (as Yeats undoubtedly would have wished) as the protection of an aesthetic purity from the sullying waters of profane needs (the politics of 'filthy' modernity). Or this gathering of creative control may be interpreted as a ruling élite manoeuvering into a position of survival via an altered state of power.[4] Either way, the end result was a much more highly controlled and hierarchical performative space; it was a space that left little room for the earlier 'broad-church' system of collaboration and exchange.

This is not merely a retrospective interpretation; at the time this re-ordering of the 'National Theatre' (as it proposed itself) gave out a clear signal that could not be ignored. For many, including Arthur Griffith, the perceived 'take-over' simply confirmed what they had long been thinking – that any theatre overseen by the likes of Yeats and Gregory would end up as the preserve of a bourgeois 'un-Irish' (or non-native) philosophy. Griffith perceived this new formation as Yeats's way of removing the theatre from its original direct contact with nationalist politics proper. As early as 1903 he had begun to withdraw his earlier support (which had been demonstrated in his reaction to plays such as *Cathleen Ní Houlihán*), distrusting the rationale for the 'non-political' national theatre that Yeats had begun to present in tandem with the new organisation:

> Mr. Yeats does not give any reason why if the Irish National Theatre has now no propaganda save that of good art it should continue to call itself either Irish or National. If the Theatre be solely an Art Theatre, then its plays can only be fairly criticised from that standpoint of Art. But whilst it calls itself Irish National its productions must be considered and criticised as Irish National productions. This is surely obvious.[5]

Griffith's criticism came, of course, in the context of a wider set of misgivings regarding the newly envisaged national theatre project, misgivings that had already caused (and would go on to cause even more) internal strife, as well as external rejection and opposition. Griffith's call for a more thoroughgoing 'Irish National' theatre would find responses from a number of different sources. As Mary Trotter has put it, those involved in what would become the Abbey 'claimed the laurel of Ireland's representative national house too soon'.[6]

Taking this kind of assertion as its starting point, much recent scholarship has sought to recover the various responses to (and rejections of) a Yeatsian dramaturgical philosophy. Most notably, the Players Club (established 1903), the Cork Dramatic Society (1908) and the Theatre of Ireland (1906) have undergone (to a greater or lesser extent) reconsideration in recent years.[7] The very names chosen by these groups (one insisting on the status of a collaborative 'club', one on regional specificity and the other suggesting a more inclusive national agenda) are indicative of the sorts of responses that greeted the turn to hierarchical professionalism at the Abbey. The nomenclature 'Theatre of Ireland' in particular highlights that group's desire to fill a position that as they saw it remained vacant. This immediate (Dublin-based) challenge to the newly 'Limited' National Theatre Society's position as 'Ireland's' theatrical space was instigated by a number of the original members of the Irish National Theatre Society (Edward Martyn, James H. Cousins, Constance Markiewicz, etc.). It was these not insignificant figures who had most strongly resisted the more centralised, less collaborative, style heralded by the move from 'society' to 'limited company' and broke away in order to search out different modes of theatrical possibility. This new company would go on to be *one* of the Abbey's strongest rivals in the years ahead. It would reject both the Abbey's organisational structure and its perceived emphasis on a ruralist canon. Indeed, one of its best-known playwrights, Fred Ryan, would later make the case that the Abbey's rural plays had 'little or no relation to the life of the country as a whole'.[8]

Ryan's comment, which opens up a space more fully occupied later by the likes of O'Casey and Denis Johnston, is particularly interesting in terms of the Ulster Literary Theatre. It highlights how the Theatre of Ireland perceived itself as playing those parts of a potential Irish canon left unexplored by the work at the early Abbey. In place of the homogeneity of an 'Abbey aesthetic', Ryan points to a much more complex web of relations, gaps and silences. Any recovery of these tensions, ambivalences and ambiguities reveals, as Trotter puts it, 'the influences all the theatres had on one another as they competed for nationalist audiences'.[9] The fact, then, that the Theatre of Ireland in effect 'poached' a number of its key creative talents from the Ulster Literary Theatre is an interesting one. Fred and Jack Morrow were central to the creative vision of the Ulster Literary Theatre (in terms of direction, design and production) and they would quickly establish themselves as equally important figures for the Theatre of Ireland (while retaining their links with the ULT). Such an exchange of talent and expertise points to a network of theatrical experimentation searching out the parts of the canon left 'un-played' by the developing Abbey coterie. While the work of these other alternative companies has received a good deal of attention recently, it seems the Ulster Literary Theatre occupies an unstable position in our ongoing recovery of this cultural and political moment. It is interesting to note, then, that Ryan's implied search for an alternative or supplementary canon goes to the heart of what the Ulster Literary Theatre was all about. Drawing on the cultural and political landscape sketched out in the previous chapters, we can now begin to re-place the Ulster Literary Theatre, and its search for a counter or supplementary canon, into the cultural landscape of the period. This kind of recuperation also reveals how the Ulster Literary Theatre's project was intricately bound up with the singular boundary situation experienced by the North in these years.

To begin the story of the Ulster Literary Theatre one must move back from 1904 (just as any history of the Abbey cannot properly start with that year either). The two key figures in the development of the Ulster Literary Theatre were Bulmer Hobson and David Parkhill, and their mission to create a nationalist theatre for Ulster began some years before its official establishment in 1904. For Hobson, in particular, the Belfast attempts to mark 1898 would remain with him as a critical cultural and political influence. Hobson came from a Belfast Quaker family; after conversion to the nationalist cause (informed by his dissenter inheritance) he would go on to be a leading figure in much of the political reorganisation of Ireland in the first decades of the twentieth century. He was to play an important role in the evolution of Sinn Féin, for example, and was on the council responsible for planning the Easter Rising (although he would withdraw support for the action some time before the actual events).[10] Unfortunately not that much is known of David Parkhill, beyond his involvement in establishing the Ulster Literary Theatre, and that he trained as an architect. In the first few years of the company's existence he contributed a number of successful plays (under his pseudonym Lewis Purcell), but sometime around 1908 he emigrated to

Australia. Not much is known of him after this time, beyond that another of his plays (*Cobber Go Halves*) was performed by the group in 1931. The reviews of his early Ulster Literary Theatre plays suggest, however, that Parkhill was for a time considered to be one of the group's most important creative influences.

What is clear is that both men had observed with keen interest as the idea of an independently minded Irish drama had taken 'centre stage' in the minds of those intent on national renewal. Most obviously the Belfast pair had taken note of the Irish Literary Theatre's first season in 1899, but they would have been aware too of other nationalist organisations' attempts to play out nationalist possibilities on stage. Bulmer Hobson had become a close friend of Alice Milligan and she had introduced him to many of those that gathered at Ardrigh. Hobson would have been well aware of Milligan and Carbery's involvement with Maud Gonne's Inghinidhe na hÉireann (Carbery was for a time vice-president). As noted above, Milligan in particular was a strong creative influence in Maud Gonne's attempts to stage nationalist *tableaux vivants* at various cultural festivals. In this same period Milligan was also involved with the Gaelic League's dramatic offerings and, of course, she would contribute a play (*The Last Feast of the Fianna*) to the Irish Literary Theatre's second season in 1900. It is just these networks of influence and contact that Mary Trotter refers to with her assertion that 'Yeats learned from Alice Milligan of the Gaelic League as well as from Antoine of the Théâtre Libre'.[11] But it was not just in Dublin that lessons were drawn from Milligan; her influence was if anything more powerful in her home-town. Indeed using the theatre for cultural exploration and experimentation seemed a particularly interesting possibility in Belfast. Here was an opportunity for Ulster's nationalists to represent themselves *directly* to their fellow men and women in the North, as well as to broader nationalist opinion in Ireland.

It was with just such an idea in mind that Hobson and Parkhill decided on a course of action in 1902: they would establish an Ulster 'sister-branch' to Dublin's Irish Literary Theatre. The reasoning for such a move is quite clear: an Ulster branch to the new 'national theatre' would allow for the performance of a specifically northern perspective within the broad church of Irish nationalism. Such an intention directly harks back to 1898 and the commemorative drive in Belfast around those years. In this regard we may view Hobson and Parkhill as 'second wave' cultural nationalists, whose project was deeply indebted to the slightly more established group that had taken shape within the precincts of F.J. Bigger's 'Ardrigh'. Indeed, Bigger's cultural contribution and patronage was later acknowledged by the Ulster

Literary Theatre, which installed him as its first president. Bulmer Hobson, moreover, acknowledged that it was the work of Alice Milligan and her fellow nationalists from Ardrigh that directly influenced his cultural and political mindset. He recalls how it was through Milligan that he first became interested in cultural renewal:

> As soon as I was old enough to take a serious interest in books, Alice Milligan, the poetess, loaned me several books by Standish O'Grady: *The Coming of Cúchulain, In the Gates of the North, Early Bardic Literature of Ireland,* and *Finn and his Companions,* which opened up for me new ranges of hitherto unimagined beauty. My world of the imagination became peopled with the heroic figures of a great literature. Balor and Lugh and The Sons of Tuireann, Mananan and the De Danaan gods, Fergus MacRoy, Cuchulain and Ferdia became my constant companions and were to me far more real than the crude town in which I lived.[12]

Beyond this first introduction to the mythography of a nascent revival, Milligan was to remain a strong influence on Hobson as he grew up. In the years before the Ulster Literary Theatre it was Milligan's journalistic career in particular that provided a constant source of material and intellectual provocation for the young Hobson. As a boy Hobson attended the Friends' School in Lisburn, but he recalls how his interest in the new cultural movements had already begun to mark him out as different from his fellow pupils. Once again Hobson recalls it was to Milligan that he turned:

> While still a pupil at the Friends' School at Lisburn I learned that Alice Milligan and Ethna Carbery were about to start a monthly paper in Belfast. After a stiff struggle with the teacher, an Englishman, who controlled our pocket-money, I became a subscriber to the *Shan Van Vocht.* It caused quite a flutter in the school and definitely marked me as an eccentric. I was not perturbed and in the *Shan* I came for the first time in touch with the new forces that were beginning to stir in Ireland.[13]

The *Shan Van Vocht* thus provided Hobson with his early model of cultural nationalism. Indeed Hobson's subsequent career appears shadowed by many of the concerns and issues disseminated by his earlier reading. Like Milligan, Hobson's writing was marked by a search for a language and a form that would cease to mark northern nationalism out as 'eccentric'. Throughout his memoirs, *Ireland: Yesterday and Tomorrow,* Hobson highlights the centenary celebrations of 1898, which he learnt of through the pages of the *Shan Van Vocht,* as pivotal in his evolution from non-political Quaker to committed Republican.

> While I was still at school the centenary of the insurrection of 1798 occurred. A new fire was kindled when I learned about Tone and Russell and the Society of United Irishmen, and their activities in my native town. Their noble aim and courage and devotion to the cause of Irish freedom were an inspiration.[14]

It was the conflation of these influences that propelled Hobson on the journey that led him to form the Ulster Literary Theatre, as an organ of northern cultural nationalism. As Hobson would have it: 'Standish O'Grady had given my mind a very definite bias in a pro-Irish direction, and the teaching and example of Tone and the United Irishmen charted my future course. So I left school in 1899, a disciple of Wolfe Tone . . .'[15] The crucial point here is that Hobson came to be 'a disciple of Wolfe Tone' through the process of re-articulation that had shaped the northern commemorations of 1898. The fact that the Belfast commemorations were so central to his nationalist conversion suggests that Hobson's version of nationalism, out of which the Ulster Literary Theatre was born, was from the very beginning informed by the problematic of the North and its place in the wider project. As we will see below, the issue of the Ulster Literary Theatre's 'peripheral' status in relation to the Abbey's claim for cultural hegemony may be read as a continuing reflection of the problems of power and control demonstrated throughout 1898. A certain kind of 'meta-representation' was, in other words, largely inescapable for the fledgling northern theatre company.

Tracing Bulmer Hobson's involvement with various other cultural and political endeavours reveals the manner in which his work was haunted by just this 'meta-nationalist' positioning. From his earliest adult years Hobson was involved with Cumann na nGaedheal and in 1904 he would join Denis McCullough's revitalised Irish Republican Brotherhood. In 1905, along with McCullough, Hobson founded the Dungannon Club and a year later he began his short-lived Belfast-based newspaper, *Republic*.[16] The Dungannon Club in particular was very much an extension of the 1898 centenary; it self-consciously drew inspiration from the eighteenth century and based itself upon the non-sectarian model of the Irish Volunteers founded in the 1780s. The nomenclature at work here is again interesting: the Volunteers were founded in a small church in Dungannon and the reclamation of this heritage was clearly designed to establish a nationalist genealogy. In the year in which the Ulster Unionist Council was officially established (1905), McCullough and Hobson's new politico-cultural organisation was intended to highlight Ulster as the keeper of a nationalist tradition (and not simply the place of most radical unionism). The Ulster Unionist Council had been established in direct response to the 'devolution crisis' of 1904/5, when Balfour's unionist government was suspected, as Patrick Buckland would have it, 'of fostering a policy of home rule by instalments'.[17] The Dungannon Club was founded to articulate a counter-Ulster position: it advocated a policy of abstention from the British parliament and was amalgamated with Cumann na nGaedhael in 1907 to form the Sinn Finn League. This in turn was merged with Arthur Griffith's National Council to form Sinn Féin. Hobson in these years also made rapid progress within the Irish Republican Brotherhood's hierarchy and was granted a seat on its supreme council. It was this progress that meant he was on the council that began planning for the Easter Rising.

Before his involvement with McCullough's IRB and the foundation of the Dungannon Club, however, Hobson had first directed his energies into the foundation of the Ulster Literary Theatre. Indeed Hobson viewed the Dungannon Club as the logical extension of his work with the theatre: 'now that the Ulster Literary Theatre was firmly established, I turned to the work of organising Ulster for the new policy. Denis McCullough and I decided to start a new organisation which would have a better chance than the National Council to make progress in the peculiar and difficult conditions in Ulster.'[18] Hobson's narrative emphasises the specific political environs of the North; 'the peculiar and difficult conditions in Ulster' refers, of course, to the hegemonic position that Ulster unionism quickly occupied in the wake of the various Home Rule crises. Hobson also positions the Dungannon Club as a political extension of the cultural motivations that underpinned the Ulster Literary Theatre. This remarkable lineage, then, locates the Ulster Literary Theatre as a significant fulcrum in the development of northern nationalism's response to the conflicting moments of crisis simultaneously occupying the North.

It is particularly apt, then, that the idea for the Ulster Literary Theatre began to take shape in the immediate wake of 1898. In 1901, just two years after leaving school, Hobson (along with David Parkhill and William McDonald)[19] established the 'Protestant National Association', a small grouping that, as Hobson put it, aimed to spread 'the ideas and principles of Wolfe Tone and the United Irishmen'.[20] The Protestant National Association was Hobson's attempt to continue with the work begun in 1898, but it was also born out of the lessons learned by Ulster's nationalists in the centenary year. The very name – Protestant National Association – recreates, indeed, many of the political intentions that had marked out Belfast's commemorative moves. The insistence upon a Protestant group based in

Belfast to celebrate the nationalist legacy of the United Irishmen obviously sought to resist the unionist hegemony at work within the North's Protestant community. It is the nature of this early twentieth-century need that necessitated a dissonant translation of the United Irishmen once again. Wolfe Tone's non-sectarian politics are here translated onto a religion-specific grouping, albeit (and paradoxically) in an attempt to denounce the polarisation of sectarian politics accompanying the Home Rule question in Ulster. This grouping was to become the genesis of the later theatre company. On Hobson's own admission, the group 'met with little noticeable success', and hence its organisers 'decided to try the drama as a vehicle of propaganda'.[21] This move, and the aims of the new drama company which arose from it, are outlined more thoroughly by Hobson in the following terms:

> The Protestant National Association had a brief and unimportant life, but brought together a group which subsequently formed the Ulster Literary Theatre, a body which exercised some influence on the cultural development of the North of Ireland. It was started by David Parkhill and myself, with the intention of writing and producing distinctively Ulster plays, which would be a commentary on the political and social conditions in the North of Ireland.[22]

Hobson's narrative, written several decades later (published in 1968)[23], presents a straightforward movement born out of a sense of northern independence, a company designed to comment on the 'political and social conditions in the North of Ireland'. In some ways, however, this manages to write over and partially disguise the more complex cultural negotiations that accompanied the actual formation of Belfast's first nationalist theatre company. The notion of a company intent on merely representing the North was complicated by the group's drive to firmly situate itself within the emerging nationalist drama project in Dublin. As with 1898, the early history of the Ulster Literary Theatre was made complex by a necessary negotiation of structures of inclusion/centre and exclusion/periphery.

Christopher Murray's suggestion that the 'theatre in the North is, historically, a mirror image of the political relationship between North and South', and that the decision to found this Belfast company 'was at once a form of imitation and a gesture of independence', nicely captures the negotiations involved in this genesis.[24] Indeed, this doubly informed moment (imitation and independence) resonates through much of the Belfast group's early existence. Once Hobson and Parkhill had made the decision to form a drama company in Belfast, for example, it was to Dublin that they turned for help. Moreover, Hobson makes it clear that, in its very earliest moments of inception, the new theatre company in Belfast was intended to be an 'Ulster Branch' of the group originally established in Dublin by Yeats, Moore, Gregory and Martyn. This original idea had much more to do with a federalist idea of a shared nationalist theatre, than it did with some form of separatist northern nationalism. Thus in 1902, after deciding on the need for a nationalist theatre in Belfast, Hobson and Parkhill set off for Dublin to meet up with many of the key figures that had been involved in the Irish Literary Theatre, in a bid to request assistance. The purpose of this visit was to request advice and material aid in forming a company imagined as a northern 'branch' to the Irish Literary Theatre (despite the fact that this entity was now all but defunct). The men had, for example, been hoping for an exchange of actors to help get their company established. In this they were partially successful: Dudley Digges and Maire Quinn, two acting mainstays of the Dublin group, agreed to come to Belfast and take part in the Ulster Literary Theatre's first productions later that same year.

The meeting, however, was not a total success from the Belfast men's point of view. The idea of an 'Ulster Branch' of the Irish Literary Theatre met with definite resistance in Dublin. Hobson recalled how the most significant stumbling block on their mission came in the form of W.B. Yeats himself: 'Everybody was most cordial and helpful except for Yeats – haughty and aloof.'[25] The major point of contention would appear to have been Hobson and Parkhill's desire to perform a certain play in the inaugurating season of their theatre company. Yeats, it seems, was very unwilling to allow the Belfast group to perform *Cathleen Ní Houlihán* (a play, of course, which demonstrated the continuing power of 1798/1898 in the imagination of Yeats and Lady Gregory also). In the end, as Hobson remembers it, Maud Gonne took him aside quietly to tell him, 'never mind Willie, he wrote that play for me and you can perform it anytime you like'.[26] The problem of Yeats was it seems, in this case at least, resolved by a strategy of reversed occlusion on the part of the Ulster men, a policy that would find all kinds of echoes in the years that followed. In an extraordinary account, Sam Hanna Bell, after interviewing Bulmer Hobson as an elderly man, reconstructs the journey undertaken by the two men returning home from this very meeting in Dublin. It is a journey that marks the founding moment of the Ulster Literary Theatre:

> One evening in the autumn of 1902, two young men were travelling homeward on the Belfast-bound train from Dublin. They had just parted company from the most remarkable group of men and women in that Ireland

> of the new century and had achieved more than partial success in the errand that had taken them to the capital.
>
> But idealists are inclined to chafe under anything less than complete success. Young Mr. Bulmer Hobson and young Mr. David Parkhill from Belfast were, above all else, idealists. It is not recorded at what point on that historic journey Hobson struck the arm of his seat and exclaimed "Damn Yeats, we'll write our own plays!" What can be said is that the blow laid the foundation of the Ulster Literary Theatre.[27]

Hobson's declamation, 'Damn Yeats, we'll write our own plays!', stands at the heart of the subsequent history of the Ulster Literary Theatre. The angry cry is both a stance of independence – 'we'll write our own plays' – but also, perhaps, an acknowledgement of a centre against which the Ulster Literary Theatre would have to define itself, the damning of Yeats revealing the metaphorical location of this centre.

Despite the obvious issues of resistance, Hobson and Parkhill carried on with their plan and on their return to Belfast established a theatre company, which they in the first instance named the Ulster Branch of the Irish Literary Theatre. As can be seen, the Belfast men held firm to their vision of a federalist national theatre network. The name not only reveals the motivating desire to feed an Ulster dimension more fully into the revivalist drama as performed by the Dublin coterie, it also proposes a version of the 'national theatre' as a space shared (and created) by a number of linked theatres. As discussed above, such a vision was strongly resisted by the centrifugal forces at the heart of the Dublin project. In the coming years, following through on these federalist intentions became increasingly complicated, but for now, on their return to Belfast, the newly formed company lost little time in staging their inaugural performances. In November 1902 the Ulster Branch of the Irish Literary Theatre staged *Cathleen Ní Houlihán* and James Cousins's *The Racing Lug* in St Mary's Minor Hall, Belfast. To aid in the staging of these performances the actors Digges and Quinn held true to their promise and travelled up to Belfast; they gave advice to the young founders and also took roles in the plays themselves. It is interesting to note that even at this stage Yeats strongly resented Digges and Quinn's decision to provide help to the new venture. As part of the later reorganisation of the INTS a new rule was introduced that prevented actors taking roles with other groups without first getting the permission of the Dublin hierarchy.

Those involved in the new Ulster Branch of the Irish Literary Theatre, however, can only have been profoundly grateful for any such assistance, even if the new company had yet to build up an audience for itself in Belfast and the numbers that attended these first performances were small. Despite the small scale, these performances represented an important early foray into a literary nationalist drama for Ulster's main city. A small stone may have been dropped into a fairly large pond, but the ripples it created were important, especially for those nationalists that had been looking for an outlet for their cultural and political thinking in Belfast. It was at this first performance, for example, that Joseph Campbell first became aware of the new theatre in his home-town. Joseph Campbell, his brother John and their sister Josephine would soon become central figures in the company. Looking back, the Campbell family seem to have been destined for involvement in the Ulster Literary Theatre. As with Bulmer Hobson, they had strong links with the Ardrigh nationalists – Anna Johnston (Ethna Carbery) was a cousin of the family and the Campbells were frequent visitors to F.J. Bigger's home. On 'seeing the drama for the first time', Joseph would later recall that he was 'especially moved by the wavering chant of Cathleen'. For Joseph Campbell, at least, *Cathleen Ní Houlihán*'s first appearance in Belfast was an epiphanic and cathartic experience: 'The drab environment of the ugly hall became transformed for me, and I headed homeward feeling that I had been cleansed and ennobled – as Aristotle argues I should be by great tragedy.'[28]

Despite such a promising start, it was to be another two years before the company found itself in a position to stage any further performances. This period was spent building up the company's resources, particularly in terms of personnel, for the group's first performances had been staged in very much an *ad hoc* manner, with actors (and audience) drawn in from Hobson and Parkhill's network of connections. Although the company would always retain this feel of a collaborative society, it was clear that they just did not have the resources to put together a more extended season during this period of development. So it was not until March 1904 that the company took to the stage for its second short season. Once again Yeats's *Cathleen Ní Houlihán* was performed; this time the bill included AE's *Deirdre.* By this time Joseph Campbell was heavily involved in the group and he and his brother John were in the cast of *Deirdre.* In addition, Jack Morrow designed the costumes for these performances, a task he repeated for much of the company's existence. His involvement at this formative stage was to be an early indication of just how crucial the Morrow family were to be in the Ulster Literary Theatre's history.

Sam Waddell (better known by his pen-name Rutherford Mayne) also became involved with the group around this time, and he recalls how he was much more struck by the performance of AE's work than that of Yeats's *Cathleen.* In particular he was impressed by the performance in *Deirdre* of 'John and Joseph Campbell. They had magnificent voices and they filled my idea of how a man should speak verse'.[29] The Campbells would later appear in many of Rutherford Mayne's own plays, plays that were written specifically for the Ulster Literary Theatre (Mayne would also marry Josephine Campbell). By this stage in 1904 many of the main players in the subsequent history of the Ulster Literary Theatre were in place. If these two opening seasons, consisting of 'appropriated' texts (written by playwrights from outside the Belfast group's ranks), marked the company out as still assuming a position of imitative dependence, then the gathering personnel would soon ensure a move towards a more independent mode of production. As it turned out 1904 would be a pivotal year for the company. Helped by the gathering together of figures like the Campbell family, Rutherford Mayne and the Morrows, this was a year that would end with a quite distinct move away from imitation to full creative autonomy.

A number of factors informed this transformation in the Belfast theatre group during the course of 1904. Firstly a series of collaborative projects bore fruit around this time, and this seems to have provided an added boost of confidence to those involved. Joseph Campbell remembers the results of one such endeavour:

> In August, 1903, F.J.B. [Bigger], Herbert Hughes, Freddy, his brother (a fine folk-song singer), and John [Campbell] went off on a trip to North Donegal. A carefree, exploratory holiday – breathing mountain ether, eating mountain food, meeting adventures as they shaped themselves on the road. I was not, alas! of their company. Herbert brought his notebook with him, and F.J.B. his camera. They came back with a rich harvest: a veritable treasure-trove of unrecorded airs and peasant photographs. Out of this trip blossomed *Songs of Uladh.* It was published in 1904 at Bigger's expense.[30]

As well as a walking trip, the friends had undertaken their journey in the hope of committing to paper old folk stories and songs kept alive in the oral tradition of the north-west. In this regard the Gaelic-speaking regions of Donegal functioned for these northern revivalists in much the same manner as the Aran Islands did for J.M. Synge at the Abbey. Herbert Hughes, destined to be a composer of international fame, also became involved in the Ulster Literary Theatre around this time. His brother Fred was already involved with the early productions and Herbert would go on to provide the musical score for many of their most popular productions. On his return from the trip Herbert asked Joseph Campbell to become involved in working on the material they had gathered along the way: 'For some of the songs he had collected no words, and my job was to supply them . . . In this way, such pieces as *My Lagan Love* and the *Gartan Mother's Lullaby* came before the world.'[31] The resultant publication (*Songs of Uladh*) was critically well received and a popular hit and seemed to confirm to those involved that there was room for a revivalist project with a distinctly northern flavour. The timing of this publication could not have been better, for Joseph Campbell had been deeply hurt not to be included in AE's *New Songs*, published the same year. Although AE's collection did include some work by Alice Milligan, Campbell appears to have felt snubbed by the general exclusion of northern writers.[32] He may also have decided that this was proof that those writing out of the north could not rely on the Dublin-centric revivalist hierarchy for recognition. The fact that AE was a fellow northerner can only have added to the feelings of hurt in this regard.

Nevertheless Campbell recognised the importance of such publications as AE's *New Songs*, describing 1904 as the year when 'the second wave of the Revival broke on Ireland'.[33] In proposing it as such Campbell may also have been recording 1904 as a key year in the activities of northern nationalists. We can see this, for example, in another formative event that took place that year: the first *Feis na nGleann* (Feis of the Nine Glens), which was held in June. At this time the Glens of Antrim, as well as the hills of Donegal, were still a significant repository of folk memory for northern revivalists.[34] As Eamon Phoenix writes: 'The Glens of Antrim formed one of the last Gaeltacht areas in Ulster up to the early 1900s' and 'as late as 1897, the Belfast Gaelic League, composed mainly of middle-class Protestants such as F.J. Bigger . . . made a field visit to Glenariff to meet and speak with the remaining native Irish speakers'.[35] From this interest was born the idea of a feis to celebrate the unique culture of the Antrim Glens, and the first such event was held on Thursday 30 June 1904. The feis's centrepiece were the various competitions, designed to promote the arts and skills 'native' to Ireland, and so competitions 'covered vocal and instrumental music, dancing, history and language, and the Feis was almost unique in having a Local Industries section'.[36] This final local industries section ensured the support and presence of Horace Plunkett, the driving force behind the popular farming co-operative movement at this time. Plunkett presented the prizes for all the competitions at a dance held on the evening of the feis. Aside from Plunkett, the panels of judges for the various sections reveal the extent of involvement of Ardrigh regulars and, more especially, those connected with the new Ulster Literary Theatre project. The 'recitation' competition was judged by Parkhill and Hobson, along with William MacDonald and Joseph Campbell, while John and Joseph Campbell also judged the literature competition and the Irish dancing section. Other significant figures involved in the events included Denis McCullough, Eoin MacNeill, Stephen Gwynn and Pádraic Colum.

The feis had a galvanising effect on many involved, and it certainly provided momentum for the decisions and actions in the latter half of 1904. The success of the feis, and the recognition it received as a cultural event of some note throughout the rest of Ireland, also confirmed a developing sense of confidence that the North could take its rightful place within the cultural-nationalist project. As Jack Magee puts it: 'The camaraderie initiated by the events and activities of the 1904 Glens phenomenon proved to be a catalyst for the cultural and literary renaissance that blossomed during that remarkable year.'[37] Joseph Campbell, for example, would in later life recall the importance of meeting Pádraic Colum at the first feis: 'Through Pádraic Colum I had connected up with the intellectuals of Dublin, and the circuit between North and South was now complete.'[38] The first *Feis na nGleann* was, then, a time of new optimism for those figures now determined to bring the possibilities of a nationalist drama to Belfast and the North. It is this gathering head of steam in Ulster, as evidenced by the *Feis*'s popular reception, the publication of *Songs of Uladh* and the emergence of an 'Ulster Literary Theatre', that may well have influenced that assertion of Campbell's that 1904 was the year in which the 'second wave of the Revival broke on Ireland'. The second wave in this case was the now more fully formed northern revival.

There was, however, still much to be done and many hurdles still to be jumped in the search for a fully co-operative and federalist revival. Just how much was revealed by an exchange that led the members of the Ulster Branch of the Irish Literary Theatre into a rethink, and a rebranding, of their project. By the time the Belfast group took to the stage again in December of 1904 its name had changed, and it is a change of name that signifies a complex web of cultural exchange and dialogue. Some time early in 1904 George Roberts (the Belfast man who was then the secretary of the Irish National Theatre Society) wrote to David Parkhill informing him that the group had no authority to describe itself as a branch of the Irish National Literary Theatre.[39] In the same letter, according to Hanna Bell's account, 'he demanded royalties from the impoverished company' for the performances given while describing itself as a sister company to the Dublin organisation.[40] The direct result of this letter was a swift change of name for Belfast's fledgling nationalist theatre. Between March and December of 1904 the Belfast group re-emerged as the Ulster Literary Theatre, having decided in the wake of Roberts's letter to drop the explicit connection with the Dublin organisation. This change of name from the Ulster *Branch* of the Irish Literary Theatre to simply the Ulster Literary Theatre is crucially important. Simply on a practical level, the move was about saving money; by avoiding royalties the new name provided economic as well as cultural independence. More fundamentally, however, the new name represented a more confident desire to express a distinctively 'Ulster' identity, rather than to simply 'import' the mythic and historical voices of the Dublin dramatic project.

After the successes of 1904 those involved now knew that they could operate as an autonomous creative force, one that would be freer to innovate if standing alone from a clearly wary Dublin group (which was at this stage preparing its new home at the Abbey). Further proof of this new empowerment is demonstrated by the fact that in 1904 the company also began publication of its own journal, *Ulad*. It was in its pages that the tensions and paradoxes associated with issues of region and nation, and the Ulster Literary Theatre's stance within these problems, were most openly discussed. Indeed the journal's main editorial remit was to explore many of the issues under scrutiny in this study: namely the network of cultural signifiers produced by the idea of revival in the North, and the series of geo-cultural negotiations that such a project necessitated. Many of the journal's pages were taken up, for example, with the call for a local 'Ulster' school of drama. Crucially, the nature of this call seemed to imply the need for a specifically Ulster-centric dramaturgy. *Ulad* made it clear that such a 'methodology' involved the reclamation of a specifically northern-centric voice, a voice that would draw on (and be born of) Ulster's historical narratives and mythic paradigms.

This refocused and ambitious project would depend on building up a talented group of people who could carry forward the mission to articulate a distinctly northern voice. In this regard Hobson and Parkhill were very fortunate. For any number of reasons, those with cultural-nationalist interests in Belfast at this time represented a fairly small and circumscribed grouping. The political make-up of the city ensured that such interests had retained much of the 'eccentric' quality noted by Hobson above. And so, as ably demonstrated by the activities at Ardrigh, the cultural-nationalist scene in Belfast was built upon a network of quite close and cross-referenced relationships. One such grouping had formed within the ranks of the city's School of Art Sketching Club, which coincidentally disbanded (1904) around the time of *Ulad*'s call for local talent to represent local issues. The Arts Club, combined with the associations forged at Ardrigh, was to provide the nascent company with a ready-made source of artistic talent in search of a new project. The Campbell family, for example, had been involved with the Arts Club (as had a number of other older Ardrigh figures, such as Herbert Hughes). It is probable that the Arts Club connection also provided the Ulster Literary Theatre with another perhaps even more significant family connection. The Morrow brothers became from the very beginning crucial to the success of the new company. Of the large Morrow family five would go on to be well-known figures in the world of journalism, literature and theatre. As an article in the *Belfast Telegraph* devoted to the Morrow family's contribution to the city's cultural life puts it:

> Five of the Morrow brothers achieved distinction in the arts. Harry, under the non-de-plume of Gerald MacNamara, was the author of *Thompson in Tir na nOg* and other plays, and Fred was the most brilliant producer of the old Ulster Literary Theatre. Norman was a fine poster artist, Eddie was a black and white artist on *The Bystander,* and George, of course, became famous for his illustrations of a series of books by E.V. Lucas and for his many cartoons in *Punch.*[41]

All of the brothers, in fact, at one time or another had a connection with the Ulster Literary Theatre, either behind the scenes in production or on stage acting.

The two most important figures, however, were Harry Morrow and Fred Morrow. Fred Morrow was to be the Ulster Literary Theatre's producer for most of its thirty years' existence. It was Fred Morrow's vision and energy that generated much of the early praise that accompanied the company's performances. As mentioned above, it was his vision and talent that was also harnessed outside of the Belfast scene as he went on to be the Theatre of Ireland's producer for many years. Harry Morrow, writing under the pen-name Gerald MacNamara, became one of the Ulster Literary Theatre's most important playwrights. His plays provided the Ulster Literary Theatre with its most popular and successful productions. Indeed it seems pretty clear that the Morrow brothers quickly became more important figures than the group's founders, Hobson and Parkhill. Hobson soon shifted his creative energies on to the Dungannon Club and his paper, *Republic,* and, while Parkhill supplied the group with three important early plays, he did not remain in Belfast long enough to dominate the Ulster Literary Theatre's new direction. In this regard it was the obvious talents and commitment of the

Morrow brothers that allowed Hobson to move his attention away from the Ulster Literary Theatre so soon after its birth. The Morrow brothers' contribution to nationalist theatre in Belfast is perhaps best summed up in Sam Hanna Bell's comparative analysis:

> If the Abbey Theatre had its Fay brothers the Ulster company had its Morrows. All the Theatre's activities without exception were affected by their energy and genius. Jack, Edwin, and Fred acted or staged or produced; Norman, another artist member of the family, contributed . . . drawings . . . to the first number of Uladh.[42] Harry, under the pen name of Gerald MacNamara, was one of the two outstanding playwrights . . . Fred Morrow . . . was its producer for thirty years.[43]

It was to be around this core group of figures that the new *Ulster Literary Theatre* set about the task of providing a nationalist representational space for the North. In December of 1904 the Ulster Literary Theatre performed its first two plays to be written, produced, directed and acted solely by its own members. On this occasion David Parkhill ('Lewis Parkhill') provided his first piece, *The Reformers,* which was paired in performance with Bulmer Hobson's *Brian of Banba.*

The implications and consequences of this move from 'imported texts' to the performance of completely 'Ulster' plays are very significant in terms of the Ulster Literary Theatre's project. To understand the full significance of this development we have to move back a little, perhaps, to those two first seasons of the Ulster Branch of the Irish Literary Theatre. In particular we need to consider more closely Hobson and Parkhill's insistence on staging *Cathleen Ní Houlihán.* The Belfast men were clearly aware of the play's nationalist potential, and its emphasis upon Ireland as 'four green fields' would undoubtedly have increased its appeal to the Ulster nationalists. The return to 1798 as a potential unifying moment would also have appealed to men directly inspired in their missionary zeal by Belfast's commemorative attempts in 1898. In these terms Cathleen as the embodiment of Ireland fits nicely into Ricoeur's model of identity crisis. In a central moment of exposition one of the characters rehearses a story he has heard: 'Do you remember what Winny of the Cross-Roads was saying the other night about the strange woman that goes through the country whatever time there's war or trouble coming?'[44] *Cathleen* here becomes an empowering narrative to be drawn upon in 'moments of danger'. It is this that Richard Kearney locates as central to the power of the play. His analysis cites *Cathleen* as an almost perfect exemplar of Ricoeur's thinking on the function of myth:

> Yeats offered the myth of Mother Ireland as spiritual or symbolic compensation for the colonial calamities of historical reality. The mythological Mother would restore the lost national identity by calling her sons to the sacred rite of blood-sacrifice whereby they would re-enter the sacred time which transcends historical time – and thus undo the wrongs of history. In short, since the reality told a story of division and dispossession, Yeats replied with answering symbols of unity and self-possession.[45]

It was in just these terms, of course, that Yeats's work would have been such an obvious and attractive choice for the Ulster Literary Theatre's founding members.[46] After all, the decision to establish a nationalist company in Belfast was an attempt to 'expand' the search for a nationalist narrative for the North.

The reception of *Cathleen Ní Houlihán* in Belfast, however, made it clear to many of those involved that its performance as a symbol of 'unity and self-possession' was in need of further interrogation. Harry Morrow (Gerald MacNamara) was present at one of the performances of *Cathleen Ní Houlihán* (it is not clear if this was 1902 or 1904); he remembers quite clearly the reaction of the Belfast audience to Yeats's symbolism:

> The Belfast public were not taken by *Cathleen Ni Houlihan.* Ninety-nine per cent of the population had never heard of the lady – and cared less; in fact someone in the audience said that the show was going 'rightly' till *she* came on.[47]

Morrow's memory (quite different to that of Joseph Campbell cited above) raises a number of key issues. He clearly felt that the play's nationalist message had by-passed the Belfast audience that night; *Cathleen's* relevance is severely undercut by the feeling that the play had been 'going "rightly" till *she* came on'. Rutherford Mayne would also later recall a similar reaction at one of these performances: 'I'm afraid I didn't quite catch what Yeats was at because the audience seemed to take it as a sort of rather funny peasant play.'[48] It was just this sort of reception that spurred on the new Ulster Literary Theatre in its new mission. This mission was now a search for a language, a style, for narratives and images, that was more attuned to the needs, sensibilities and politics of its northern audiences. The fact that *Cathleen* 'didn't play in Belfast', in other words, haunted the search for a northern nationalist alterity seen most explicitly in *Ulad* (discussed in the next chapter). If the journal sought to engage directly with this issue, then pretty much all of the group's early plays were an oblique exploration of its tensions and/or potential. The play's reception in Belfast usefully demonstrates some of the motivations behind the group's search for different myths and historical narratives informed by the specificity of northern nationalism. The quite different boundary moment occurring in the North at the turn of the century found little reflection in Yeats's vision. The Belfast audience intuitively perceived the need for a different response to a different kind of crisis.

The task for the Ulster Literary Theatre was to find the mode and voice that would articulate this northern boundary situation. However, this task was doubly complicated by a further negotiation: the Ulster Literary Theatre, with its nationalist intentions, was faced with exploring this difference while still retaining its central aim of inclusion within the larger nationalist project. This doubled and doubling need may shed some light on Harry Morrow's description of the early years of the Ulster Literary Theatre:

> The nucleus of 'The Ulster Theatre' was a band of serious minded young men and women (none of them out of their teens) who, in the first years of this century were enthusiasts in the 'Irish Ireland' movement.
>
> Although their sympathies were with the Gaelic League they were not attached to that organisation in any official way. They were absolutely 'on their own' – what might be called an 'Ulah Sinn Fein'.[49]

As we have seen, the evolution of the Ulster Literary Theatre was indeed connected (if loosely) to the later founding of Sinn Féin. Morrow's description of the group as an 'Ulah (sic.) Sinn Fein' is more striking, however, as it appears to inscribe the Ulster Literary Theatre in terms of a separate Ulster identity, or perhaps even a form of cultural partition. In a sense this was exactly the negotiation to be undertaken by the Belfast group, particularly in its early years. These are years that saw the Ulster Literary Theatre battle to articulate a particular brand of northern nationalism, at once different from – but also part of – the wider Irish sense of nationalist endeavour. It is a battle that we can see very clearly in the content of *Ulad,* the subject of the next chapter.

CHAPTER FOUR

'Draw It Not Too Rigidly': Ulad *and the 'Position' of Ulster*

You had to prove
Your permanence.
You scored the ground

With a sharp brooch,
Mapped your first
Hillfort.
'Macha', Paul Muldoon

I mean by deep life that men put into their writing the emotions and experiences that have been most important to themselves. If they say 'I will write of Irish country people and make them charming and picturesque like those dear peasants my great grandmother used to put in the foreground of her water colour paintings' then they had better be satisfied with the word 'provincial'. If one condescends to one's material, if it is only what a popular novelist would call local colour, it is certain that one's real soul is somewhere else.
W.B. Yeats, *Samhain*, No. 4, December 1904

The aim of this society is to produce literary and artistic plays, and to encourage in Ulster a school of writers and actors of such plays. Those interested in the development of a native and local dramatic art are invited to become members or subscribers.
The Secretary, Ulster Literary Theatre, 1904[1]

The first issue of *Ulad: A Literary and Critical Magazine* appeared in November 1904. As with most else connected with the Ulster Literary Theatre, the emergence of this journal traces out a complex web of intentions and propositions. While clearly modelled on Yeats's

Samhain, Ulad also sought to respond to some of its more hegemonic claims. The choice of name is once again telling in this regard; in place of Yeats's temporal abstraction, the Belfast group opted for a regional preciseness – this was a literary organ for Ulad (Ulster). The committee responsible for its production was drawn from the members of the Ulster Literary Theatre and consisted of David Parkhill, James Winder Good, John Campbell, W.B. Reynolds (who wrote under the pen-name William Donn) and Bulmer Hobson. Reynolds was appointed as editor, while John Campbell filled the position of manager; Joseph Campbell designed the cover of the journal, signing himself (as he often did) Seosamh MacCathmhaoil . The scale of this operation would remain quite small in comparison with the journal's Dublin counterparts; and throughout its existence the editorial committee for *Ulad* had to function on a very small budget. Their meeting place, for example, was usually at Loretto, the Campbell's family home, and Bulmer Hobson recalls how their working capital was never more than five pounds.[2] The journal in the end was to last for only four numbers: Number One, November 1904 (the *Samhain* issue); Number Two, February 1905 (the *Féile Bridghe* issue); Number Three, May 1905 (the *Bealtaine* issue), and Number Four, September 1905 (the *Lughnasa* issue). Whilst short-lived, *Ulad* nevertheless made a major contribution to the task of giving a voice to (nationalist) Ulster, a voice that spoke to the rest of Ireland but also spoke to Ulster of itself.

Although drawn from a group of theatrical amateurs, *Ulad*'s committee had the benefit of much useful professional experience, and it was this that allowed the group to produce a high-quality journal from the first issue. James Winder Good was a journalist on the staff of the *Northern Whig;* he would later also contribute to Hobson's *Republic* and assist AE in editing the *Irish Statesman.* Under the pseudonym 'Robert Harding' he would also contribute a play to the Ulster Literary Theatre in 1908, a popular piece entitled *Leaders of the People* (now lost). He would also go on to write a fairly withering attack on unionist practice in the years after the First World War (*Irish Unionism,* 1920). W.B. Reynolds, *Ulad*'s general editor, was equally experienced and was for many years the music critic for the *Belfast Telegraph.* In addition to contributions from the committee members and others directly involved in the Ulster Literary Theatre, *Ulad* also published essays by figures such as F.J. Bigger, Roger Casement and the nationalist MP Stephen Gwynn.[3] This range of talented writers when aligned with the graphic skills of figures like the Campbell brothers combined to provide the Ulster Literary Theatre with an eloquent, incisive and imaginative printed voice. Its content was varied and at times a little eccentric; as well as articles on the theatre, in particular reviews of the Ulster Literary Theatre's performances, the journal published articles on wider issues of culture, politics and history. David Parkhill, for example, in an attempt to explore issues of cultural specificity, published a number of essays discussing the correct architectural style for an Ulster home and the appropriate manner in which such a home should be decorated.[4] *Ulad* was also used as an outlet for creative work: its four numbers contain poetry by figures such as Bulmer Hobson, Alice Milligan and Pádraic Colum – in addition to the early plays of Joseph Campbell and 'Lewis Purcell'.

The first number opens with a signature poem by Hobson entitled 'Ulad'. The poem, designed to establish the cultural thrust and political outlook of the journal, relies on delayed decoding to reveal its full meaning. Its first verse runs as follows:

> In the north is the strength of the wind, of the whirlwind;
> In the south there are murmuring waters;
> The east has a *caoine* for its song;
> In the west is strengthless love.

With the North thus described as the origin of the wind's power, the poem is not fully decoded until its final didactic line: 'The wind is your master, is strongest!' This insistent image of the North as the possible, and perhaps even rightful, leader of the island sets up one of the major themes of the journal. The North's position within the cultural and political dynamics of the island would be discussed and unpacked throughout *Ulad*'s four numbers. Crucially, the journal imposed no editorial line, a decision that resulted in an open and energetic debate on this potentially divisive and antagonistic topic (a practice that I have attempted to leave intact in the discussion below).

Hobson's insistence on a kind of revelation is particularly apt in terms of the revivalist project. His sense that the true potential of the North (as cultural and nationalist leader) had to be uncovered or reclaimed establishes a familiar revivalist dialectic between historical narrative and 'true' identity. That said, if Hobson's poem fits neatly into this model, it also points to *Ulad*'s more specific mission to ground this revivalist practice firmly in the context of an altered and altering northern geo-cultural/political landscape. The problematics of such a project established the critical landscape explored in the future issues of the group's journal. In its pages the group's earliest members, as well as other interested parties, openly debated the aims and objectives born of their initial desire to expand the Irish Literary Theatre's (and later the INTS's) project to the North. By the time of *Ulad*'s publication, of course, this federalist vision of nationalist drama had been clearly refused by the Dublin grouping, and the group now known as the Ulster Literary Theatre had made the decision to focus its energies on the production and performance of works by Ulster writers. And so *Ulad*'s pages functioned as an introduction of the Ulster Literary Theatre's aims and objectives to a wider audience, as well as an internal 'discussion board' allowing members to question the full implications of their complex project.

Perhaps most importantly, these debates would also help shape the group's sense of its own material. It soon becomes clear that at the heart of the energetic exchanges there stood one central driving motivation: how to re-imagine a dramatic space that would feed into the wider nationalist search for amenable representations but that would also provide an arena for the singularity of northern life. In these terms the selection of narratives to be told, and the kinds of voices through which they could be presented, became fundamental issues. The reaction of Belfast audiences to *Cathleen Ní Houlihán* had already demonstrated to the group that other narratives (mythic and historical) would have to be presented if a meaningful impact was to be made on the people in the auditorium. After that early chastening experience, only one conclusion was open to those who had most fully realised the extent and profundity of Ulster's quite particular situation: that the representation of its ontology could not easily fit into the narratives finding space on stage in Dublin. This is a conclusion that haunted many of the key articles to appear in the journal's four-issue run. In the end what is perhaps most interesting are the slippages that occur as a result of this haunting presence in the subsequent debates. As we will see, some articles seem intent on proposing various aspects of northern history as a means of bypassing contemporary political 'blockages'. Moments such as the eighteenth-century Volunteers and the United Irishmen are all returned to as possible models for recasting the still emerging north/south dynamic concerning Home Rule and Ulster unionism. Other articles sought to demonstrate that this same reclamation process could operate as a warning function, rather than an obvious model for the present. Some contributors seemed to fear that on too close an inspection the North's history would simply reveal the contemporary problems of Home Rule and Ulster difference as somehow essential and inevitable. All the while, a contingent debate continued regarding the Ulster Literary Theatre's position within the revivalist project. As such, the pages of *Ulad* contain one of the most remarkable contemporary debates on the various relationships between a nationalist Irish history, the construction of political/cultural discourse and the position of the North at the crossroads of competing hegemonies.

In an article entitled 'Art and Culture in Old Belfast', for example, F.J. Bigger draws on the familiar models of the eighteenth century to consolidate his vision of Ulster's cultural importance. It was just this centrality in the past, according to Bigger, that led to Belfast's title of 'Athens of the North':

> It gave rise to the Volunteer movement which flooded the North with a spirit of patriotism that had been hitherto unfelt and has never since been surpassed. All classes were affected by this spirit. The histories of other nations that had acted on similar lines were studied and lauded. Craven races were despised and held of no esteem. (*Ulad*, no. 1, p. 11)

The echoes of 1898 are obviously still strong in this narrative, particularly with the now familiar paradigm of the North's key role in the history of Irish resistance movements. However, the real focus here is on Belfast and the North as the place of an advanced learning and culture: Bigger assures his readers that 'the Athens of the North was worthy of its name. It was quite abreast of the age in culture and learning.' His article in this inaugural issue of a new cultural venture was intended to demonstrate the necessity of the job in hand; the piece concludes with a Yeatsian flourish on the primacy of art in the face of a corrupting modernity:

> To bring about a healthy state of affairs art and literature must have a foremost place in any community, no matter how commercial that community may be. Otherwise life becomes sordid and mean, the enrichment of a few is accomplished and the degradation of the masses assured. (p. 12)

Bigger's contribution helped establish the twin interests of reclaimed history and renewed contemporary culture, and their linked potential for circumventing internal conflict. The indication that art and literature must be given a foremost position, even (or especially) in a commercial city, reveals Bigger's concern that too many people thought Belfast a lost case in this regard. For Bigger, *Ulad* and the Ulster Literary Theatre were perfect forums for addressing this problematic. Such hopes, and the problems inherent in their fulfilment, would receive much attention in the journal. Indeed much of the point of Bigger's article was to provide an early impetus in the process: his appropriation of the Volunteer movement recalls a moment in history when Ulster's religious factions were brought together in a common cause. The boundary moment of the late eighteenth century is presented as providing a common communal code, through which the North's population is read as a single community experiencing the same crisis. As an example of a very particularly Ulster cultural nationalism, Bigger's retreat into history clearly sought to circumvent the late nineteenth/early twentieth-century crisis that had resulted in a greater polarisation of/in the North.

In a sense this represents the more optimistic side of the cultural politics informing the early Ulster Literary Theatre; Bigger's is a perfect demonstration of the idealism that shaped the northern revival at this point. Not everyone was sure that the case was so straightforward. Bigger's article was to be countered, or perhaps supplemented, by a 'warning' in the very next number. Stephen Gwynn's article 'The Northern Gael' provides a different interpretation of northern history to the unifying potential described by Bigger and others. For Gwynn, the story of the North had been one of separatism and isolationism. In place of a model to be replicated, he proposes Ulster's history as a warning for the present. It is interesting that a Home Rule Member of Parliament should present this argument most forcefully. Gwynn was clearly attracted by the possibilities of cultural renewal; he was heavily involved in London's Irish Literary Society (acting as its secretary for some time) and he published a number of historical romances. However, in the end it is his political sensibility that leads him to recognise the potential dangers of a project so heavily centred on an Ulster difference (even if this difference is couched in nationalist rather than unionist terms).

Gwynn's article is in effect a call for nationalists to keep their more romantic inclinations in check; one must not get so carried away, he reminds his readers, as to get myth and history confused. So he opens by claiming that any proposal of the North's leadership can only really be sustained in that realm that exists somewhere between the mythic and history proper:

> Northerns in all countries count it natural that the North should lead; and far back in Ireland's history we find the North leading. Outside the limit of ascertained history, yet on the hither side of fable, deeds of the Red Branch heroes rise up, like a range of mountains on the furthest verge of sight. (*Ulad*, no. 2, p. 9)

Here, briefly, is a return to the vision of Hobson's 'Ulad', but Gwynn is quick to deflate such romantic musings. For Gwynn these hazy pseudo-historical narratives have been permanently overwritten by subsequent events that stand firmly within 'ascertained history'. These are events that reveal Ulster as isolationist and slow to come to the aid of the rest of the island. His point is to reclaim the primacy of *real politic* over discursive reinvention, and he takes for an exemplar moment the Elizabethan plantation:

> That is why it helped Ireland little, that Ulstermen, the strongest and most obdurate of Irish fighters, drove back the English time and again, till in Elizabeth's day, while the rest of Ireland had been partitioned out, and much of it occupied and re-occupied by men from overseas, scarce an acre of Ulster had passed out of Irish hands. Behind the Gap of the North, they were secure for the moment.
>
> Only then – only when the rest of Ireland had been brought to a point at which resistance slackened – did the North realise that its turn would surely come next. Only then did the North take up its function, and begin to lead.

His message cites northern history as a nexus of tension and paradox rather than a unifying example. The article is clearly intended to dampen any temptation to oversimplify the possibilities of a 'northern nationalism'. In essence, however, this is a supplementary rather than a completely counter argument to that proposed by Bigger. The two do not disagree regarding their aims and objectives, only on the best methods to see these brought about. Like Bigger, Gwynn argues that Ulster must be included and include itself in the new cultural and political movements in Ireland. His point is that emphasising a northern difference (or special position) is not the best way to achieve this goal. In this regard he concludes pointedly (and, as it turned out, poignantly):

> And certainly if Ulster, or even Belfast, is finally divorced in spirit from Ireland, it is a pity of pities; for Ireland, wanting the hand of the North, will go maimed; but Belfast divorced from Ireland will be squalid, undignified, and contemptible. (p. 12)

The image of the North divorced from the rest of Ireland opens up a debate on northern difference that was to recur throughout the journal's run of four numbers. It is a debate that directly impacted on the journal's positioning of the Ulster Literary Theatre within wider cultural-nationalist contexts.

Indeed James Power, writing about the Ulster Literary Theatre in the fourth number, proposes a really quite startling image of northern difference. It is one that comes close to a partitionist view of Irish culture: 'North is North, and South is South, irrevocably, and though the line of demarcation be not so firmly drawn as between the Occident and the Orient, it nevertheless demands recognition' (p. 5).[5] He goes on to draw on the singularity of the North's historical experience to back up such claims:

> It seems to me that if Ulster be true to its instincts it must necessarily have a somewhat different point of view from the rest of Ireland. And, at a time when the more genuinely Celtic provinces are casting off the intellectual misfits of generations to clothe themselves in native thought, it is surely unreasonable to ask that the North should continue to cloak its individuality with alien modes of expression.

For Power, if Ireland is seen as casting off its alien intellectual forms, Ulster must also avoid 'cloaking' itself in alien forms. But in this case the alien forms are, presumably, those associated with a cultural nationalism born out of (and thus appropriate to) other parts of Ireland.[6] There is no point in thinking of Ulster, in other words, as a place that simply needs to reconnect with some still extant cultural homogeneity. Rather, Power suggests, Ulster must embrace its own historical (and thus cultural) specificity and find strategies to give voice to this experience.[7]

Debates such as these provided the backdrop for the journal's other central concerns: namely the relationship between the 'regional' and the 'national' within revivalist practice. This issue was often aired as a debate about the Ulster Literary Theatre's primary motivating force. Time and again the debate returned to a series of central questions: was the Ulster group engaged with creating a distinct Ulster 'school' of drama, or in making a home in Ulster for the 'National' vision at work on the stage in Dublin? Notably, the journal also openly discussed the difficulties involved in trying to create *any* form of theatre company in Belfast. This discussion reveals a central tension within the journal as the differences (cultural/political) between north and south are unpacked in an effort to negotiate the problems of staging nationalist plays in the North. The problem of staging identity locates, for those involved with the Ulster Literary Theatre, a more fundamental problem concerning the nature of northern identity itself. W.B. Reynolds's editorial to the first number immediately engages with this precise formational dynamic. In this case his remarks are directed at a fairly basic level of definition: the problem of speaking of Ulster, or Ulad, as a coherent territorial entity at all:

> Ulad means Ulster. It is still often necessary to state as much; we intend to insist. Draw an imaginary line across Ireland from that great bight, Donegal Bay, in the west, to Carlingford Lough, on the east, and draw it not too rigidly; north of that you have Ulster. This Ulster has its own way of things, which

> may be taken as the great contrast to the Munster way of things, still happening on Irish lands. (p. 1)

This description (in both senses) of the geographical territory of Ulster and of the Ulster 'way of things' is based on an inside/outside dynamic, at once establishing the notion of a distinct northern identity containable within the broader Irish spectrum. In a sense it is Ulster's liminal position that provides the perspective that calls for a more federalist conception of Irish identity. The claim that 'Ulster has its own way of things, which may be taken as the great contrast to the Munster way of things, still happening on Irish lands' would go on to shadow much of the Ulster Literary Theatre's early work. At this point, however, there was still much to be determined in terms of just what such a claim could mean:

> Exactly what the local temperament and artistic aptitude are *Ulad* wants to discuss. *Ulad* would also influence them, direct and inform them. And as the Theatre is the most essential of all art activities, and the surest test of a people's emotional and intellectual vitality, *Ulad* starts out as the organ of the Theatre, the Ulster Literary Theatre, but proposes to be as irrelevant to that movement and its topics as is deemed necessary.

This opening stance once again establishes the Yeatsian relationship between theatre and nation (each a function of the other). However, the question at work here relates to the role of a specific Ulster identity in the theatre, and the implications of this for the relationship between northern drama and the rest of Ireland. Essentially Reynolds proposes that, in place of some unifying essential truth, those involved in cultural renewal should be more interested in a spectrum of regional variations:

> We recognise at the outset that our art of the drama will be different from that other Irish art of drama which speaks from the stage of the Irish National Theatre in Dublin, where two men, W.B. Yeats and Douglas Hyde, have set a model in Anglo-Irish and Gaelic plays with a success that is surprising and exhilarating. Dreamer, mystic, Gaelic poet and propagandist have all spoken on the Dublin stage, and a fairly defined local school has been inaugurated.

The work of the Irish National Theatre in Dublin is recast as a localised school of drama, a move that denies the Dublin group the status of central national representational space that is implicitly claimed by the company. Instead the Irish National Theatre Society is re-presented from the North in terms of one local school within a network of many other possible schools.

As Reynolds goes on to state: 'We in Belfast and Ulster also wish to set up a school; but there will be a difference' (p. 2).

The nature of this difference, it becomes clear, is still to be negotiated or discovered. *Ulad* leaves this issue – the distinctiveness of artistic sensibility in Ulster – mostly open-ended, again, perhaps, seeking the avoidance of closure inherent in that image of drawing the line 'not too rigidly'. Reynolds does, however, indicate one possible generic area of difference, a difference that he suggests will become crucial in any relationship between the northern school of drama and others:

> At present we can only say that our talent is more satiric than poetic. That will probably remain the broad difference between the Ulster and the Leinster schools.
>
> But when our genius arrives, as he must sooner or later, there is no accounting for what extraordinary tendency he may display. Our business is, however, to plod along gathering matter for his use, practicing methods, perfecting techniques, and training actors.

The fact that this 'genre map' is sketched out in terms of a network of 'local schools' is key to its importance. The scope and inclusive embrace of the Irish National Theatre Society is drastically reduced, becoming in Reynolds's terms simply a representative of the 'Leinster school'. Interestingly the discussion of difference does also admit that (as opposed to the Dublin group perhaps) the Ulster school had yet to find the genius that would fully give voice to this 'satiric difference'. The final chapters of this study argue that this voice did arrive, in the figure of Gerald MacNamara, but was never fully recognised. Moreover, as it turned out, that idea of 'satiric difference' is indeed vital to any discussion of MacNamara's work. That said, throughout his introductory editorial Reynolds argues that the arrival of an Ulster genius is not essential to the success of the Ulster Literary Theatre: the real job at hand is to give an honest voice to the North. Finding the best way to do just this leads Reynolds towards a concluding vision that clearly counters the Abbey's insistence on the primacy of the West. While the Ulster Literary Theatre may never produce world-changing art, it will 'at least attain to something unique in Ulster, smacking of the soil, the winds on the uplands, the north coast, the sun and the rain, and the long winter evenings' (p. 2). The manifesto thus set out, Reynolds makes it clear that it is these concerns that will make up the 'broad propagandist lines' along which *Ulad* and the Ulster Literary Theatre are to be run.

Perhaps unsurprisingly, positioning this project in 'Ulster propagandist' terms caused some confusion at the time. In particular the call for the establishment of a 'local school' in Ulster and the relegation of the Dublin company to a 'Leinster school' instigated a thoroughgoing debate on the nature of art, provincialism and nation. In this sense the idea of an Ulster 'school' raised many of the same issues indexed by the vision of Ulster isolationism that Stephen Gwynn had warned against in his article. Reynolds's proposal for an 'Ulster school' was interpreted by some as simply repeating the separatist 'failings' inherent in certain elements of Ulster's history. The next number of *Ulad,* for example, ran an article appearing above the name 'Connla' that strongly resisted the principles established by Reynolds.[8] In turn, this same number also contained a second editorial by Reynolds responding to the criticism. The presentation of strongly opposing views within the same issue perfectly demonstrates the openness that characterised *Ulad*'s mission. While there is no doubt that such exchanges reveal tensions and instabilities within the Ulster Literary Theatre's project in these early years, they more fully point to the drive for inclusive dialogue upon which the company was founded. In his piece Connla argues strongly against the concept of provincial schools in favour of embracing an overarching nationalist vision. The article begins, however, by affirming that there is indeed a gap to be bridged between Ulster and the rest of the island:

> Those of us who have lived and been educated in Ulster are only too well aware how far the greater portion of the province has drifted from the life and thought of Ireland as a whole, and notably that portion where the means were readiest to hand for centralising anything in the way of intellectual and artistic life. (*Ulad,* no. 2, p. 13)

However, acknowledging this gap is the exact basis of his argument against provincialism; Ulster's drift must be retarded not by the formation of a distinctive school of drama but by the holistic counter-embrace of a national sensibility:

> The great and lamentable hiatus is being bridged over in part by the Gaelic League; the decay of a century has been arrested by its work in the last decade; retrogression has stopped, and we are now moving forward.
>
> For all that, Ulster has not yet reached the marching line; has not yet sufficiently assimilated the rudiments of *national* culture on which she must base the development of her best *provincial* characteristics.
>
> Until that point is reached, until Ulster has absorbed the same genetic

> spirit that today is moving the rest of Ireland, until she has acquired the more notable marks of national homogeneity, all merely provincial development will run to seed.
>
> If we accept the broad fact that Ireland, of which Ulster is part, is *a nation*, we must recognise that provincial differences will be quantative [*sic*] rather than qualitative.

In a manner which strongly echoes Stephen Gwynn's earlier contribution, Ulster's history is cited here as fundamental to why the 'national homogeneity' was required evermore in Ulster, if the province was to attain the 'genetic spirit' at work in the rest of the island. As already noted above, just one month before this number of *Ulad* was published the Ulster Unionist Council had been officially inaugurated, providing the most significant ideological locus within which Ulster unionism was to be institutionalised. It is against this form of radical political Ulster difference that Connla is here writing, concluding that nationalists in Ulster should not also embark on a route of institutionalised difference, but should instead strive to more completely embrace the 'genetic spirit' of national identity.

Connla's piece does, however, acknowledge the applicability of some of the earlier arguments presented by Reynolds:

> This implies on our part no slavish imitation of method in Dublin, Cork, or Galway, as applied to literature or art, prose, poetry or drama. Local temperament and artistic aptitude will, inevitably, and of themselves, evolve new means and manners of expression.
>
> The provincial self-consciousness which would arbitrarily define a 'school', while the elements of a possible 'school' are still in a state of flux, is less a matter for encouragement than deprecation, and to proclaim that attitude aloud to the four winds of Erin is scarce becoming to our modesty.

Connla's articulation of a 'local temperament' does point to a partial *rapprochement* between his vision of the national and Reynolds's vision of the provincial. Indeed, Connla concludes by writing: 'To mould their plays from their experience of humanity as typified in the Ulster Irishman is indeed a worthy aim; better defined as an attempt to realise Ulster to the rest of Ireland than to set up a new "school" of dramatic art' (p. 14).

As mooted above, it is clear from this published response that the first issue of *Ulad* had been suspected by some of declaring a *de facto* cultural partition. The second issue, as well as containing Connla's article, also contains a clarification from Reynolds. Reynolds makes the case that this second editorial is 'for the benefit of readers who may also have misunderstood what exactly our objects and ideals are' (p. 1). The nature of this misunderstanding revolves around the issue of provincial partitioning:

> We have not striven to erect a barrier between Ulster and the rest of Ireland; but we aim at building a citadel in Ulster for Irish thought and art achievements such as exists in Dublin.
>
> If the result is provincial rather than national it will not be our fault, but due to local influences over which we have no control, but which we shall not deliberately nourish and cultivate.
>
> That the work in Ulster will for some time be of a critical and destructive nature, as well as constructive and creative, no one who knows the conditions will deny.
>
> Here our satire will come in (p. 1).

While this is an undoubtedly a heartfelt rejection of any suggested schism, Reynolds's response does also reveal a certain ambiguity in his thinking. His editorial for the first number had quite clearly indicated that the nourishing and cultivating of 'local influences' was precisely the aim of the new company. As Mary Burgess has noted, those involved in the Ulster Literary Theatre 'maintained a sometimes awkward tension between a hard-won sense of provincial difference and a simultaneous claim to be part of the national movement'. At moments such as these we can see the ways in which the problems inherent in such a position led 'representatives of the Ulster drama to slip into a potentially divisive mode of expression'.[9] Reynolds's responding editorial is haunted by an acknowledgement of just such a danger. Despite this, Reynolds seems unable to fully rid his thinking of this oppositional tension:

> We have not attempted to define a school. To say that our talent in drama will be more satiric than otherwise is not defining a school, but merely stating what may be, and, indeed, is a ruling characteristic. We do not deliberately sit down to write that way; but we do write that way, and our most vital work, little as it is, is of that kind. (p. 2)

The defining of a school had been one of the primary aims set out in the previous number, yet this position is retracted, presumably under the suspicion of an artistic and cultural partitioning. More than anywhere else, perhaps, it is here that we see the difficulties faced by the group as it attempted to negotiate the precise nature of its inside/outside relationship with the broader revivalist project.

Such ambiguity is further evident in *Ulad*'s consideration of the actual functioning of a northern 'difference', particularly in terms of the performance of nationalist plays in the North. The problems inherent in the staging of an Ulster identity predicated upon this 'same but different' dynamic are explored in a series of articles by James Winder Good focusing on the Ulster Literary Theatre itself. Taking up the debate outlined above, much of Good's analysis concerns exactly this issue of Ulster's relationship to the rest of Ireland (he would later write a full-length study entitled *Ulster and Ireland*), in terms of the difficulties of staging the types of play envisaged by the Ulster Literary Theatre. Discussing the performance of the plays 'imported' from the Dublin company, for example, Good argues that the major problem in acting and staging these pieces was located in the peculiarities of the various Ulster identities and sensibilities:

> Frankly, the performances given so far by the Belfast company of players have been creditable, but, at the same time, very bad. What do I mean?
>
> In order to understand our difficulty it is necessary to remember that we live in Belfast, that we are Presbyterian, or that we are Catholic, or Episcopal, with a hard layer of Presbyterian crudeness and repression upon top of that; and crudeness and repression are not good for the stuff out of which actors are to be made.
>
> Where every national impulse has been dried up at its inception, all gaiety eyed with suspicion, all good-will withdrawn lest it commit one to a little generous feeling, and all forms and ceremonies deemed unprofitable and vain, how can the necessary forgetfulness and self-abandonment exist that mimicry and pantomime demand? (*Ulad*, no. 1, p. 7)

Essentially the problem to be overcome by the new company, Good argues, is the specificity of Ulster – ironically the very thing that the company wished to embrace and give a voice to. The tensions inherent in the North's conflicting communal identities, Good contends, result in the inability of northern men and women to take on new 'roles' which represent the possibilities of the North as envisaged by the company. The 'necessary forgetfulness and self-abandonment' needed to construct the new relationship is blocked in this argument because the North is too much ever present. Good's is an interesting thesis, as it establishes the 'specificity of the North', with its internecine tensions, as the major barrier to a true representation of the 'specificity of the North'. It is the overcoming of this internal and self-reflective conflict that Good sees as central to the success of the new company:

> What with Philistinism and Puritanism hand in hand, the Scotchman always with us with his self-consciousness, the Cockney with his slang and vulgar tastes, and our willing imitation of these – we in Ulster have had a great deal to contend with. Fortunately, the Scotch element has neutralised the Cockney to some extent; and in this way there is still left some native grace and worth. But this, too, will have disappeared if we do not hasten with the new impetus to work along native lines, and cast off this deadening, suffocating Puritanism.

These inhibiting factors are posited as very different from the situation in Dublin, where, as Good puts it, 'they have not this temperamental difficulty to contend against, and their results in a short time have been proportionately satisfactory'.[10] Indeed Yeats would appear to back up this reading of things in the edition of *Samhain* published two months after this number of *Ulad*. In the course of discussing the emergence of stage talent to work with, Yeats suggested that Ireland was the natural home of fine acting: 'whatever they play, they will have one advantage the English amateur has not: there is in their blood a natural capacity for acting'.[11]

A northern provincial difference in this regard, Good seems to suggest, is exactly that which will have to be negotiated if the province is to truly speak of itself to itself and to the rest of Ireland. He argues, moreover, that this situation is a result of a historical divergence, writing that: 'In Dublin the project for a national theatre was bound to find many supporters from the first. There the drama has always been a force, and new ideas, even in the darkest days of reaction, have been granted a hearing' (p. 4). This putative openness to new visions/versions on stage of Irish nationalism is presented as a stark contrast to the situation in Belfast, where the even more palimpsest-like identity has contrived to negate such possibilities. Good nevertheless concludes his piece with an assertion of the potential power of the Ulster Literary Theatre to renegotiate the terms upon which these fundamental relationships were built:

> It may seem absurd to imagine that a handful of enthusiasts can accomplish a revolution, but in Ireland it is not always the large movements that have left the enduring record.
>
> The Ulster Literary Theatre may never produce an epoch-making play, or evolve a distinctive school of acting; but if it aids, even a little, in breaking down the barrier that has so long divided the North from the South, its work will not have been in vain. (p. 5)

Thus the Ulster Literary Theatre sought not only to 'Irishise the North' but also to 'northernise Ireland'. While this was obviously a highly contested dynamic for those involved in the group, it is also clear that it was this conflict of inclusion/exclusion that gave the company its early energy and creative drive.

A short story by Joseph Campbell published in the first issue indicates a number of the routes that were to be explored by the Ulster Literary Theatre in its early attempts to negotiate this double relationship. The story, entitled 'The Sleepers of Aileach-Neid', is in many ways a response to Harry Morrow's memory that the Belfast people had 'not taken to' Yeats's *Cathleen Ní Houlihán.* Campbell's story reworks the myth of Cathleen, or the poor old woman, in a specifically northern context. The story is of a young Ulster man who dreams of an old woman calling him to arms. The description of the figure is couched in the classic terms of the 'Shan Van Vocht':

> I looked around fearfully, and beheld a haggard old woman before me. She was the very picture of misery. Her face was fleshless, wan, and furrowed with innumerable wrinkles, they told all too plainly the sorrow and the suffering she had seen in her time. Her hair was thin and hoar, and partly covered by the long blue cloak that hung about her spare form. She had never a shoe to her foot, and as she approached me, hobbled with difficulty over the stones that strewed the pathway at this point. Her wretched appearance moved the soul of tears within me. (*Ulad*, no. 1, pp. 5–6)

In the dream the old woman calls to him – 'The time is upon us' – initially causing much confusion. The subsequent dialogue between the two once again echoes Bulmer Hobson's vision of the North as a dormant nationalist space in 'Ulad'. Campbell presents an image of the Fianna heroes of the North called up from their subterranean place of rest:

> "What time?" I enquired, struck with wonderment at her strange words.
>
> "The time for the heroes to ride forth", she said. "I wandered just now in the cave that pierces this hill at its foot. I saw there the heroes of the sons of Niall. Many think they are dead; but they are not dead. They are not dead, I tell you. They are lying trance-bound, as in sleep, their right hands upon their swords, and their left hands upon the bridles of their horses. Aodh, their leader, awoke as I entered, and lifting his helmeted head, he asked me wearily – 'Is the time come?' I answered: 'Yea, is it come, truly, O Aodh, son of Feardorach. Uladh, go forth! That is the command I speak to you. Uladh, I say, for in you lives the quenchless fire of the northern men. Go forth, go forth, O Valourous Lights of the North! The spirit of Action calls ye'".

If Hobson's 'Ulad' was an apt opening shot by the new journal, then Campbell's short story about a northern Cathleen Ní Houlihán provided an equally suitable concluding demonstration of the journal's central dynamic. The story not only makes a home in Ulster for the nationalist vision of Cathleen Ní Houlihán, it also repositions the North to the very centre of the nationalist vision. The dynamic of critical and creative expressions promulgated via the journal established the cultural landscape explored on stage by the company in subsequent years. The northern 'Cathleen' was, moreover, merely one sign of an ongoing negotiation as northern nationalism sought to accommodate and give expression to its emerging inside/outside position regarding the wider nationalist project. It is this double movement that was to occupy much of the intellectual territory of the early Ulster plays in the years during and immediately after the life span of *Ulad*. In the end the journal provided a kind of proto Ulster Literary Theory to be performed by the Ulster Literary Theatre.

Chapter Five

The Ulster Literary Theatre's Early Myths

I inclined
To lose my faith in Ballyrush and Gortin
Till Homer's ghost came whispering to my mind
He said: I made the Iliad from such
A local row. Gods make their own importance.
Patrick Kavanagh, 'Epic'

While the politicians situate their action in actual present-day events, men of culture take their stand in the field of history.
Frantz Fanon[1]

Ulad's setting out of the group's aims and motivations coincided with the Ulster Literary Theatre's first productions of plays written, directed, produced and acted solely by its members. Indeed many of the articles discussed in the previous chapter contained calls for new writers to come forward with plays born from knowledge of Ulster's unique qualities. In these works, then, we find the beginnings of a distinctly 'Ulster nationalist drama', with all the complications that this term implies. The period 1904/05 saw the Ulster Literary Theatre first put its 'Ulster literary theory' into practice. These earliest Ulster Literary Theatre plays are a significant expression of Ulster's relationship to the complex project that was in the process of finding its 'home' at the Abbey. This chapter (and the one that follows) examines the Ulster Literary Theatre's first performances of its own 'Ulster plays'.[2] The nature of these early attempts to intervene into, and thus help define, the national dramatic space reveals the ways in which the Belfast group remained intent on pursuing the possibility of a federalist nationalist dramatic project. In response to the kinds of narrative presented on stage at the Abbey, the Ulster Literary Theatre worked on its own counter or supplementary narratives. These were narratives that focused on historical (or pseudo-historical) narratives particular to Ulster, on scenes and scenarios revelatory of northern social realities and tales based explicitly on Ulster-centric mythic paradigms. A central contention of what follows is that the Ulster Literary Theatre's recuperation of these narratives was an attempt to adjust the 'horizon of expectation' of Irish nationalist drama. More ambitiously, perhaps, these early plays are also indicative of the Ulster Literary Theatre's broader attempt to re-imagine Irish nationalism's terms of reference. This chapter examines the ways in which this process involved the search for a mythic frame of reference amenable to the needs of Ulster's cultural nationalists. We will see that the nature of the Belfast group's project necessitated that from the very beginning this representational strategy engaged with forms of 'meta-mythology'. The next chapter examines those early plays that demonstrate a more social realist attempt to produce narratives and images conducive to Ulster's engagement with a federalist nationalist drama.

As noted above, the first two 'independent' plays staged by Belfast's theatre practitioners were written by its two founding members: in December of 1904 the Ulster Literary Theatre staged *The Reformers* by Lewis Purcell (David Parkhill) and *Brian of Banba* by Bulmer Hobson, in St Mary's Minor Hall, Belfast. The script for Purcell's *The Reformers* is regrettably lost, but contemporary reviews describing it as a 'smart, spicy, comedy exposé' certainly suggest that it was very well received.[3] Such reviews also suggest a critical reception that was quick to spot Purcell's talent and potential importance to the new venture. Fortunately Hobson's piece had been published some time earlier in the *United Irishman* (2 August, 1902; all quotes below are from this source). Although a slight piece, it cannot have lasted more than thirty minutes in performance, *Brian of Banba* does reveal the cultural politics driving forward Hobson's version of northern revivalism at this point (see below). Although the attendance at these first performances was still relatively small, certain sections of the Belfast press did pick up on the new movement and pointed to its potential importance. the *Northern Star,* for example, published a review of the plays that also linked them to the politico-cultural stance of *Ulad:*

> The young men behind the revival movement in this city – that is, those in the Ulster Literary Theatre and the contributors to the periodical *Uladh* – in preaching in the courageous fashion they are in the principles of broad

> Nationalism deserve the warmest support of every Irishman who wishes to see an elevated, prosperous, and free Ireland.
>
> With such talent in their midst as the Messrs. Purcell, the Campbell brothers, the Morrow brothers, Bulmer Hobson, and other cultural aspirants in the new school of National thought operating in our midst, there is every reason to look with feelings of confidence and hope to the future of our city, socially, intellectually, and nationally. (9 December 1904)

Nevertheless, the overtly nationalist stance adopted by the new company – and demonstrated most clearly in Hobson's work – did cause some unease, most obviously and naturally within the broadly unionist sections of the city's press. The *Belfast Newsletter,* while reviewing these first performances, pointed to the inherent dangers in the group's project:

> The aim which the members of the Ulster Literary Theatre have set before them – namely, to produce literary and artistic plays, and to encourage in the province a school of writers and actors of such plays, is a highly meritorious one, but there is a distinct danger that enthusiasm may outrun discretion, and there may be allowed to creep in a spirit of partisanship which will infallibly stifle the enterprise in its infancy...
>
> If the project is developed on broad, tolerant, and generous lines it will attract to itself an equal measure of generous and hearty support, but if, on the other hand, it is kept subsidiary to the furtherance of a particular propaganda or limited set of ideas, it will alienate the sympathies of those who take a wider and more comprehensive view of human affairs. (9 Dec 1904)

From the very start, then, the work of the Ulster Literary Theatre was received in terms of cultural tensions with which it had to negotiate. While the initial impetus behind the company's foundation may have been a drive to give voice to the North within the revival, quite clearly here the problematic of the company's relationship to sections of the community unsympathetic to a nationalist motivation is highlighted. In the end the company appears to have realised that their long-term success could not lie in the direction of obvious nationalist propaganda. Nevertheless, this sense of a multi-pronged negotiation was to become ever more embedded in the Ulster Literary Theatre's work in the years that followed these first performances.

Spurred on by the generally sympathetic (if at times cautious) response, the company returned to the stage in May of the following year (1905) with two more new Ulster plays. These next performances comprised *The Enthusiast,* again by Purcell, and *The Little Cowherd of Slainge,* by Joseph Campbell; both of these plays were also published in different numbers of *Ulad*.[4] The company was to take a short break to prepare new material before reappearing in December 1906 with Lewis Purcell's *The Pagan* and Rutherford Mayne's first play, *The Turn of the Road*. The performance of these works also marked the Ulster Literary Theatre's first visit to the Abbey in Dublin. This was a truly significant event for those involved in the Ulster Literary Theatre. Here they were returning to the site of their initial exclusion, performing plays born out of that very federalist ideal that had been so flatly rejected. Bulmer Hobson could not contain his delight and satisfaction at this turn of events, writing in *The Republic* (28 March 1907):

> The gulf that had divided Ulster from the other provinces is due more to the lack of knowledge than to essential differences of outlook or temperament, and the theatre striving to bridge that gulf is engaging in a work of vital importance to the Irish nation.

While Hobson's commentary does reveal a certain distance between the one-time founder and the subsequent direction of the Ulster Literary Theatre (a group now ever more dedicated to constructively exploring differences in outlook and temperament), it also reveals the gathering power of the group's mission and its reception beyond Belfast.

As well as its first visit to the Abbey, the production of these plays occasioned another significant first for the group back home: in December 1906 the company performed both plays in the Examination Hall of Queen's College, Belfast. The performances were to raise funds for the Queen's College Literary and Scientific Society, the secretary of which was Lawrence Lynd, whose brother Robert had become involved in the Ulster Literary Theatre. This event was important for the group in a number of ways: firstly, as the *Northern Whig* comments, the plays were performed before a 'larger and perhaps a more critical audience than [the ULT had] ever been favoured with' (5 December 1906). More significant than this, however, was the actual venue that played host to these performances. As one reviewer writes:

> Especially significant is the fact that the inaugural performance of this winter's session took place last night under the roof of Belfast's Queen's College. When such an institution lends a helping hand to Irish drama much, indeed, may be expected of the result. In any country enjoying a healthy national life there would be nothing surprising in any college patronising native drama and dramatists, but in Ireland – and especially Belfast – such patronage accorded by an [institution] like Queen's is a remarkable sign of the times.[5]

The boundaries between the intellectual and cultural life of an institution like Queen's and the aims of the revival were exactly those that the Ulster Literary Theatre sought to break down. The above review goes on to suggest that groups like the Scientific Society, with its connections to the Ulster Literary Theatre were undertaking exactly this task. The critical link established in the review ambitiously proposes the Ulster Literary Theatre, as an intellectual site of mediation between the different political viewpoints in the North. The reviewer goes further, indeed, making the case that the members of these groups:

> realise that even though a man may be a Presbyterian or an Episcopalian and in politics a staunch unionist , he does not sacrifice an iota of principle in supporting and encouraging this movement for an Irish stage in Ireland: for a theatre which will be typical of the people of the country.
>
> So it came that the great dim portraits of [past] professors and presidents looked down from the lofty walls of the Examination Hall last night upon such a scene as they never before had seen within that imposing structure.

Rhetoric of this sort, proposing the Ulster Literary Theatre as the site of a possible *rapprochement,* only reinforced the landscape of multiple negotiations outlined in *Ulad.* The reviewer's insistence that a 'staunch Unionist' would not sacrifice any element of his principles in supporting the evolution of an 'Irish stage in Ireland' is crucial in these terms; the piece's reasoning for such an assertion is that 'a theatre will be typical of the people of the country'. Implicit here is an assurance that 'an Irish stage in Ireland' could not really be so if it did not reflect all elements of Irish society: if it failed to do this, then it would not be 'Ireland on stage'. This could be read as a veiled attack against those who attempted to exclude the experience of Home-Rule Ulster from the articulation of possible Irelands. The Ulster Literary Theatre, it is suggested, is engaged, perhaps more than any other grouping, with a process of geo-political inclusivity in place of representational exclusivity. Moreover, the review appears to acknowledge that the group's position as a nationalist company operating in Belfast made this undertaking more necessary than for those groups operating outside the North. The visit to Queen's was to be a unique occasion in the company's history, but the pathways of ambition that it opened up remained significant. Once again it was (the admittedly biased) Bulmer Hobson, looking back some months later, who would highlight the broader importance of such moves (*The Republic,* 16 May 1907):

> There are few more striking proofs of the reality of the Irish movement in Ulster than the heading it had made amongst the students of Queen's College, Belfast. Ten years ago, if Irish affairs were not despised they were decidedly ignored, and the remnant, who ventured to look to Ireland instead of to the 'Empire' were dismissed as toy-shop revolutionists or hopeless cranks.

It is a piece that obviously sets out to clear up any possible misreadings of the Ulster Literary Theatre's aims and objectives. The Ulster Literary Theatre was to do for Belfast what the Abbey was doing for Dublin: turn the cultural gaze of the Irish away from the models of Britain and Empire towards more specifically Irish narratives of identity. Implicit in Hobson's comments, of course, is the sense that this task was most difficult, and thus most necessary, in the northern province.

Another key year in the development of the Ulster Literary Theatre was 1907: in December of that year the company first took to the stage with a play written by Gerald MacNamara (Harry Morrow). MacNamara's first work, *Suzanne and the Sovereigns* (written with Lewis Purcell), marked the debut of the company's most remarkable playwright. It also provided the group with its first truly popular hit. Following on from the enthusiasm that greeted MacNamara and Purcell's play, 1908 saw the first production of the Ulster Literary Theatre's second popular success. Rutherford Mayne's *The Drone,* performed in April 1908 during the Ulster Literary Theatre's second visit to the Abbey, was an instant hit and was to become one of the company's keynote pieces in the years that followed. That year also saw the production of Robert Harding's (James Winder Good's) work, *The Leaders of the People.* The piece, judging from its reviews (the manuscript is lost), would seem to have been a sharp and well-observed political satire. Later in that year a second Rutherford Mayne piece, *The Troth,* was presented. Finally, in this early stage of the ULT's development, Gerald MacNamara's second play, *The Mist That Does Be on the Bog,* was performed in 1909.

In the first few years of its existence, then, the Ulster Literary Theatre made a strong impact on the new nationalist literary scene; it was not just in Belfast that people were forced to take note. Yet this is an impact and a reception that has been somewhat lost in the critical biography of this period's cultural-nationalist milieu. This chapter, and the one that follows, attempts to recuperate the significances of these early plays, their performance history and their broader cultural impact. As mooted above, the group's output during these first years, like that of the early Abbey, divides into two reasonably distinct categories: plays that drew on narratives broadly mythological, and those more realist (or, at least, socially mimetic) in form. We begin with those early plays that appropriated Ulster-centric myths. These are works that entered into a powerful debate with the 'neomythicism' of the Abbey, while simultaneously articulating a distinctly northern voice. Although short-lived, the 'mythic stage' of the Ulster Literary Theatre opened up a fascinating performative moment in the history of northern revival.

Mythic Revisions: The North in Search of a Different Time?

In the first two years of its independent existence the Ulster Literary Theatre staged three new works based on mythic themes: Hobson's *Brian of Banba,* Joseph Campbell's *The Little Cowherd of Slainge* and *The Pagan* by Lewis Purcell. Each of these works developed from an attempt to carve out a specifically northern space within the 'myth-work' of the revival. Born from the call in *Ulad* to find narratives and spaces amenable to presenting the cultural component of a northern nationalist outlook, in these early performances we find a return to myth that displays the ideological traces shaping its very existence. Judged on purely literary or aesthetic criteria none of these three plays is a great success; there is nothing quite to match the fully realised pathos of Yeats's Cúchulain or the grand ambition that it represents. But what these plays do perform for us is the record of a very unique politico-cultural project. Working in the same years as the early Abbey, here is evidence of the Ulster Literary Theatre's attempt to vie for representational control over the direction of the new Irish mythology, and thus, of course, of the new myth of Ireland.

Even read in these terms, however, it is perhaps fortunate that the Ulster Literary Theatre would only stage one play by its co-founder, as Hobson's work is certainly not the most subtle or well-structured piece of stagecraft. The interest very definitely in this case lies in the revelation of meta-political intent rather than in any kind of dramaturgical intricacy. At the most obvious level, *Brian of Banba* is a classic piece of early revivalist drama, recounting the last actions of an ancient Irish king and the consequences for his two sons. However, this familiar *mise-en-scène* only barely manages to disguise an obvious critique of the forces within Irish politics that sought to make Ulster a special case within the Home Rule question. The piece opens in the 'death-chamber of Cennedigh McLorcan, King of Thomond and heir to the Kingship of Caiseal', wherein the dying king is joined by his two sons, Mahon and Brian. Before dying, the father wants to sort out his sons' inheritance. Mahon is content to be made King of Thomond and thereafter King of

Munster, but Brian shows no interest in such business. Refusing all offers, Brian instead declares that all he wants is 'An Hundred men to fight the Northmen, my father'. Brian's pronouncement is followed by a fairly clumsy piece of explication that allows the audience to understand that the Kingdom of Ireland is under threat from this invading force known as the 'Northmen'.

While these alien foe are a putative invading force of northern Europeans – 'the Danars' (a mythic synecdoche for various Viking forces) – it is clear that the play is really concerned with an alienating northern force within the Irish body politic. Mahon is unsure of how to react to his brother's fighting talk and seeks advice from his father. His parsing of the situation reveals a concern for pan-Irish unity in the face of a disruptive divisive force: 'My father, ought I not also to aid Brian against our foes? Is it right to let him go – a boy with a hundred men against their hosts?' In the end Brian sets off to face the Northmen with his own force, only to return some time later disguised as a beggar to update those in the royal court of his mission and to gain an insight into their thinking without fully revealing his identity. The play ends with Mahon committing to aid his brother (now revealed) in his fight against this common enemy: 'Much glory hast thou won, O Brian! by thy valiant warfare, and greatly hast thou ravaged the Danars. No longer shalt thou be without aid, not again shalt thou go with a hundred men, but we will together face the Northmen with the brave Dalcassians. *Brian of Banba* plays out a kind of a parable (in much the same way as *Cathleen Ní Houlihán*) about the need for Irish unity in the face of those 'northern forces' which sought to disrupt the functioning of 'native Irish' systems. Hobson's play was a coded call for nationalists throughout Ireland to remember, and thus not leave isolated, their northern 'counterparts', who were feeling ever more squeezed by the ideological pressures building around them.

Cathleen Ní Houlihán had clearly demonstrated to Hobson the possibility of using drama as a call to action (if not a call to arms) – he published *Brian of Banba* just months before the 'Ulster Branch of the Irish Literary Theatre' performed Yeats's piece in Belfast for the first time. While the model is certainly discernible in the shape of *Brian of Banba*'s narrative, Hobson's play indexes a different problem in need of urgent action, namely the developing sense of a northern difference in opposition to the nationalist call for a renegotiation of the Union. As it turned out, *Brian of Banba* and *Cathleen Ní Houlihán* had more in common than their sometimes over-obvious engagements with the politics of myth. Unfortunately for the Ulster Literary Theatre, Hobson's play was also something of a flop in front of its first Ulster audiences. Joseph Campbell recalled watching the audience at a performance for the Gaelic League *feis* in Toomebridge in August 1905. Campbell was disappointed to note that the play bored the farmers and fishermen present; it was, he noted, in terms reminiscent of Cathleen's entrance on the Belfast scene, 'over their heads'.[6] A change of tack was clearly needed. This came in the form of Campbell's own work, *The Little Cowherd of Slainge*, a piece that was much more interested in the aesthetics of mythic drama than in using it as a vehicle for overly obvious political campaigning.

The performance of his first play for the Ulster Literary Theatre was one facet of an impressive output from Campbell in these years and he would quickly establish himself as a well-known figure in revivalist circles (James Joyce would early on nickname Campbell 'Mountainy Mutton'). In 1905, as well as the performance of his first play, he published a first book of poetry, *The Garden of the Bees;* the collection and the title had been inspired by the garden that surrounded Ardrigh. Soon after its publication, Campbell, acting on the advice of his close friend Roger Casement, moved to Dublin to take up a post with the Forestry Department. However, the move did not end his connection with the Ulster Literary Theatre; in fact it provided Campbell with a larger network through which to disseminate the Ulster Literary Theatre's message. In November of that year he published an article in *The Nationist* describing the vital nature of the project in hand and the necessity of drawing Belfast into nationalist imaginings:

> Once Belfast begins to become conscious of the national soul, once she begins to be 'moulded by the environment which has moulded the majority of the people', once she has in her 'something of the will of the race', there will be hope for her. Then and not till then, will she produce good pictures, good statues, good books, good plays – good anything, in fact, that makes for a clearer understanding, a more perfect expression, of the life that is of her and about her. (2 November 1905)

Central to Campbell's project was the use of northern settings and voices within a revivalist writing mode. His collection, *The Garden of the Bees* contains poems such as 'A Northern Love-Song' and 'The Nine Glens of Aon-Druim', which describes the differences between each of the Antrim Glens. This latter was written in honour of the first *Feis na nGleann* in 1904 and details the qualities of each of the Glens; in turn it presents the Antrim Glens as keepers of a hidden knowledge. This is a knowledge that is essentially native and untouched by the politics of modernity, much like the west coast of Gregory and Synge. The second verse runs as follows:

> Gleann-taise sings the faery-songs she knew of yore;
> Thro' Gleann-seasg exalting the blue-streamed runnels leap;
> And stirred by the seaborne breath that fills her bosom hoar
> Gleann-Duine looks up from her sleep

Heavily marked by the revivalist search for an unsullied source of native Irish identity, this kind of work is a now familiar romantic rendering of Irish landscape. It also reveals more than a trace of Yeatsian stylistic influence. What makes it more noteworthy is the privileging of specifically Ulster subjects couched within this revivalist register. Indeed Campbell would recall how his use of northern dialect and local names had caused confusion and puzzlement. His description of these various reactions also nicely captures the particularity of the north's historical narrative:

> Being a Belfast man, hearing the half-Scots, half-Irish speech of my neighbours about me daily I could not escape so lusty an environment. Indeed, if the truth be told, I grew up with three languages: a legacy from father's side of the family of a memory of Border Gaelic, the Chaucer-cum-Burns of Co. Down, the classic English of my schoolbooks, and the literature I read – not with any system but always discursively. This, perhaps, explains the use of strange idioms and odd words, a polyphonic, polymorphic jargon, which dogs my style even yet and puzzles and irritates my readers.[7]

Perhaps even more than Ulster's landscape, the idea of capturing a 'subaltern' voice is placed by Campbell at the heart of his project. He would suggest, in somewhat unusual terms, that he was 'a poet of the Prakrit (the vernacular speech) rather than of the Sanskrit (the speech of the sheltered elect)'.[8] Campbell's notion of a northern polyphony is a particularly useful one, suggesting, as it does, the idea of the voice as yet another keeper of singular historical experience. Indeed, this is a concept that will find particular resonances in the next chapter's discussion of the Ulster Literary Theatre's realist productions. Campbell attributed this interest in Ulster language and myth, and the links between the two, to his mother:

> From mother I got my interest in folklore. She spoke the vernacular of the north-east counties (using in her talk lovely words like 'thrawn' and 'thraveless' and 'throughother', 'menseful', 'genteel', 'disabil', and the like, of Scotch and French vintage).[9]

In 1906 Campbell published a second book of poetry, *The Rushlight,* and in this year he also moved to London, where he joined the Irish Literary Society, acting as its secretary for some time. He would also work with

Eleanor Hull at the Irish Texts Society, a group dedicated to publishing canonical texts of early Gaelic literature. His involvement in the London scene brought him into contact with Ezra Pound and HD (Hilda Doolittle), and by 1909 he was established as a member of the Imagist group in Soho, Ezra Pound referring to him as 'the dark man from the north'.[10] By 1912, however, Campbell had returned to Dublin and joined the staff of Pádraic Pearse's St Enda's school as a teacher. Later still he would adopt a staunch anti-Treaty stance and fight on that side during the Civil War, an involvement that led to his imprisonment with other Republicans in 1922.[11]

Campbell's first play for the Ulster Literary Theatre was, then, an important event at the beginning of a career dedicated to providing a powerful voice from, and of, the North within Ireland. This despite the fact that Campbell would soon regret his early foray into the theatre as a writer instead of actor, describing *The Little Cowherd* as his 'first attempt (and a foolish one) at drama'.[12] Nevertheless, *The Little Cowherd* does represent an interesting moment in the development of the Ulster Literary Theatre's dramaturgy in these first months of existence. For one thing, Campbell's piece stands out as the play that most clearly reveals traces of Yeatsian influence in the approach to matters mythological. In this regard the true significance of this play lies in the fact that it is a retelling of a putative myth from the Carlingford Lough/Cooley Mountain region.[13] This area had been an important place for the young Campbell, who had spent much of his early childhood making extended visits to his grandfather's farm near Flurrybridge in south Armagh. It is here, he argues, that he got to know 'the hidden Ireland, an idea then only faintly understood. For this was Muirthemhne, Cúchulain's soil'.[14] As with the Antrim Glens, this region on the very edge of Ulster was an important imaginative homeland for northern cultural nationalists, not least because 'Irish was still spoken on the border in these days: there was quite a smattering of it among the hillfolk of Annaverna, and further north, at Omeath'.[15] Perhaps most pertinent to this area's cultural attraction was that sense of it as 'Cúchulain's soil'; after all, the entire narrative action of that canonical revivalist text *Táin Bó Cuailnge* is played out across its territory.

By setting his first play in this region Campbell hoped to send out a strong message: the Ulster Literary Theatre was no longer a merely imitative organ. No straightforward copyists, the Belfast playwrights were prepared to acknowledge the influence of their more famous contemporaries but wished also to develop a nationalist recuperation born out of the North, which would in turn speak of the North to the rest of Ireland. This was a delicate line to tread, and the play is perhaps only a partial success on these terms. It did, however, stand in for a newly confident message that was key to the group's new independent outlook. The vehicle for this message is a mythic figure named Boirche, who was 'a magical cowherd, who exists only in the minds of the peasant-people, and in the hearts of maidens he lures to madness by his youth, beauty of person, and skill in playing on the bagpipes' (taken from the version of the play found in *Ulad*, no. 1; all further quotes below are from this source). The central story retold involves Ros Ruadh, the red king of Crioch Slainge; his daughter Fionnghuala, who becomes enchanted by the vaporous cowherd; and Aodh MacEoghain, a foster son of the king who falls in love with Fionnghuala. While a slight piece, Campbell's play manages to reveal some fascinating tensions and paradoxes in the Ulster Literary Theatre's attempts to free itself of the tag of inferior copy to Dublin's Abbey theatre. In the play's verbal register, for example, we can hear a distinct echo of the syntactic stylised precision found in Yeats's dramatic versions of Irish myth. The opening dialogue between the king and his foster-son perfectly displays this sense of a retrospectively stylised mythic landscape (Irish myth via the Renaissance). As the scene opens, the two men are playing chess:

> ROS: It is thy move, see.
>
> AODH: Yea, O father.
>
> ROS: It is thy move, O foster-son. Dost not hear my little board, *Ceann-caomh,* say it? Thou art in love, methinks, O Aodh. Thy heart is not in the game.
>
> AODH: The game is thine, O father. See, my king is in perpetual check. It may not move, or, haply, it is taken. Ah, father, thou speakest rightly. I am in love.

As well as the language heard on stage, visually the piece also draws on the techniques made familiar by earlier efforts at nationalist dramaturgy (and here we can include the work throughout the 1890s of Alice Milligan as well as Yeats and Gregory). The final ceremonial entrance of Fionnghuala's body, for example, is played out in a ritual that distinctly references the developing conventions of cultural-nationalist drama. Fionnghuala has drowned herself as a result of the demented state brought on by her love of the magical cowherd. The scene is set out by the following stage direction:

> Enter bearers with pall, and Fionnghuala's dead body upon it. Youths carry torches on either hand, and mourning-women follow behind. The 'caoine' is raised, and all join in it. The pall is set down: Eithne throws herself upon it.

These stylistic traces of influence are, paradoxically as it turns out, much of the point of the piece. On the one hand, there is little doubt that Campbell sets out to demonstrate the applicability of a revivalist dramaturgy within a northern context, yet this is not simply a piece of 'Abbey drama' that happened to be written and performed in the North. The reclamation and re-presentation (or invention) of a northern mythology is the primary aim of this slight work. But this is not an example of a mythology born out of northern separatism; rather, this is a play dedicated to showing the holistic possibilities of an original pan-Irish network of mythological narratives. *The Little Cowherd,* read in these terms, is about the importance of recovering all of myth's spaces and geo-cultural meanings. It is for this reason that the, 'wise man', Seanchan time and again reinforces the myth of the cowherd as one rooted to (born out of) the Ulster landscape:

> Maids that love the cowherd are not like to trouble the world for long. He is a beauteous youth, half sprite, half mortal, who sits upon the windy carn of Slainge, piping to imaginary herds. His house is in the rock hard by where Slainge, son of Partholan, lies buried. They say he is as old as the hills, but by some strange power he owns, he keeps the form and figure of a boy. Ros the Yellow, King of Uladh, fostered him a thousand years agone.

While this kind of narrative is most obviously attempting to bring the revival northward, the insistent rehearsal of a precise *mise-en-scène* may also be read as a recuperation of myth from the rather more 'hazy' locale of its Yeatsian incarnation. Or, perhaps more accurately, the insistence on a northern mythology seeks to reinsert that which was largely occluded in the Abbey's early work. Thus the Abbey playwrights' (Yeats and Gregory most notably) performance of the mythic as a utopian space (in that etymological rendering of utopia as 'no-place') is countered by the Ulster Literary Theatre's vision of myth as very definitely inscribed with the concerns of region, location and place.[16] The play thus operates along two main pathways of intent. Its style places it firmly within the revivalist model and hence demonstrates that this model is usable within the Ulster context. At the same time, the specificity of the play's location and material seeks to make Ulster the nexus of a nationalist mythology. Rather aptly, perhaps, the mythology of a place destined to become the border region not so far in the future is used here to bring Ulster to the revival as much as to bring revival to Ulster.

Lewis Purcell's work, *The Pagan,* continued with this early Ulster Literary Theatre mythic form. It was first performed in the year following *Little Cowherd,* during the December 1906 season, in a double bill with Rutherford

Mayne's *Turn of the Road*. As noted above, very little is now known about Lewis Purcell/David Parkhill beside his early involvement with the company he helped establish. George Morrow (the nephew of Harry Morrow/Gerald MacNamara) recalls that Parkhill left the Ulster Literary Theatre shortly after the production of his collaborative piece with MacNamara, *Suzanne and the Sovereigns* (1907), and soon thereafter emigrated to Australia.[17] Many years later, in 1931, the 'Ulster Theatre' produced one last play by Purcell entitled *Cobbers Go Halves,* but it is not clear if David Parkhill had returned from Australia with this script or if he simply sent it over by mail to some of his old acquaintances. The loss of Purcell's creative energy so early on must have been a severe blow for those involved in the Ulster Literary Theatre; reviews for his first performed work, *The Reformers,* suggest that Purcell was thought of as the Ulster Literary Theatre's first real discovery. A review of the play in the *Northern Star,* for example, concluded that: 'Such productions as *The Reformers* disclose . . . that we have young men of brilliance, like "Louis Purcell" [*sic*], in our midst' (9 December 1904). Another reviewer in the *Irish News* begins by warning against over-inflated praise, 'as some of the more mediocre of latter-day English writers have suffered from the over-enthusiasm of reviewers who wrote fulsomely of "another Walter Scott", "another Dickens", and so on', but he goes on to conclude: 'Lewis Purcell, however, will produce good work no matter what is written of his efforts. In him the Ulster Literary Theatre has its premier dramatist' (23 December 1904).

With this kind of praise ringing in the ears, Lewis Purcell's third play for the Ulster Literary Theatre, his first to deal with a mythic theme, was something of an early 'event' in the company's short history. *The Pagan,* along with *The Turn of the Road,* was first performed in December 1906 in Belfast and again in April 1907 as part of the Ulster Literary Theatre's first visit to the Abbey Theatre. The work is set on Cave Hill in 'about the sixth century' and explores the tensions and conflicts in a society undergoing schism as it shifts from paganism to Christianity. The play also explores a specific conflict between Ulster 'factions' as the chieftains of the Uí Néill and Cruithni tribes clash; the conflict concerns the marriage of the former's daughter to the latter. Its setting and plot suggest Purcell's play as a partial *homage* to that earlier northern writer, Sir Samuel Ferguson. In particular the idea of returning to the setting of Cave Hill at a time of conflict between paganism and Christianity recalls Ferguson's story 'Corby MacGilmore'. Like Purcell's play, Ferguson's story involved a clash of ideologies and clans on the slopes of Cave Hill ('Ben Madighan'). In addition, both works centred on an illicit love-match that crossed the new religious boundaries of

Christianity and a recalcitrant paganism. It is not surprising that a key figure from the Ulster Literary Theatre should return to a figure such as Ferguson. Samuel Ferguson had been amongst the leading writers of his generation, a key literary forefather for W.B. Yeats, and would be remembered by James Cousins as 'the Irish Wordsworth and the father of the Irish Literary Movement'.[18] The fact that he was a Belfast man would have made him all the more attractive for those involved in the literary renaissance (as with Standish O'Grady, Ferguson's actual politics were sidelined in preference to his imaginative powers).

Moreover, it may well be through James Cousins that we can trace a line of influence to Purcell's piece. Inspired by Ferguson's work, James Cousins set about writing his own homage to Cave Hill with his long poem *Ben Madighan,* in which he too revisited Cave Hill as a seminal space for northern cultural nationalists. Cousins's introduction to this work (first published in 1895) was a call to action for the nascent revival in the North. Key to that call was his insistence that, while those in Ulster had their own inspirational landscape all around them, its full potential had yet to be tapped in a proper fashion:

> How few people relatively have seen the beauties of our Northern Coast or the Vale of Glenariff. To come nearer home, how many of the citizens of Belfast have looked upon the Valley of the Lagan from the Castlereagh Hills, climbed the slopes and stood upon the summit of Divis Mountain or Ben Madighan, or know aught of the historic interest attached to them or to many other places in the vicinity of Belfast![19]

Cousins's preface also makes clear once again the influence of Ardrigh and F.J. Bigger in his own journey towards cultural enlightenment: 'I have also to record my obligations to Mr. Francis Joseph Bigger, M.R.I.A., on whose historical notes and suggestions the main portion of 'Ben Madighan' is constructed.'[20] Later in life Cousins would suggest that the publication of this first collection was something of a cultural bell-wether, if not a popular hit, for Belfast's engagement with the new literary movements:

> The book disturbed no hornets. Rather it aroused much appreciation – not as poetry, for it had none, and there was no one in my world who knew the difference any more than myself; but because in a city which, as far as I knew, literature was a subject in Queen's College but nowhere else, a writer had apparently arrived, and had lifted the self-respect of the city by transforming the common place Cave Hill into the historical and romantic Ben Madighan.[21]

So it is apt that Lewis Purcell's first 'mythic' play for the Ulster Literary Theatre should return for its sources and inspiration to two of the key figures in the development of a sustainable revivalist position in Ulster. It is apt, too, that he should select as his setting a place that had been so vital to Belfast's commemorations in 1898: Cave Hill. Briefly, the story of *The Pagan* involves Crimall Ruadh, 'petty chieftain' of the Uí Néill, his daughter Nuala, and Gorman MacRory, the 'petty chieftain' of the Cruithni. Ruadh has converted faiths and now follows the 'new God', while MacRory and his clan still hold faith with the 'old gods'. Despite the fact that the Cruithni and the Uí Néill tribes are ancient enemies, when MacRory arrives injured at the gates of the Uí Néill's camp Ruadh gives him shelter and orders that his wounds be treated. While this action takes place the audience discovers that Ruadh's daughter, Nuala, is in conflict with her new Christian faith. Her servant-boy, Feilech, has spotted her visiting Dicho, the same druid to whom he is still loyal. Feilech talks to Nuala about her obvious worries and finally enquires if Turlough, her suitor, has changed allegiance to the new gods:

> FEILECH: Then you too worship the new gods only with your lips, but your heart is still with the gods that Dicho serves. Ah, those are my gods. *They* glory in great and noble feats of arms. Fell me, does Turlough worship the new gods – I mean in his heart?
>
> NUALA: I think he does.
>
> FEILECH: (*Thoughtfully*) It is strange for a fighting man to forsake the Gods of Cuchulain and Conchubar.[22]

Feilech's enquiries posit the action of the play precisely at an imagined foundational moment of instability. By linking this instability with the figures of Cúchulain and Conchubar, Purcell subtly reveals a certain meta-dramatic intent within the piece. While Feilech questions the position and applicability of Cúchulain to the new religion, and also the appropriateness of the new religion to his way of life, Purcell may be seen to question the transferability of one historical moment onto another. The slippage that such a reading reveals locates *The Pagan* as a play that utilises the mythic form in order to question the validity of the mythic form. Such a 'meta' reading is reinforced by the play's plot development. The dénouement involves Nuala and Gorman MacRory falling in love. Nuala has also discovered that her mother was from the Cruithni and that her father had raided the Cruithni camp in order to steal her mother away, injuring the girl's father in the process. In the last moments of the play, Nuala steals away to join MacRory. The reason for her flight is left unresolved. One reading suggests that Nuala flees in order to join her true love. However, another site of slippage is left half-open, for Nuala may be seen as taking flight in order to save her father from the same fate visited by him on her maternal grandfather, for MacRory has threatened to take Nuala by force if necessary.

It is this final element that Sam Hanna Bell isolates in his analysis of the play as one primarily concerned with the modern condition rather than with pre-historic Ulster:

> On the evidence of Purcell's earlier plays, an interpretation equally plausible is that *The Pagan,* a satire rather than a tale of heroes, deals with problems nearer in time; the 'mixed marriage' and the collision between parsimonious puritanism and 'the sweet wild times' that the Ulsterman, with a vague unease, feels must have existed sometime, somewhere.[23]

As with Campbell's piece, then, Purcell's *Pagan* deals with the use of mythic material in order to address a specifically Ulster issue. The 'meta' trajectory of this work, however, may be read as establishing a more complex reading of the inter-communal problematic than that proposed by Hanna-Bell above. The play's temporal ellipse does not necessarily perform the task of circumventing modern problems; indeed, the play may be read as a coded warning against the cultural vision that reads myth in those terms. Rather, the temporal framework of the play, the intersection of a major cultural schism, allows Purcell to explore the manner in which a simple calling back of pre-colonial times may not necessarily operate to negate present day difficulties. *The Pagan* is in many ways a creative exploration of Stephen Gwynn's point about the instability of drawing on Ulster's politicised past as a model for contemporary resolution. In these terms, *The Pagan* functions as an early indicator of the 'meta-nationalism' that would find its final northern embodiment in the writings of Gerald MacNamara.

This sense of Lewis Purcell doing 'something other', particularly given the proximity of *The Pagan* to pieces such as Yeats's *On Baile's Strand,* is reinforced by *The Pagan*'s form: satirical comedy. *Ulad* had, of course, predicted satire as the key revelation of the Ulster genius, and Purcell openly discusses the power of satire within the piece. This explication on the power of satire takes the form, naturally, of a satire on the power of satire; Congall, Ruadh's 'bard', discusses the waning influence of the bard and his own inadequacies:

CONGALL: Often I am sad at my own efforts when I think of the great poets that my house has given to Eire. Fiachra was the most cunning weaver of a story that was ever known. Kings and champions would sit whole nights listening to his manner of telling the Tain-Bo-Cuailnge, and Berach, his grandson, was a most powerful satirist. It was said of him that when he was a young man he had four rivals in love, and he satirised them, till the whole world was laughing at them. And at last they went and drowned themselves in the sea.

Purcell's use of the satiric form places further emphasis on *The Pagan*'s meta-mythic framework. Moreover, it is the specificity of the northern province, a place engaged in the most radical of dialogues with its history and its effects, that drives Purcell's vision of an Ulster difference concerning the possibilities of negating history through myth. *The Pagan*'s satiric motivation and doubled frameworks locate the North as a place where mythic reclamation does not necessarily translate into a vision of historical homogeneity. In these terms the play's stance as a comedy of history becomes doubly embedded within its northern origins and the history that shapes that location.

Reviews of the first performances in Belfast and Dublin suggest that this comic element was indeed located by a number of critics as central to the import and success of the play. Concerning Purcell's mythic vision, and its relationship to the kinds of work found at the Abbey, the *Northern Whig* wrote:

> He sees it differently, however, from the majority. It is not in his eyes the decorative dream-world of Mr. Yeats, where frail figures murmur beautiful words in a world of shadow, but a world of coherent ideas, bright, various, and many-coloured, where blood runs in men's veins and on occasion ginger is hot in the mouth.
>
> Greatly daring, he does not even exclude humour in a study of the conflict of ideals between Pagan and Christian Ireland, but it is subtly and cleverly managed without clowning or offensiveness.
>
> He sees the subject, too, from the dramatic, and not the dogmatic, point of view, and this helps him to avoid arid discussions that lead nowhere. (5 December 1906)

It is this specific reclamation of 'northern-ness', along with Purcell's selection of representative characters, that the reviewer locates as essential to Purcell's drive to represent the normally occluded. Moreover, for another contemporary reviewer it is the comic element that enables Purcell to explore and present the normally silent spaces of the mythic form:

> *The Pagan* marks an entirely new departure. We have had historical and quasi historical plays go leor in Gaelic and English; we have have [*sic*] had Mr. Yeats's poems in dramatic form which he called drama; we have had several 'Deirdres' (including AE's beautiful play of that name); we have had King Charles in a barrel; the French on the sea, and similar works by enthusiastic Gaedhilgaoir: - but not until now has anybody had the temerity to adventure on a comedy of ancient Ireland. This is what "Lewis Purcell" has done in *The Pagan.*
>
> The scene is laid within the enclosure of Crimall Ruadh, a free ceile of the tribe of Ui Nial, on the slope of Cave Hill, and the period is the sixth century. Furthermore, the comedy is remarkable for the fact that there are
> NO ROYAL PERSONAGES NOR GREAT CHIEFTAINS IN IT.[24]

The review goes on to point out that two of the main figures are 'petty chieftain' and 'none of the other characters are of higher social standing'. In a manner that recalls Joseph Campbell's insistence on recording the full possibilities of a northern polyphony, Purcell is here read as performing an act of subaltern recovery. In response to the privileging of great figures such as kings, poets and champions, Purcell is credited with giving voice to figures from 'outside' history. It is this different direction that marked Purcell's dialogue with the early Abbey's search for mythic models. In a much more developed way than either Hobson or Campbell, Purcell was here engaged in a form of meta-mythology.

The above reviewer, for example, was quick to pick up on the possibility of Purcell's play as a direct commentary upon the form and intent of the Abbey's work:

> The acting last night was very good, even for the Ulster Literary Theatre players. But then, in each play that had congenial flesh and blood characters to enact, not merely shadows mouthing platitudes in prose, or reciting long poems. 'Lewis Purcell' has sketched in every figure in his little play with a firm assurance that makes it a living, breathing entity.

The comparative structure at work here, between the northern playwright's 'realist myth' and the 'shadowy' symbolism of his Abbey contemporaries, most notably Yeats, indexes a recurring critical motif that surrounded the Ulster Literary Theatre at the time of its first visit to the Abbey. Reviews of these first performances, and of other plays subsequently brought to Dublin by the Ulster Literary Theatre, often describe the work of the northern company as a counterpoint to the perceived flaws and indulgences of the Abbey. Using the Ulster Literary Theatre as a salutary example for its southern counterpart was most prevalent amongst that wing of Irish nationalism that had begun to read the Abbey as a decadent and dangerous place of bourgeois values and 'un-Irish' sentiment. In particular the *United Irishman* would become a significant champion of the northern company in these years. Thus the Ulster Literary Theatre, the company that had its origins in an act of exclusion by the Dublin company, rapidly began to be described as the grouping most fully creating a truly 'Irish theatre'.

Picking up on many of the points raised by the *Northern Whig*'s review (above), the *United Irishman* writes of the first visit of the Ulster Literary Theatre to Dublin (April 1907) in terms of the northern company providing a 'lesson' for the Abbey playwrights:

> There has been no better demonstration of the artificiality of the school of Dublin writers, who are endeavouring to establish a National drama in Ireland, than the visit of the U.L.T. This company, from Belfast, put on the boards of the Abbey Theatre on Saturday night, two plays, one dealing with heroic life; and the other with contemporary peasant life. But the outstanding fact, and the predominating merit of both plays, as compared with those produced by our Dublin dramatists, was their essential humanity.
>
> They were crude and raw in many respects. The acting was slovenly at times, and sometimes even showed signs of coarseness. But always the spectator felt the one great redeeming fact – so wanting as a rule in the Abbey Street playwrights – that here, whatever their defeats, one was at least face to face with humanity, and with the facts of life. (6 April 1907)

The call for the Ulster Literary Theatre to be recognised as an exemplar of Irish drama is echoed in the review of these April performances published in *The Peasant.* In this case the sense of cultural negotiation is heightened even further by the metaphor that shapes the review, which presents the Ulster group as more able to provide creative criticism exactly because of its 'outside' position:

> It is to be hoped that Saturday's visit of the members of the ULT to Dublin is the beginning of a long series. We would all be glad of many such Ulster 'raids' . . . The Dublin audience was genuinely pleased with the Northerners, and we hope set thinking. (6 April 1907)

The fluidic inside/outside dynamic established with the image of an 'Ulster raid' perfectly summates the critical construction of the Ulster Literary Theatre at the time. The company's 'outside' stance is cited by many as crucial to its ability to counterpoint the Abbey and provide a missing element in the dialogue searching out a more thoroughgoing and inclusive cultural nationalism. This ability to be simultaneously inside and outside is cited by W.J. Lawrence (in his review of *The Pagan*'s Dublin unveiling) as propelling the Ulster Literary Theatre forward in its dual mission to 'northernise' Ireland and 'Irishise' the North:

> The hardy little band that adventured upon the seemingly Quixotic enterprise of storming the citadel of fastidiousness and preciosity returned to the North with the cheers of the conquered still ringing in their ears, full of the assurance that the praises of their own province had not all been partial and theirs too was the right to don spurs.
>
> To have worn down the silent opposition and inward skepticism of a coldly critical and thoroughly representative audience; to have captured the intelligence and aroused the sympathies of those who came (more or less) to scoff – all this constitutes an achievement as rare and notable as it is epoch-making.
>
> Not only did the ULT Society return home in full consciousness of the righteousness of their work and the honesty of their mission, but it was their due to take with them the knowledge that they had provided a salutary object lesson to the Irish National Theatre Society . . .
>
> Between North and South it is well-nigh time there should be a rapprochement, and artistic intercourse will tend to bring it about.[25]

Such reviews make it clear that *The Pagan* was marked out as a significant contribution to the cultural-nationalist movement at the time. Moreover, its conflation of forms and genres, as well as its specifically northern setting, are indicative of the ways in which the Ulster Literary Theatre had begun to embrace its exclusive/excluded position. This is not to suggest that the Ulster Literary Theatre was operating within a programme of cultural isolationism; rather, in these early years its playwrights became more aware of the possibilities afforded by its 'de-centred' locale. The years to follow would see the company even more fully embrace the potential of a meta-nationalist position. The next chapter will explore how a number of these same issues concerning dramatic representation and 'nationalised space' were also investigated through more social-realist methods. The plays discussed in the next chapter, indeed, were amongst the earliest in the twentieth century to take the realities of the north of Ireland as their main subject.

CHAPTER SIX

Dramatic Federalism: Representing the Not So Mythic North?

Do I contradict myself?
Very well then I contradict myself,
(I am large, I contain multitudes).
Walt Whitman, 'Song of Myself'

Declan Kiberd concludes his seminal *Inventing Ireland* with a proposal for Ireland's properly realised postcolonial condition; it includes an updated image for Ireland of the 'seamless garment once wrapped like a green flag around Cathleen ni Houlihan' replaced by 'a quilt of many patches and colours, all beautiful, all distinct, yet all connected too' (p. 653). As we have seen, the Ulster Literary Theatre had as early as 1904 isolated the iconic Cathleen as an inadequate symbol for the diversity of identities at work 'still on Irish lands'. It is of note, then, that Kiberd links his image of a patchwork identity with a projected new role for the Abbey theatre:

> If 'Ireland' is recovering an interest in its constituent parts, that may be all to the good: writers nowadays are more alert to the dangers of overriding real differences of class, region or language. While the peripheries seem ever more vital, the Abbey Theatre . . . has found it increasingly difficult to reconcile its 'national' duty to perform a large ruralist canon with its 'civic' desire to service its immediate hinterland. Perhaps by redefining the National Theatre as an abstract, federal entity, encompassing vibrant regional companies who might play parts of that canon, the Abbey could be freed to move in that direction. In this way the idea of a national theatre could be defended and updated. (p. 653)

The idea that the 'National Theatre' has to be redefined and updated in order to be defended, and that this process could take the form of a more abstract, federalised and 'decentred' model, opens up a crucial space in terms of this study. In many ways Kiberd's vision is a rehearsal of the principal ideals upon which the Ulster Literary Theatre was founded. As we have seen, the Ulster Literary Theatre's journal *Ulad* was much occupied with the idea of a federalised national space that was shared and created in co-operation by regional schools of drama. Similarly Kiberd's proposal rests on the idea of a multivalent set of spaces created out of a network of realities, each engaged with telling their own part of the national story. The Ulster Literary Theatre had from the very beginning invented itself in just such terms, presenting itself as 'playing part' of the national canon; or, at least, it envisaged giving voice to the North as key to the formulation of such an inclusive canon. The Ulster Literary Theatre is, then, a still interesting performance of pre-partition possibility.

Following on from the exploration of the group's northern mythology, the focus here is on the more social-realist expression of Ulster life undertaken in the Belfast theatre. This chapter's opening and sustaining contention is that the Ulster Literary Theatre's search for a more 'naturalised' expression of northern identities corresponds to and supplements the project focused on the West of Ireland undertaken most famously by Synge and Lady Gregory at the Abbey. In addition, looking back more closely at these often forgotten plays may reveal that the move from under-representation to canonical status achieved by the West (what Kiberd describes as the 'return to source' model of cultural nationalism) may have occluded other possibilities at this time. This partial or full occlusion, one could argue, has been reinforced and recreated in much of the modern-day critical practice that attains to this moment. Just maybe the recovery of these other narratives and voices presented by the Ulster Literary Theatre in the same years as the ruralist works of Synge, Gregory et al. could aid our re-placing or reforming of this critical landscape. After all, it is not just that the Ulster Literary Theatre's model of federalised identity and national drama suggests itself as a prototype to Kiberd's (postcolonial) vision of a patchwork identity. More specifically it is in the group's earliest attempts that we find the only dramatic space dedicated to the political and social dilemmas experienced by Ulster communities split by the Home Rule issue. The nature of the Belfast group's mission, and the context out of which it operated, necessitated that Ulster unionism as well as nationalism be given a voice on stage. The Ulster Literary Theatre, born out of the necessities inherent in its home-place, negotiated with and gave voice to the multivalent identities at work in the North. While the final form that these plays took was informed by the company's nationalist sympathies, its work undoubtedly attempted to deal with the complexity of northern identities at exactly the moment when the fundamentals of what 'Ulster' should and could be were under political and cultural consideration. The difficulties involved in giving voice to such ideas are traced across the surface of the Ulster Literary Theatre's realist works; fortunately such traces have also left us with one of the most fascinating records of this key moment in the elaboration of diverse identity codes on Irish stages.

And so in the same years that saw the performances of Joseph Campbell's *Little Cowherd* and Lewis Purcell's *The Pagan,* the Ulster Literary Theatre also produced plays dealing with life in contemporary Ulster. In 1905 the company produced Lewis Purcell's *The Enthusiast,* a work concerned with inter-communal tensions in the North, investigated through the idea of farming co-operatives. The following year saw the performance of Rutherford Mayne's first play, *The Turn of the Road,* which explores the relationship between 'art' and 'economy/capital' within a small Co. Down farming community. Their attempt to write Ulster ruralism into the revival from its northern wing was key to the Ulster Literary Theatre's federalist project. The fact that these attempts are more often than not missing from critical overviews of the revival's achievements could suggest that this was a failed project. The truth is somewhat more complex. Back in 1917, for example, Ernest Boyd had claimed that Rutherford Mayne's rural dramas had 'done for the North of Ireland what Synge had done for the West'.[1] The force of such a claim has certainly dwindled in the intervening decades and, while this can be partly explained by the process of critical and aesthetic judgement over the years, it does not account completely for such a sharp decline in fortunes. It would seem that the realist work of the Ulster Literary Theatre has fallen between the gaps of competing hegemonies, most notably the Abbey's claims to representational dominance and the historical force of partition as a defining event in Irish identity.

Thinking about much these same problems, Seamus Heaney has described a certain dissonance between the process of imagining nation and the resultant political reality:

> The political arrangement which incorporated Northern Ireland into the United Kingdom of Great Britain and N. Ireland was not one allowed for in the envisaging minds of the Irish Literary Revival. Yeats, Synge and Lady

> Gregory constructed an imagined place that gave eternal life to Gaelic country people of the west and their Anglo-Irish lords and ladies, while Joyce made a divine comedy out of the urban tumult of Dublin. So, both Joyce and the Revivalists, in their different ways, prepared cultural paths for the political fact of independence; and indeed when that independence came it included only those constituencies who the writers of genius at the turn of the century had written into the imaginative record.[2]

Heaney's is a curiously paradoxical description, one that seems to battle with the tensions of its own conclusions. Implicit is the image of the nation as a 'reverse construct', with the eventual independent state casting its shadow backwards, privileging those factors and elements out of which it was born. 'Ireland' the imagined nation, in this sense, becomes the shadow cast back by 'Ireland' the nation-state. Heaney's formulation of an axis running from the 'urban tumult of Dublin' to the 'Gaelic country people of the west' neatly summates the occlusion from the 'imaginative record' of the northern cultural-nationalist voice and vision. In this regard the Ulster Literary Theatre's realist plays may be read as revealing a vital dialogical process. As noted above, this part of the group's repertoire set about negotiating in particular with contemporary representations of the West; its purpose was to represent 'Irishness' more fully as a dialogue continually in process.

The group's focus on the role of place in the making of identity was often framed by a related interest in the relationship between identity and history. The life on stage (or, at least, the way of living) is often explicitly indicated (particularly in Purcell's *Enthusiast*) to be the result of the historical narratives that coincide in Ulster. In this way too the peasant rurality and Gaelic purity of the Abbey vision finds a natural correspondence for the Ulster Literary Theatre in the small farms of (Counties) Down and Antrim. Of course, as with much else connected with the Belfast group, the nature of this geo-cultural process is multivalent. While the representation of Ulster's rural life obviously 'answers back' to the Abbey by presenting a 'mirrored' vision of identity, at work also is the notion of a 'co-response', in the search to present Ireland on stage. Read in this manner, the Ulster Literary Theatre and the Abbey may be seen as providing localised co-responses to the same problematic. Instead of a counter or challenge to the Abbey's peasant drama, the Ulster Literary Theatre's rural work operated as a kind of supplement to it. This is, of course, exactly what the writers in *Ulad* had hoped for, and this co-response model certainly reaffirms the Ulster Literary Theatre's own proposed schemata of Irish identity as composite and a constantly shifting dialogue. And so, in response to Synge's drive to translate the rhythms and cadences of spoken Irish into English, these early works by Purcell and Mayne, as with Joseph Campbell above, sought out the specificity of northern speech with its particular brand of Ulster-Scots, Irish and English registers. Ulster dialects, with their singular phrases, cadences and words ('loaning' for lane, 'tay' for tea, 'weans' for children, etc.), provided the Ulster Literary Theatre with a counterpoint and/or supplement to the proposed hegemonic 'real Irish folk' on the Dublin stage.

The articulation of different voices ('still happening on Irish lands') and the polyphony of accent and vocabulary apparent in the works from north and south corresponds, in this sense, to the broader articulation of a multi-reality composite Irish identity. What quickly becomes apparent is that these polyphonic characters are 'shadowed' on stage by a historical discourse out of which the northern voice is seen to emerge. As such, the performance of this relationship between language and world is presented as the result of the historical narratives 'passing through' the bodies on stage. In providing a space on stage for the stories of its rural characters, the Ulster Literary Theatre sought to present a form and outcome of history that was not easily accommodated by the historical calibrations of the Abbey.

Bringing It All Back Home: Rutherford Mayne's County Down Kitchen

If the Ulster Literary Theatre set out to take the revival home to Ulster, then the home that most often awaited it was that of Rutherford Mayne's Co. Down cottage. Seamus Deane, discussing, as he puts it, another 'later Irish Revival' (one that included Austin Clarke, Patrick Kavanagh and Sean O'Faolain), suggests that its writers 'made a virtue of its localism, of its deep insider's knowledge of the life of the mass of the Irish people, contrasting this with the shallower if more cosmopolitan attitudes of the Revival'.[3] What this study has been arguing all along is that this potential for a more localised set of responses was in fact very much alive within the Irish literary revival the first time round. In a curious way those cultural-nationalist writers working out of the North in the years either side of the turn of the century were engaged with constructing just such a post-revival sensibility, a 'post' sensibility that was contemporaneous to the movement itself.

Central to this dynamic within the Ulster Literary Theatre's project was the figure of Sam Waddell, known to the Irish theatre world as Rutherford Mayne. While still at school Waddell had become friends with David Parkhill and this friendship led Waddell to his involvement with the Ulster Literary Theatre. Indeed, he remembers that the first night he went to an Ulster Literary Theatre performance had been as a result of Purcell's insistence: 'One night in digs Purcell suddenly appeared and induced me to buy tickets to go and see the society that he was interested in.'[4] Sam Waddell's connection with the Belfast group was to last for the rest of the company's existence, although after moving south (working for the Irish Land Commission) his role became less direct in the actual running of the group. From the very beginning Waddell's commitment was evident and his activities were not confined to that of a playwright – he was for many years one of the company's leading actors, taking roles in his own plays and those of his contemporaries. The first of Mayne's plays, *The Turn of the Road,* was performed in Belfast in December 1906; in April of the following year the play made up half the bill during the Ulster Literary Theatre's first visit to the Abbey. Mayne's second piece for the company, *The Drone,* was performed for the first time at the Abbey in April of 1908 as part of the Ulster Literary Theatre's second visit to the Dublin theatre. *The Drone* was an instant success and would become one of the Ulster Literary Theatre's keynote pieces in the years to come. These Dublin performances would turn out to be especially significant for Mayne; he was amongst the cast for *The Drone* at the Abbey and this exposure resulted in an approach to join the well-established William Mollison company. While he did indeed agree to join Mollison's group, he also remained a member of the Ulster Literary Theatre. Importantly one of the conditions of his new association, however, ensured that Mollison's company retained first option on any of Mayne's new plays; and so it was that his next play, *The Troth,* was first performed by the Mollison company at the Crown Theatre (Peckham) in October of 1908. The Ulster Literary Theatre would perform *The Troth* later that same year.

The success of Rutherford Mayne's and Lewis Purcell's social realist work for the Ulster Literary Theatre only confirmed what had quickly become evident in the previous months. Pairing the more realist works of Mayne and Purcell with the mythological pieces discussed above merely highlighted that the strength of the company was in the former kind of drama. Audience reactions had also only served to reinforce this gathering sense. Joseph Campbell may have noticed that the farmers of Toomebridge had little time for the pseudo-ancient musings of Hobson's *Brian of Banba,* but he also noted that when it came to Purcell's *The Enthusiast* they 'entered into the fun and the homely touches of type, local idiom and situation with the greatest enjoyment'.[5] Cathal O'Shannon, who would go on to become a writer and journalist of some note, remembers well his reaction as a thirteen-year-old to these 1905 performances. For him the real triumph of the Ulster

Literary Theatre was in *The Enthusiast,* and the way it captured the life of those that watched from the audience:

> For the first time I saw the kind of people that I knew and lived among and sprung from in Co. Antrim and Co. Derry were there alive and talking as they talked at home and round about home.[6]

Embracing this widely perceived strength added greatly to the company's claims for cultural importance. Indeed by the time a 1908 number of *Samhain* came around W.B. Yeats was forced to admit, in the course of an article criticising other Dublin theatres, that 'the Ulster Players are the only dramatic society, apart from [the Abbey] which is doing serious artistic work'.[7] It seems that even Yeats had to concede that in the Ulster Literary Theatre Ireland had a serious company. Here was a talented group of writers dedicated to putting on stage the kind of life that they could see being lived every day outside the auditorium's doors in Ulster.

The fact that they had become so accomplished at just this work was acknowledged by a growing popularity amongst audiences in Dublin as well as Belfast. A performance of Rutherford Mayne's *The Drone* would guarantee a large and appreciative audience. The action of *The Drone,* as with most of Mayne's early work, takes place exclusively within the bounds of a small kitchen in rural Co. Down. The story concerns an 'old bluffer', Uncle Dan, who will do anything to avoid work. To this end he manages to convince his brother with whom he lives that he is working on an amazing new invention – 'Fan-bellows' – which will make them all rich. The play is most notable for its use of regional dialect and mannerisms. On hearing, for example, that Dan wants money to go to London to seek a patent for his 'invention', a visitor to the house comments (to Dan's niece, Mary):

> ALICK: That uncle of yours, Mary, heth he's as canny a keoghboy as I've seen. It's the queer tears he'll be taking to himself in London if I know anything.[8]

Mayne's knowing use of local idiom and speech patterns, as well as the abstract mapping involved in the idea of London as a place unsuitable for Uncle Dan, all contrive to write this part of the island into the 'imaginative record' of the nation. Uncle Dan becomes a kind of benign 'playboy', employing bluff rhetoric and fake technical terms to avoid admitting that his persona of great inventor is a fake. Just as with Synge's *Playboy,* Mayne's piece explores the relationship between language and action (or, perhaps more accurately in both cases, the relationship between language and a lack of action). The work's importance lies in the fact that it is a northern linguistic landscape that is projected on stage and as such may be read as a co-response to Synge's writing of the West into the imaginative landscape of revival.

The poster issued by the Ulster Literary Theatre for its visit to the Abbey with *The Drone* is of note here for its presentation of just such a corresponding, but particular, northern voice. The Belfast group advertised Mayne's play in the following terms (the original typography has been retained):

> <u>Irish Plays</u>
> The Irish of the Northern Province are a type distinct from any other in Ireland. They are as far apart from the Scotch peasant as they are from the men of Galway: they are the product of the strange history of Ulster, but one cannot see these plays and players, and understand the people they portray, without recognising once and for all, and despite many peculiar distinctions, they are **intensely Irish**.[9]

The poster graphically demonstrates the manner in which the Ulster Literary Theatre was not simply attempting to write back against the construction of a northern difference, but was, rather, engaged with the possibilities of a more complex sense of Irish identity. That said, the rather insistent typography and tone also retain a strong echo of Hobson's foundational cry ('Damn Yeats, we'll write our own plays!): the poster reveals not just the work being done, but the work the group felt still needed to be done.

Interestingly it was precisely this proposal of a decentred 'localised knowledge' that was highlighted by many of the contemporary reviewers sympathetic to the Ulster Literary Theatre's response to the Abbey's work. The *United Irishman,* for example, posted the following response to the visit of *The Drone* to the Abbey:

> An invasion of the men of Ulster carries the imagination back to heroic days and some still untarnished glory of the epic, I could almost believe, hovers about the band of players who unfolded the delightful humanities of Ulster life in these two plays. (1 May 1908)

The articulation of an Ulster humanity is pinpointed here as the power of the Ulster Literary Theatre's contribution to the reawakening of 'heroic days'. Implicit in the review is the notion that it is Mayne's knowledge of his locality and his desire to give life to its specificity that operate as the most salient lesson to the decadences of the Abbey. *The Peasant,* moreover, highlighted the productivity of the northern company as another sign that the Ulster Literary Theatre was producing the most energetic and 'true' Irish drama. This productivity, and its supposed inverse at the Abbey, is used once again to point out the Dublin group's decadence and, perhaps, 'shallow cosmopolitanism':

> The visit of the Northern playwrights and players should serve as a stimulating example to our local society with the pretentious name, which apparently exists to talk and to hold rehearsals of plays that have been produced before, but gives little evidence of any capacity to add new work to the movement. (1 May 1908)

This reviewer's suggestion that the nomenclature of the Dublin company (its claim to be the 'National' theatre) reveals a certain 'pretentiousness' is clearly also intended to support the Ulster Literary Theatre's claim for a more regionally sensitive (and thus perhaps less élitist) cultural nationalism.

The reaction to Mayne's first piece, *The Turn of the Road* (1906), had been delineated along similar lines. Once again set in a Co. Down farm kitchen, the plot concerns a young man, Robbie-John Granahan, and his love for music – particularly the fiddle, which he plays with great flair. The play portrays the clash between the creative Robbie-John and the rest of his family, who are more concerned with the practicalities of making a living from their small farm. The nature of this clash, between 'culture' and modernity's post-industrial work ethic, engages the play with very familiar revivalist intellectual territory. Like many of its contemporaries, Mayne's play suggests the necessity to recover the primacy of 'art' and 'culture' in the face of a dehumanising economic modernity. Crucially, the performance of this dialectic is couched in terms also concerned with the relationship between cultural production and place: in the end, Mayne reminds his audience of the importance of locally grounded culture in the face of a homogenising tyrannical modernity. The play opens with the mother shouting at Robbie-John to stop playing his music. Her chastisement firmly establishes the central problematic of the play as the tension between artistic creativity and economic necessity:

> MRS GRANAHAN: I wish some one would stop that boy's fool nonsense wi' his fiddle. He's far too fond of playing. It would stand him better to mind his work. (*Calls*) Robbie! (*Louder*) D'you hear me, Robbie?[10]

This clash between the concerns of economy and 'industry' against those of creativity becomes doubly important in terms of the northern context. In what follows, Mayne defies the vision of the North as an industrialised cultural wasteland. This was a vision that had been drawn on time and again during this period to denigrate the North as a place lost to the darker desires of modernity – a place thus not in touch with the 'soul' of 'real Ireland'. In place of this Mayne provides a counter-vision of an underlying cultural potential that is in search of an expressive, performative framework.

Mayne's quest to highlight an as yet unrepresented but culturally valid voice is embodied here (as is so often the case) by the figure of the visiting 'tramp'. Robbie-John's brother has taken the man home as a warning of what lies in store for those who follow the creative life, for the tramp is also a great fiddler. It comes as no great surprise when the tramp turns out to have been a great and famous musician who has fallen on hard times. He offers to play some music for the father of the house, William John, but of a different kind to that expected:

Tramp:	Perhaps with your permission I may venture to play you a few extracts from my repertoire. I can play to suit all tastes from a simple country ballad to a concerto by Brahms or the great Russian composer Tschaikouski.
William John Granahan:	(*open-mouthed*) Them Rooshians has the tarr'ble names!

Placed in the context of the Ulster Literary Theatre's mission, the figure of the tramp opens up a performative space, similar to Hobson's poem 'Ulad', of a region with a vast untapped cultural potential in need of recovery or unearthing. Implicit here is a rejection of the North as simply the land of shipyards, factories and mills, an image that had been used by Irish unionists and British conservatives to demonstrate Ulster's integral position within the economy of Britain and Empire.

As suggested above, the search for an authentic use of dialect, as seen in William John Granahan's response (above), is also crucial to the play's significance within the Ulster Literary Theatre's project. Most of the piece, as with the later *Drone,* is played out in this particular dialect that Mayne worked so hard to capture. Robbie-John's grandfather, for example, warns him against following his heart and the music, telling him he will end up like the tramp; his speech is saturated in the rhythms and cadences of rural Co. Down:

Grandfather: Take heed till yourself. I know what's going on better nor you. Take an ould man's advice. Settle yourself down and give up that string instrument. Coorse, I dare say you may go and become a great man with it, but you are more like to become a cratur like thon that was in as not. There's no good running risks. And your father, I heerd him say himself, if you make your bed you'll lie on it, for he'll never help you out once you take to the fiddling.

In the end though Robbie-John can see no path to redemption and runs away from home to pursue his music. In the final moments of the play the grandfather chastises William John for being too harsh; and in the course of this dénouement it emerges that Robbie-John's father had once been a great fiddler as well but had given it up to focus on his work. The grandfather's chastisement in the closing moments reveals the double codes upon which the piece has been built:

Grandfather: Ye thought he was wasting time and money. D'ye think there's nothing in this life beyond making money above the rent. I tell you it's not the money alone that makes life worth livin.
It's the wee things you think nothing of, but that make your home a joy to come back till after a hard day's work. And you've sent out into the could and wet the one that's making your home something more than the common.
D'ye think the proud city folk will listen to his poor ould ballads with the heart of the boy singing through them. It's only us – it's only us, I say, as knows the long wild nights, and the wet and the rain and the mist of nights on the boglands – it's only us I say could listen him in the right way, (*sobbing*) and ye knowed, right well ye knowed, that every string of his fiddle was keyed to the crying of your own heart.

This refusal of a 'philistine' work ethic, and the promotion of cultural creativity as a fundamental necessity, finally position the play firmly within the revival's worldview. It is apparent too that *The Turn of the Road* in these final moments also becomes about the need for a cultural life that attends closely to the ontology of regional variance. We may read, then, in the grandfather's final chastisement a kind of 'performing back' to the revival's perceived occlusion of the North. Mayne points to the need for culture to represent with sensitivity the specific place (and history) out of which it is born (even if this place does not necessarily conform to the model of pre-colonial Gaelic 'purity'). That the 'proud city folk' would not be able to properly appreciate and 'listen to his poor ould ballads with the heart of the boy singing through them' also casts a sceptical eye over the metropolitan/cosmopolitan motives of those who turn country life into a spectacle for city dwellers.

Reviews of *The Turn of the Road* reveal that it was acknowledged as a significant contribution to the new drama. The *Irish Times* review of the Abbey performances, for example, declares that '*The Turn of the Road* . . . is beyond question one of the most sterling products of the Irish Literary revival ever seen at the Abbey Theatre' (1 April 1907). The response in the North was also for the most part positive, and perhaps more knowing with regard to what Mayne had set out to capture. The *Ulster Guardian* (30 November 1907), in the course of reviewing the Belfast performances, parses exactly the nexus of identities and intentions discussed above as central to the success of the piece:

> It is of the nature of a paradox that the Ulster type of character which has stamped itself so definitely and completely on every part of the civilised and uncivilised world should lack its adequate expression in literature. It is something, then, of a triumph for Rutherford Mayne, of the ULT, to have written a play which brings the very soul of Ulster before us.
>
> Distinctly Irish, yet owing as little to the Celt of the Western seaboard as to the cotter of Ayrshire, I venture to assert that two out of every three men in Belfast on seeing or reading *The Turn of the Road* will unconsciously exclaim – 'That's exactly it; I was reared that way myself'.

The insistence on an Ulster uniqueness – equidistant from the West of Ireland and from the cottages of Ayrshire – while still 'distinctly Irish', locates the play firmly within the network of cultural exchanges found at the centre of the Ulster Literary Theatre's project. Implicit here is the idea of uniqueness not predicated merely on the nature of geographical terrain, but also radically informed by the specific historical discourses that coincided there. By outlining the network of 'multi-cultural' narratives coinciding in the 'Ulster type', the reviewer sees the characters on stage as tropes of history as well as regional peculiarity. That this play was judged to be important because it made room for an identity that had previously gone without 'adequate expression in literature' thus becomes more significant. The play is here judged as performing the northern historical experience, and this role is intrinsically embedded within the broader search for a newly invigorated Irish identity.

It was precisely *The Turn of the Road*'s double expression outlined by the *Ulster Guardian* – distinctly Ulster while remaining distinctly Irish – that Whitford Kane would remember as key to his conversion to cultural nationalism. Kane would become a regular actor for the Ulster Literary Theatre before becoming a famous figure on the stages of England and America. The fact that Kane cites this piece as the theatrical experience that triggered for him a further investigation of just what it meant to be northern Irish reveals that the play was a major success for the aims of the Ulster Literary Theatre. Kane, indeed, remembers that it was Mayne himself who took him to the Ulster Literary Theatre's production:

> Up to this time my entire theatrical experience had been English playhouses and I hardly knew anything about the Abbey or the Ulster theatres . . .
>
> It is for my introduction to the Ulster Literary Theatre, and to Rutherford Mayne in particular, that I am indebted for finding myself. One evening during one of my summer vacations, he took me to see his first play – *The Turn of the Road* . . . This performance must have struck some chord in me, for I went again next night; after that I was asked to join a gathering at the Arts Club. There I heard for the first time some of the beautiful folksongs and poems of my own country, and as I listened to them, I realised how Irish I really was, and also how intensely Irish Ulster was in spite of its many peculiar distinctions.[11]

Thus *The Turn of the Road* records a valuable instance in the mediation of the Irishness of Ulster to Ulster, and of the specificity of Ulster to Ireland, while still managing to embrace the 'many peculiar distinctions' in the process. Mayne's first play was an almost perfect expression of the desire expressed in *Ulad* to make the local the proper carrier of authentic identity, and to reveal the network of authenticities, each valid in their own way, that could play their part in the larger puzzle of what it was to be Irish.

Purcell's *Enthusiast* and the Problem of History

Aptly for the playwright who, with *The Pagan*, would push the boundaries of the Ulster Literary Theatre's mythic form, Purcell's *The Enthusiast* (1905) was the group's most radical examination of the contemporary problems of history and society in the North during these early years of development. As with the work of Mayne, Purcell's piece was an attempt to make room within nationalist drama for those 'northern bodies' that were the result of a quite particular history. Even more overtly than Mayne's work, moreover, Purcell's second play is one of the very earliest twentieth-century attempts to represent the intercommunal tensions of the North on stage. *The Enthusiast* is the story of a young Protestant idealist, 'James McKinstry', who returns from Belfast to his family home in rural Antrim planning to establish a farming co-operative in the area. The piece is a powerful exploration of the communal tensions, bisected along religious and political lines, just below the surface of farming life in this part of Ulster. Born along by the same attempts to capture local dialect and accent that had marked out Mayne's work for such praise, and motivated too by the spirit of the previous year's feis, Purcell's play seems intent on replacing Synge's Glens of Wicklow with the Glens of Antrim. Much more than a mere expression of local curiosities, however, Purcell's work is a serious (and controversial) exploration of the multivalent relationships between history, identity and place that informed the political landscape of the North in the years of the Home Rule debate.

The piece opens with James's aunt sounding off about the transformation in his dress sense. James's adoption of city fashions in this early exchange foreshadows his much more 'worrying' conversion to an ideology alien to the closed farming community:

> AUNT: He's a bigger swell ivery time he comes hame. Last year it wuz a white, india-rubber tap coat. This time it's yella' boots. But maybe he'll be wantin' a drop mair tay.[12]

The aunt's speech also nicely demonstrates Purcell's efforts to articulate a distinctively Ulster 'language-scape'. What may at first seem like an over-use of local idiom does nevertheless correspond well with the similar emphasis on Irish-English at the early Abbey. The vital difference in this case is that the reclaimed voice is that of an Antrim woman – a character who later in the play will give voice to the concerns of a community distrustful of 'Home Rulers' and suspect 'outside' ideas. The play's central concern is quickly outlined as James tells his father (William John) and brother (Sam) of his 'great idea'. James has been, as he tells them, 'reading and thinking a lot lately about the old village communities' and has come to wonder what would happen if the same 'sort of co-operation' were applied in the area once again. James's idea is essentially for the sort of farming co-operative that had played such a large part in Horace Plunkett's schemes for the benefit of smallholders around the turn of the century. Plunkett had founded the 'Irish Agricultural Organisation Society' (IAOS) in 1894, in the wake of the mass land reforms that marked out the final decades of the nineteenth century. As P.J. Mathews outlines:

> Although the majority of Irish farmers now enjoyed fixity of tenure, most of them lacked the expertise to compete in an increasingly sophisticated and

> mechanised agricultural market. For this reason the IAOS was set up to educate farmers in modern agricultural practices and encourage them to benefit from economics of scale by farming co-operative societies and credit unions.[13]

Purcell was an admirer of Plunkett and his ideas, and the two had also met just the previous year when Plunkett had been the guest of honour for the prize giving at the *Feis na nGleann* (June 1904). From James's description of his ideas, it is obvious that he has been influenced by exactly this sort of thinking on his 'travels'; it is clear too that his father and brother remain completely bewildered, forcing him into a further explanation of his plans:

> JAMES: As it is at present everyone is working blindly for himself. Everyone has more work to do than he can accomplish, if he wishes to get the best results from his land. Suppose now that a dozen farmers agreed to combine their farms and work them on a large scale, as they do, for instance, in America. You would find that, with properly organised labour, it could be made to pay with one-half the sum of work that is expended on the separate dozen farms. Do you follow me?

Crucially, James's vision of farming co-operation can only really work if it is in the context of a broader communal *rapprochement*. The importance of the play is mainly tied to this dynamic. Drawing on the framework of farming co-operatives, Purcell embeds his staging of northern rural life within the political framework of its time (most particularly, the issue of Home Rule and the power of the Orange Order). Just how easily could Plunkett's vision of co-operation be transplanted to a small Antrim community seems to be one of the main questions posed by the play. As befits one of the founders of the Ulster Literary Theatre, Purcell comes down firmly on James's side in his enthusiasm for intercommunal co-operation, but in the end Purcell's is a somewhat sceptical and pessimistic conclusion.

Nevertheless its combination of plot and concern for the remarkable language of this part of the world establishes *The Enthusiast* as a significant co-response to the ruralism presented on the Abbey's stage. While the work of Synge and Lady Gregory by no means completely removed rural life from political reality, there is a sense in their work of a return to a more pure 'sacred' image of pre-modern Ireland: as Synge would write in his *Autobiography,* 'Everything Irish became sacred'. Purcell writes back to this vision of a sacred peasantry with a play based entirely on the political and economic engagement of the farming communities. Thus the image of a rural but none the less politicised life is heightened as James discusses with his family his plan to call a meeting so that the farmers of the area may hear his idea. It becomes clear that even a decision on the meeting's location cannot escape the invasive dynamics of the Home Rule issue in Ulster:

JAMES:	But *I'm* sure about it father. I intend to call a meeting of the countryside and lay the scheme before them.
FATHER:	A meetin'?
SAM:	In the orange hall?
JAMES:	No, no. It can't be in the orange hall.
FATHER:	But the's no other hall hereabouts.
JAMES:	You see, it wouldn't do to have it there. We want *everybody* into this. Neither Home Rulers nor Catholics would come to it. I'll hold it in the big meadow.
SAM:	Home Rulers in it?
AUNT:	(*throwing down "Christian Herald"*) An' Catholics? Lord a' mercy!
FATHER:	Jamie, lad, I doubt – doubt–
AUNT:	A meetin' o' Home Rulers in *our* meadow. Lord 'a mercy.
JAMES:	(*exasperated*) Oh, how long is this damnable division of the people to last? This miserable suspicion!

Fraught exchanges such as these repeatedly demonstrate the particularly heightened brand of politicisation that northern life experienced during these years. James's family cannot help but place the discussion of farming co-operation within a context of politico-religious communal boundaries. The above debate also reveals the play's concern for the problems in Ulster attendant to any attempt to re-imagine space and place. The choice of field for the meeting thus becomes a microcosm of the wider northern problematic of how to re-imagine national, as well as intercommunal, spaces. It is a reminder (aimed perhaps at the Abbey coterie) that the remapping of the nation's sense of self required a negotiation with more than one set of historically informed identities. *The Enthusiast* is thus simultaneously a representation of the multiple historical narratives that coincided most powerfully in the North, and a partial deconstruction of dramatic techniques that sought a more straightforward (and singly calibrated) historical construct.

In the end the meeting does go ahead and, as seemed inevitable from the outset, descends into a mass brawl delineated by sectarian divisions. 'Rab', a worker on the McKinstry farm, attends the meeting and on his return to the house tells the aunt about its progress: 'Oh, it wuz a gran' meetin'. I niver seen a better fight.' When the aunt asks him to explain his meaning, Rab relates the scene:

> RAB: Oh, aye – Weel, as I say, I wuzn't botherin' my head much, at the start, but as far as I mind, about a dozen got up in turns an' said as it might be a good thing an' it might not, they had no knowins. Then Andy Moore got up – 'no young Andy, the oul' man – an' he said they were goin' till upset the Crown and Constitution. An' at the wind up he axed Jamie if he cud gie scripture for it, an' Jamie as much as said he cudn't. Then somebody shouted 'Socialisms', and Ned Grahme – he wuz drunk – he shouted it wuz a Fenian thing, an' he kep' shoutin' that the whole time. An' sez I to myself, this is goin' to be the warm meetin'.

On one level Purcell may be seen to attribute the failure of co-operation to Orange Order religiosity ('if he cud gie scripture for it') and distrust of anything ideologically other ('Socialisms', 'Fenian thing'), and there is certainly something of this in the play's progress. But perhaps too we can read in the play a kind of response from Purcell to those of his fellow nationalist playwrights who found so little room for the North and its specificity in their work. In *The Enthusiast* the North defiantly remains as the most radical expression of the historical problematics within Irish identity; and they are problematics, Purcell seems to suggest, that nationalism needed to negotiate with rather than simply occlude.

The ending of the play (which proved controversial) locates the contemporary problem faced by James in terms of the skein of competing ideologies that informed northern life. James's brother Sam relates how some of 'the boys are away to bring out the drums', and the final moments of the play are dominated by the sound of the Lambeg drums beating outside the cottage. James has escaped the violent crowd and sits once again in the cottage kitchen listening to the sounds from outside. As he sits, James momentarily begins to feel that all is not lost and that he may try again, but the sound of the drums puts an end to such optimism:

> JAMES: A nice ending to all my dreams! (*Pause*) I wonder if I *could* have done anything? Was it an accidental failure? The first attempt is often a failure, that's a fact. (*sitting up suddenly*) God! I wonder if I am a coward for giving in my gun at the first reverse? (*Pause*) I might carry it out yet –

in spite of everything. (*sinking back*) I might – I might – I might.

(*There is a sound of distant cheering, and then of drums. James starts and sits up straight, listening intently*)

JAMES: (*slowly*) Listen!

(*A pause. Then the sound of talking becomes louder in room, and Rab laughs loudly. Then silence, except for the distant drums*)

JAMES: (*sinking back slowly in chair*) No – no.

The hopeful young Protestant idealist is in the end defeated by the ideological interests represented by the sound of drums. His aunt wants no part of Home Rulers in the family meadow, the crowd suspects a Fenian plot and in the end it is the Orange Order that provides communal cohesion rather than James's vision of co-operation.

While the ending remains pessimistic, the overall plot movement concerns the need for strategies that allow for a representation of complex identity patterns. The field of the meeting (and fight) symbolises the contested nature of Ulster as imagined space. The North thus becomes the location of complexities that must be resolved if a proper Irish nationalism is to be enacted and performed. The play in this way presents the North as the keeper of a nationalism that through necessity has a more acute understanding of the dynamics of history and identity. The task in hand, Purcell seems to suggest, is to arrive at strategies that can accommodate the various oppositional moments of danger apparent on the island rather than constructing a series of fanciful images that seek to write over such tensions. It was in this way that the Ulster Literary Theatre strove to fill the perceived gap articulated by both Mayne and MacNamara when they recognised that *Cathleen Ní Houlihán* did not adequately speak to the North. In such moments we can perhaps see a foreshadowing of Declan Kiberd's image of Cathleen's shawl replaced with a patchwork quilt. Much of the point, after all, of this pre-partition northern cultural nationalism, speaking from its peculiarly inside/outside position, was to highlight the need for just such a re-imagining. Returning to such plays demonstrates the ways in which the Ulster Literary Theatre sought a cultural mode that could negotiate with the inside/outside dynamic of the North within/without the wider cultural-nationalist project. Re-placing these plays in their original context also reveals how the Ulster Literary Theatre used its singular position within revival to unpack many of the assumptions found at the heart of the Irish cultural-nationalist vision. In the end these first plays can be read as an early demonstration of the northern revival's 'meta-nationalist' position. Read or reread in this way, they may be seen as preparing the ground for a playwright who would extend the potential and possibilities inherent in such a position. The work of Gerald MacNamara will occupy the last chapters of this study.

CHAPTER SEVEN

Gerald MacNamara's Other Space: Myth Writes Back

'We should have thought of it a million years ago, in the nineties'.
Vladimir, in Samuel Beckett's *Waiting for Godot*

Now, the first thing to be said about Parody is that it plays with the gods.
Arthur Quiller-Couch, 'Preface' to *Parodies and Imitations Old and New*

If, as Martin Esslin has famously asserted, the theatre is 'the place where a nation thinks in front of itself',[1] it is clear, even after the most cursory glance at recent histories of Irish theatre, that the thinking of Gerald MacNamara has been somewhat forgotten.[2] The following chapters seek to re-establish MacNamara as the Ulster Literary Theatre's most significant creative figure. It is in his work that we find the most complete articulation of the cultural position that had informed the Ulster Literary Theatre's foundation and early performance history. Indeed, MacNamara's work extended and developed the philosophy of a 'northern revival' in ways that managed to interrogate almost every implication of that very idea. Thus *Ulad*'s predicted arrival of an Ulster writer who would reshape the meaning of that term was fulfilled with Gerald MacNamara's intervention into the Irish theatre scene. His first three plays represent the greatest achievements of the Ulster Literary Theatre's early years (achievements the group would never really match in its later history). As well as bringing the cultural project of the Ulster Literary Theatre to its most complete and radical expression, moreover, MacNamara's plays also complete the critical logic that has informed this study of northern revivalism. Resituating his work within its cultural and historical context reveals MacNamara's plays as examples *par excellence* of a northern cultural nationalism. Each of them is a performative negotiation with Ulster's specificity in the nexus of political and cultural exchange that mark out this period. MacNamara develops to a remarkable degree the discursive duality that we have seen as the defining quality of 'Ulster Literary Theatre plays'; his plays are born out of, but also interrogate, the North's multivalent relationships with the revival's evolving 'Ulster question'.

Gerald MacNamara was the pseudonym of Henry Cooke Morrow, known to his friends and Belfast at large as Harry Morrow. Born in Belfast on 27 August 1865 (he died on 11 January 1938), Harry was one of the elder sons in the well-known Morrow family. As noted above, the Morrows were crucial formative members of the Ulster Literary Theatre, and Harry Morrow's contributions as playwright and actor were particularly critical to the success enjoyed by the Belfast group. His contribution as playwright, indeed, spans pretty much the lifetime of the Ulster Literary Theatre: his first play was produced in 1907 and his last first took to the stage in 1934. This period of theatrical productivity marks MacNamara out as an almost exact contemporary of W.B. Yeats, a neat conjunction that seems all the more appropriate for a playwright who spent much of his career writing back to the nationalist imaginings articulated by his more famous contemporary. Yeats's relationship with the northern company had, after all, been somewhat ambiguous, and MacNamara's comments on *Cathleen Ní Houlihán* appear representative of his perception that Yeats's vision was unsuitable for the northern context. Although varied in subject, MacNamara's project to 'write back' often took the form of a constructive scepticism, a sceptical eye that was often cast over the mythic and historical technique inherent in the Abbey's drive to re-present the Irish nation on stage.

Gerald MacNamara began his career as a playwright in 1907 with a remarkable intervention (co-written with 'Lewis Purcell') onto the Belfast theatre scene: *Suzanne and the Sovereigns. Suzanne* was in some ways a natural extension of the method and concerns of Purcell's other mythic work, *The Pagan.* Like *The Pagan, Suzanne and the Sovereigns* reproposes historical narrative as a complex nexus of slippage and dysfunction. While the piece was a collaborative project, there is evidence to suggest (discussed further below) that MacNamara was the senior partner in this extraordinary burlesque. The plot of *Suzanne* reworks Ireland's position in seventeenth-century European politics; it also reworks the role of this history in early twentieth-century Ulster. In the course of the play, events such as the Siege of Derry and the Battle of the Boyne are recast as parodic farce, and as a consequence the narrativised nature of historical discourse is laid bare and unravelled. It is a piece that sought to deconstruct those dramatic tendencies that explicitly used and reshaped historical narrative in terms of a particular political moment (MacNamara also acknowledges within the piece that its performance could not fully escape this process either).

Two years later MacNamara followed up the success of *Suzanne* with another parodic *tour de force* entitled *The Mist That Does Be on the Bog* (1909). In this MacNamara takes on another revivalist icon, the *idea* of the rural peasant (rather than the actual people) that had become so important to the material of Synge and Lady Gregory in particular. As the plot develops MacNamara relocates the concerns of the North of Ireland in a traditional Syngian landscape symbolised by a cottage in the West. This second work from MacNamara also re-plays revivalist approaches to modernity and place, as the traditional dynamic of the romantic West versus northern modernity is unpacked, exposed and unravelled on stage. It is also simply one of the funniest parodies of Synge ever staged. As Mary Burgess has put it, 'to read MacNamara's play is to alter one's sense of Synge forever'.[3] Then in 1912 came the play for which MacNamara was (and remains) best known, the riotously funny (and potentially just plain riotous) *Thompson in Tír-na-nÓg*. The play involves the story of an Orangeman (the eponymous Andy Thompson) wandering around the precincts of Tír-na-nÓg. *Thompson* was the Ulster Literary Theatre's most successful production, rivalled only in popularity by Rutherford Mayne's *The Drone*. Although this was the only one of MacNamara's plays to be published in his lifetime, the significances of this proto-modernist tale have – as with the rest of his work – been largely overlooked and/or undervalued. It is these first three works that will form the main body of the analysis that follows. They represent (of those plays still available to us) MacNamara's most radical intervention into pre-partition northern nationalism. These first three works also reveal MacNamara as a supreme parodist with a really quite unique voice.

Gerald MacNamara's extraordinary burlesques on the political and cultural machinations of the Home Rule/revival period return us anew to the productive inside/outside dialectic that characterises northern cultural nationalism in these years. It is this now largely overlooked playwright who drew most radically on just this northern specificity, and it is through his work that its cultural logic finds both its most profound revelation and a conclusion of sorts. As with the other Ulster Literary Theatre playwrights, it was just this northern nationalist 'duality' that propelled MacNamara towards his very specific dramatic vision. In almost every way, though, it seems that MacNamara took this enabling position further, with much more radical consequences. His work simultaneously assumed a coherence with the methodology and philosophy of the Abbey's performance of revival, whilst also undertaking a deconstruction of the philosophical underpinnings of that very project. As a result MacNamara's work occupies an empowered position: while it clearly functioned within a revivalist framework, his work also managed to undertake the kind of commentary and unpacking normally reserved for those writers who arrived in the wake of the revival. It seems somehow all the more apt, indeed, that a writer so obviously fascinated by the qualities of time and its manipulation in narrative should occupy this temporally unstable position. Or, to look at it another way, perhaps it is just this obsession that enabled MacNamara to occupy such a strangely uncanny locale of meaning and representation, producing plays firmly situated in a revivalist framework, yet also pointing to a 'post-revival' deconstructive technique. Whether in terms of his re-visioning of Synge's West, or exploding the mythical pretensions of Yeats, Gregory et al., MacNamara extended and fulfilled the Ulster Literary Theatre's reputation for 'seeing it differently'. It was just this ability that has led Mary Burgess to invoke MacNamara as the Ulster Literary Theatre's 'most unusual and pioneering playwright . . . whose early attempts at expressionist drama pre-empted those of several later playwrights by years'.[4] The chapters that follow examine the forms and strategies that facilitated this different sight. Key to any such analysis is MacNamara's search for a parodic 'other space', which allowed him to explore the limitations and innercontradictions of any *Nationalist* position. In this regard it soon becomes clear that, as well as exploring the localised functioning of Ulster unionism, MacNamara's work also speaks about the more generic operation of *Nationalism* – and here we may include Ireland's cultural and advanced nationalisms.

Given such strong and far-reaching claims, it seems especially curious that the name and work of Gerald MacNamara should remain so relatively little known. Until really quite recently this Belfast playwright has been almost completely lost from the canon, and perhaps even 'sub-canon', of twentieth-century Irish drama. Yet in the first two decades of the Ulster Literary Theatre's existence, MacNamara's works were amongst the most popular on the Irish theatre scene; and this popularity was not limited to Belfast but also included Dublin audiences. MacNamara's work was performed in Dublin theatres, including the Abbey, where it received warm appreciation and approval for what was seen as a much-needed deflation of the pretensions of the 'Abbey school'. Despite this powerful cultural voice, there would appear to be little room for MacNamara's vision within modern-day critical practice. Indeed it may be argued that, if anything, MacNamara's work has in recent times fallen through the gap created by the oppositional tensions within the field of Irish studies. His plays are presumably included in Edna Longley's approval for David Kennedy's summation of the Ulster Literary Theatre and its plays as 'dim giants from the Irish sagas [declaiming] in blank verse to blanker halls' and, indeed, as a 'slavish clone' of the Dublin movement.[5] (As we will see, 'imitation' was indeed central to much of MacNamara's work, but its deployment was of much greater power than Kennedy and Longley's dismissal of the Ulster Literary Theatre would suggest.) Furthermore, the *Field Day Anthology of Irish Writing*, in the course of its one-paragraph reference to the Ulster Literary Theatre's achievements, concludes that 'The first consequential Northern playwright was St John Ervine'.[6] Such assessments have marginalised the Ulster Literary Theatre's achievements and muted its potentially strong voice in the record of northern nationalism in the years before partition. One of the main objects of this study has been to reclaim and recuperate playwrights like MacNamara from their position of critical marginalisation. Key to this reclamation is MacNamara's lifelong project to construct and give voice to a parodic 'other space'. It is in this much overlooked work, finally, that we may detect some of the earliest possibilities of an Irish 'post-nationalist' voice; and crucially it is out of the North's uncanny revival *doppelgänger* that such a possibility emerges.

A *parody*, a *parody* with a kind of miraculous gift to make it absurder than it was
Ben Jonson

Re-establishing MacNamara as one of the great parodists of the revival (in both senses of that phrase) requires a closer examination of the idea and function of parodic practices. As Gérard Genette points out, 'parody' (*parodia*) is one of that select band of literary terms that reaches down to our own age from the Greek classical period: 'At the origins of its use, or very near its origin . . . is Aristotle's *Poetics*.'[7] Genette is reminding us that parody is as old as the cultural practices it seeks to rework; no mere afterthought, parody is actually one of the primary motors of cultural development and progress. Seen in this light, we can begin to rescue parody, as Linda Hutcheon puts it, from that sense of 'ridiculing imitation mentioned in the standard dictionary definitions'.[8] While imitation is important in the parodic act, to suggest that it only this is to limit its ideological and critical potential.

Parody is a mode of transformational possibility precisely because it acts as a form of 'authorised transgression' in terms of that which is normatively dominant. Taken in these terms, parody enacts a kind of regulatory surveillance, providing a safety valve and outlet for those pressures that build up in any cultural system. Most importantly, perhaps, the parodic is one of the ways in which 'newness enters the world'.

Parody is, then, an act of transformation and translation, and it operates across a series of interpretative and performative levels. At its heart parody operates as a critical function, performing a kind of commentary on that which is its 'target'. It is this, in the first instance, which lifts the parodic beyond the merely imitative; as Simon Dentith puts it, parody is 'part of a range of cultural practices, which allude, with deliberate evaluative intonation, to precursor texts'.[9] What is conjured here is a rather specific relationship between targeted 'text' and parodic reworking, a relationship Genette describes in terms of the *hypotext,* as the original or preceding text, transformed into the parodic *hypertext.* Dentith's insistence on an 'evaluative intonation' also usefully indexes the parodic as an innately critical move. The parodic in these readings is that which makes intertextuality not just visible but the very point of the cultural act. Indeed the extent and range of intertextual exchange revealed by the shift from *hypo*text to *hyper*text is central to our positioning of parody and its critical power. At one rather reductive level intertextuality 'denotes the myriad *conscious* ways in which texts are alluded to or cited in other texts: the dense network of quotation, glancing reference, imitation, polemical refutation and so on in which all texts have their being'.[10] Taken on these terms, parody, and indeed most cultural production, could be read simply as an act of recycling or cannibalism (and while the postmodern artist in particular may well be a knowing *bricoleur,* this reading of intertextuality is not adequate to the job at hand).

To fully understand the parodic and its importance, we have to extend our reading of intertextuality beyond that concerned with obvious exchange and cannibalisation. Rather we must take intertextuality as something much more fundamental, as something which reveals the 'dense web of allusion' out of which all texts and indeed all utterances emerge.[11] Instead of obvious referential quotation, intertextuality reveals itself as speaking to, out of, and against the very linguistic fabric that makes up any and all discursive systems. It is this latter more invasive reading of intertextuality that informs our discussion of parody here. It is this position too that shapes Linda Hutcheon's discussion on the nature of the parodic, a discussion that extends this mode's politicality in useful ways. Hutcheon moves away from Genette's specific reading of the parodic as something focused on the relationship between one *text* and another, whereby the hypertext is read as in a direct relation to its target. We might read this conceptualisation, for example, as more fully informed by the first reading of intertextuality, as that which directly consumes and transforms other textual instances. Hutcheon, while taking this first level of intertextual relation as a given, also reads the parodic as an operation with more generic or expansive potential. In place of the 'direct target' model, Hutcheon reveals in parody a relationship between parodic *hypertext* and *world* (or world as text). Clearly working from a more invasive reading of the intertextual, she locates in the parodic the capability to interrogate, reshape, translate and transform the fabric that makes up discourse itself. We need not always look for an exact original hypotext, in other words. For Hutcheon, parody (particularly in its postmodern phase perhaps) may be seen to take as its target a more generic cultural or discursive practice and the rules that allow it to function.

In the work of Gerald MacNamara both levels of parody's functioning may be seen at work. In the chapters that follow we will see how MacNamara's plays situate themselves, quite explicitly at times, as hypertexts that reveal in performance a clear 'evaluative intonation' in their relation to targeted hypotexts. These originating hypotexts include Yeats's mythological plays, the sacred peasantry of Synge and Gregory et al., and the historiography and iconography of a re-empowered Orange Order. But what will also become clear is that MacNamara's parodic method has higher ambitions than this straightforward and targeted performative commentary would suggest. Gerald MacNamara's plays are not simply parodic responses to particular cultural and political artefacts; rather, his work seeks to re-examine the fabric of discourse out of which such artefacts emerge. In his response to Yeatsian mythology, for example, MacNamara's parodic transformation is not simply concerned with the actualities of Yeats's dramaturgy but with cultural nationalism's drive to designate certain narratives as sacred. The same applies to his parodic unravelling of the Orange Order: it is the search for a sacred history that MacNamara seeks to parody as much as the precise hypotext of the Boyne battle or the Siege of Derry. Parody did not simply allow MacNamara to target certain artefacts, in other words; he was instead concerned to reveal and re-examine the very networks and frames of reference that produced such artefacts as keepers of meaning in the modern world.

Key to MacNamara's importance to this study is the contention that it was his position as a cultural-nationalist playwright writing out of Ulster, and thus performing from the perceived periphery of revival, that allowed him to undertake this parodic commentary on the revival from within/without. Position is, after all, important to how parody works, its very etymology revealing an operation that is 'multi-directional'. While *parodia* is usually recalled to explain parody as 'counter-song', as in a response to or against some hypo-utterance, this reading occludes another cultural role. As well as 'counter', *para* also suggests 'beside', as in a parallel co-response (and here we can already begin to see how useful the parodic mode would have been to a grouping such as the Ulster Literary Theatre). In this reading the relationship between hyper and hypo utterance is not solely one of oppositional response, it can also be a symbiotic co-response: parody as 'supplement' to that which is parodied. It is here that we can pinpoint parody as revealing the silences and gaps inherent in any dominant cultural system. This twin reading of parody as 'counter' and 'beside' (or supplementary) is particularly useful in terms of MacNamara's relationship not only to revival but also to the political culture specific to Ulster at this time. It is this function of parody, as a multi-directed synthesis, that provided MacNamara with the representational facility demanded by his particular cultural location and attendant needs. The specificity of his northern cultural-nationalist position allowed MacNamara to appropriate and relocate sites of meaning from various discursive spaces, creating in the process new spaces of interpretation and critical meaning. It is of note, then, that Linda Hutcheon should isolate the key formulations of parody as 'repetition with critical distance' and 'ironic inversion'. Such a reading – ironic inversion facilitated by 'critical distance' – fits neatly into the network of cultural relations between northern nationalism, its southern counterpart and Ulster unionism established in the course of this study. The 'critical distance' inherent in northern nationalist cultural production was harnessed and utilised most radically by MacNamara's parodic deconstruction of the very terms upon which nationalist and unionist discourses were based.

The relationship, finally, between 'parodic play' and audience is crucial. In a sense, the parodic codes used to construct this 'other' discursive space can only fully operate when co-ordinated with the decoding participation of the audience (or reader). The re-presentation of parodic meaning thus depends on the interaction between performance and the nexus of knowledge held by the audience/reader. Hutcheon's work usefully situates this interactivity as akin to the functioning of metaphor:

> In some ways, parody might be said to resemble metaphor. Both require that the decoder construct a second meaning through inferences about surface statements and supplement the foreground with acknowledgement and knowledge of a backgrounded context.[12]

MacNamara's plays depend upon precisely this form of interaction and communal interpretation; it is in the decoding process that MacNamara's works are most fully parodic. The codes of Irish nationalism and Ulster unionism are reprocessed and re-presented on stage; in the exchange of meaning, interaction and interpretation, meaning becomes 'recontextualised' (and thus made new or different). It is in this parodic process that we may detect MacNamara's drive to construct a 'third space' of meaning. Indeed, it is in this move that MacNamara approaches a series of proto (post) modernist articulations. Linda Hutcheon has suggested, for example, that the parodic form is vital in the movement away from Romantic ideology to an embracing of modernist potential; as she puts it:

> It [parody] is a part of a move away from the tendency, within a Romantic ideology, to mask any sources by cunning cannibalization, and towards a frank acknowledgement (by incorporation) that permits ironic commentary.[13]

MacNamara was able to engage in such 'ironic commentary' precisely because of the critical distance built into the inside/outside position of northern nationalism as it sought to engage with the practices of revival. Yeats would wait until 'September 1913' to declare that 'Romantic Ireland's dead and gone'; MacNamara's embrace of parodic irony would suggest that many in the North had known this all along.

Missing Texts, Missing Interpretations:Some Problems with MacNamara

Given this chapter's central contention that MacNamara's oeuvre marks the most significant achievement of the Ulster Literary Theatre, it is all the more unfortunate that a significant portion of MacNamara's work is lost to the modern-day scholar. This is a problem that has undoubtedly contributed to the neglect suffered by this writer in recent times. Much like Alice Milligan, Gerald MacNamara was extremely modest when it came to his own work and status as a writer; as a result, most of his work was never published nor indeed collected in any methodical fashion. Rutherford Mayne, as long ago as 1938, highlighted this as a problem in need of rectifying if MacNamara's contribution was to be fully recognised:

> It is unfortunate that so little of his work has found its way into print. Beyond the publication of his best-known play *Thompson in Tir-na-nOg* by the Talbot Press, and a number of sketches and short plays published in *The Dublin Magazine,* the great bulk of his work exists precariously in manuscript. One can only hope some one in Ulster may rescue it into safe keeping. His own neglect to ensure this is only another example of his extreme modesty. He never bothered to look seriously on himself as a playwright that mattered. So with the decline of the Theatre he served so loyally, and the scanty material left in print, there is little showing nowadays of this courageous old Irish jester.[14]

This warning shot from the 1930s was for many decades ignored; MacNamara's work was not to be collected in any methodical fashion until the 1980s.[15] However, due to (as Mayne would have it) MacNamara's modesty and neglect of his own reputation, a significant portion of his achievement is lost. Of his later plays, we have no manuscripts for *The Throwbacks, Sincerity* or *Thompson on Terra Firma;* all that is left of these works are some tantalising comments and reviews.

The scant publication of MacNamara's plays coupled with the unfortunate loss of manuscripts goes some way to explaining the lack of interest in this remarkable and subversive revival figure. It does not, however, completely explain the major gap left in modern-day records concerning the role the North played in shaping and criticising the direction of revivalist drama. Something more complex is evidently at work. As has been noted above, MacNamara's work spans a clearly formative period in northern Irish history. His works were played out against the backdrop of Ulster's Home Rule problematic, and as such they sought to feed into the revivalist aesthetic while also negotiating with divergent and powerful political forces in the North. That this crucial record, through which the North's negotiation of its primary 'moment of danger' may be read, is largely missing from modern-day critical discourse points to a wider problematic than simply availability of primary material. This deeper problematic may be connected with MacNamara's search for an uninhabited space from which to unravel the logic of nationalism. As such, he stands outside many of the critical frameworks attached to this period in Irish drama by modern-day critical practice. Sam Hanna Bell, while commenting on MacNamara's reputation as a writer of inconsequential comedies, hints at the extra-mural importance of these plays:

> In so far as Gerald MacNamara has come down to posterity as a laughter-maker first and foremost, his genius has been unfairly diminished. Behind his

> writings is discernible a serious and informed political intelligence familiar with the intricacies and paradoxes of whatever period of Irish history he has chosen as a backcloth to his satire. Indeed it is this exhaustive knowledge that kept his pilloried audiences suspended in a state of bewilderment and laughter. He knew their sacred cows by name better than they themselves did.[16]

In many ways it was not simply the 'sacred cows' of his own political milieu that MacNamara knew so well. In the articulation of his 'post-nationalist' sensibility MacNamara decodes many of the critical sacred cows that were to emerge in his future. The nature of MacNamara's 'third space' will occupy the final chapters of this study.

Chapter Eight

Cathleen Who? *Suzanne and Her Dangerous Moments*

He died for love of me: many a man has died for love of me.
W.B. Yeats, *Cathleen Ní Houlihán*

Hegel remarks somewhere that all the events and personalities of great importance in world history occur, as it were, twice. He forgot to add: the first time as tragedy, the second time as farce.
Karl Marx, *The Eighteenth Brumaire of Louis Bonaparte*

Stately, plump Buck Mulligan came from the stairhead, bearing a bowl of lather on which a mirror and a razor lay crossed. A yellow dressinggown, ungirdled, was sustained gently behind him by the mild morning air. He held the bowl aloft and intoned:
Introibo ad altare Dei
. . .
– For this, O dearly beloved, is the genuine Christine: body and soul and blood and ouns. Slow music, please. Shut your eyes, gents. One moment. A little trouble about those white corpuscles. Silence, all.
James Joyce, *Ulysses*

Buck Mulligan's entrance in the opening passage of *Ulysses* establishes Joyce's text as a work of immense parodic power.[1] Joyce's subversion of religious symbols in this moment interrogates the ritual-based drive of Judaeo-Christian history, re-creating its meaning in personalised farce. Mulligan's morning ablutions become a parody of the ritual and commemorative practices of Christian history's god-sacrifice centre. The crossed mirror and razor and the sacramental articulation of the shaving bowl conjure, at this point at least, Joyce's representation of historical narrative seen anew as a farce of personal revisions and counter-revisions.

This opening scene, from one of modernism's central textual expressions, articulates the internal workings of historical process as predicated upon moments of farcical reinterpretation.

Ireland's high modernist drive to open up and reveal history as (faulty) process is usually read as a reaction to many of the revival's central concerns and methodologies (modernism, including of course the later work of Yeats, sets about slaughtering the revival's 'sacred cows'). The argument to be pursued here is that this parodic inclination was already present within the fabric of revival, or, at least, at its fringes. More especially, in terms of this chapter, I want to argue that Joyce's parodic explosion of history (as some essential given 'truth') was foreshadowed some years earlier in the work of Gerald MacNamara for the Ulster Literary Theatre. This is an idea seen most effectively perhaps in two of MacNamara's earliest plays, *Suzanne and the Sovereigns* and *Thompson in Tír-na-nÓg*, both of which deal with the political retreat into the mythic. This chapter focuses on the first of these to be produced, *Suzanne and the Sovereigns,* and explores the ways in which modernism's concern for the internal contradictions of any hegemonic history was (pre)-echoed in this piece of proto-modernist drama (first seen in a Belfast theatre). It is a dramatic event that marks a radical intervention by the Ulster Literary Theatre into the very core of the revival's philosophy, a parodic performance that takes as its target the allocation of certain historical events as 'sacred'. In so doing (as mooted by Burgess above) Gerald MacNamara may be seen to open up a space that we more fully associate with later Irish writers and their (post)modernist interventions.

It was in December of 1907 that the Ulster Literary Theatre unveiled *Suzanne and the Sovereigns,* a radical (and potentially radicalising) exploration of the importance given to certain historical figures within political and cultural discourse. The play explores the power retained in communal memory by James II and William of Orange, and the events for which they have been continually commemorated. The role of historical narrative within political discourse thus forms the hypotext (or discursive fabric) that MacNamara sought to recontextualise and, in the process, 'open up' in terms of new loci of meaning and paradox. The parodic 'rehistoricising' of narratives held sacred by Ulster's political communities becomes a multi-directional exploration of the fabric and frames of reference of political discourse. *Suzanne and the Sovereigns* explores not only the historical commemoration operating at the centre of Irish nationalism and Ulster unionism, it also examines the cultural pathways (or fabric) that facilitate and structure these identity processes. This first play of

MacNamara's opened at the Exhibition Hall, Belfast, on 26 December 1907. The work was credited as a joint production by MacNamara and another of the Theatre's founders, Lewis Purcell (David Parkhill); and indeed, as suggested above, *Suzanne* does demonstrate a number of similarities with Purcell's *The Pagan*. A number of MacNamara's friends, however, recall how *Suzanne and the Sovereigns* was actually an extrapolated version of a sketch which he and his brothers used to perform in their family home for many years before this first formally staged production.[2] It would seem that it became something of a Morrow family tradition, as it was performed for a number of Christmases in a row. With every passing Christmas the piece would get longer and more elaborate until, presumably, it had almost reached the stature of a full-blown stage production.[3] There is no record of at what exact stage Purcell became involved in the full play's birth, but it does seem very likely that MacNamara was the major partner in getting *Suzanne* to the stage.

The main characters of the play are William (Prince of Orange), King James II, Lundy (that arch-villain of Protestant mythology) and Wilhelm Van Tootil (the court banner painter to William of Orange.[4]) The 'plot' (more a montage of events) is a reworking of William's involvement in Irish affairs. The eponymous Suzanne, it turns out, is the love object of both William of Orange and James II (as well as some other characters in the piece). The audience never actually sees Suzanne; rather, she is held off-stage, for-ever imagined as the 'ultimate beauty'. In the course of the play the audience will 'discover' that the Siege of Derry occurred because William placed Suzanne (the love of his life) in the city for safekeeping. In turn, James's forces are seen attempting to breach the city's defences in order to reclaim Suzanne for their king. As the play develops, the Battle of the Boyne is also replayed as a way of finally deciding who should have the girl's hand in marriage. On one level, then, the play remains a fantastical burlesque, with its pantomime quality sending strong signals to its audience that here is a night at the theatre not to be taken too seriously. But there is more at work than this reductive (although still curiously correct) reading would allow. As well as the nature of political identities in Ulster, MacNamara's piece also engages with intertextual play in relation to writing emerging from the Abbey coterie at this time. Out of this duality MacNamara manages to parody not only the specifically northern processes of historical contestation, in particular the iconography of the Orange Order, but also the forms of pseudo-historical recuperation engaged with by the Abbey's playwrights.

Indeed it is this latter function of the play that may prove the most fruitful as a starting point. In one of the more overt instances of interplay, *Suzanne and the Sovereigns* reworks a number of plot devices employed by Lady Gregory's play about the Battle of the Boyne, *The White Cockade. The White Cockade* was first produced at the Abbey Theatre on 9 December 1905, almost exactly two years before *Suzanne* took to the stage. The two plays share some similar plot moments, but the end results are quite different. Both plays purport to tell the 'true story' of the Battle of the Boyne and the two works contain some common structural elements. In each play, for example, soldiers swap sides, the kings disguise themselves in certain situations and the two kings also appear to have no real interest in the execution of war. MacNamara, like Lady Gregory, situates some of the post-battle analysis in a small inn, where the violence can be translated into a bloodless contest for meaning. In both plays these situations are used for comic effect, but the extramural intentions informing them are quite different.

Lady Gregory's play proceeds along a fairly standard cultural-nationalist (if, in this case, very specific) line of argument; the Battle of the Boyne's 'untold story' reveals King James as a coward at heart with no emotional interest in Ireland. In a comic scene the audience first discovers James after he has 'run away' from the scene of the Boyne battle (James's lack of desire for the fight is a recurrent trope in Gregory's piece). Importantly, throughout these scenes James is accompanied by Patrick Sarsfield, and it is Sarsfield who persistently encourages him to rejoin the theatre of war at another location. Sarsfield would, of course, become a key figure in the later battles at Aughrim and at the Siege of Limerick. In the company of such renowned tenacious heroism James appears all the more inadequate to the job in hand. Time and again James is only interested in his own safety, commenting to Sarsfield in quick succession: 'I wonder if this wood is quite safe' and 'I hope the little bridge we crossed that last river by has been broken so that no one can follow us'.[5] Later in the same scene when Sarsfield once again cajoles James to rejoin the endeavour for the sake of Ireland, James is shown up as a weak man of duplicitous nature: 'I would prefer to be elsewhere. It is all very well for those who have a taste for fighting. I had it once myself – when I was a boy. But it has gone from me now with the taste for green apples.'[6]

Gregory's narrative – and, in particular, its treatment of James – is born out of the classic tensions and paradoxes that haunted the Ascendancy's engagement with nationalist politics in this period. On the one hand, James is displayed as a duplicitous British monarch with no real concern for the interests of Ireland, a move which is admittedly in some ways a diversion from Irish nationalism's recalling of James's intervention as a lost moment of hope. More importantly, though, Gregory's reworking of James's involvement allows her to illustrate the futility of nationalist commitment along religious lines of demarcation; Irish nationalism's recalling of a Catholic monarchical intervention is presented as self-defeating, and James is seen to have no actual understanding of Ireland and its problems. As the play progresses it becomes obvious that the real hero on the side of James was Patrick Sarsfield; Sarsfield is time and again presented as the Irish warrior who will never give up the fight for Ireland. Indeed later in the play Sarsfield is mistakenly assumed to be the king, while James in Sarsfield's company is assumed to be a lowly servant. It is a moment that nicely highlights one of Gregory's central purposes: in the place of a confessional national identity ('native Ireland' as essentially Catholic), the mix-up reveals an Irish lineage as the guardian of Ireland's true identity. *The White Cockade* may be read, then, as a dramatic defence of the kinds of Ascendancy figures who stood at the heart of the revival.

Suzanne and the Sovereigns makes it clear that MacNamara was deeply suspicious of just this kind of ideological performance of history. In this regard one key moment may be isolated in the interplay between MacNamara's and Gregory's staging of identity. It is the scene in *The White Cockade* when Patrick Sarsfield instructs James on the nature of monarchy: 'to be a King is to be a lover – a good lover of a beautiful sweetheart'.[7] In *Suzanne* MacNamara transforms this metaphor of political desire and conquest into the 'actual' (in the sense of openly stated) reasoning behind historical events, with James and William each trying to be good lovers to 'Suzanne' (read ironic 'Ireland'). The metaphorical layerings of cultural nationalism and Ulster unionism are thus transformed in *Suzanne* into a system of farcical personal revision and inversion. The move, as we will see, is reminiscent of Joyce's parodic transformations in the opening passage of *Ulysses*. As with Joyce's replaying of the sacrificial cult of Christianity (within the personal farce of Mulligan's ritualised shaving), MacNamara reworks the historical narrative of the Williamite intervention in Ireland into a farcical narrative of personal love and confusion.

The post-nationalist (and post-colonial) deconstruction of the links between imperialism, nationalism, conquest and desire are thus foreshadowed by this northern playwright, who we might begin to think of as proto-post-nationalist. If it was modernists such as Joyce, O'Brien and O'Casey who most fully exposed the internal dynamics and contradictions of revival, MacNamara's work might just be a signpost on the road, born out of an 'internal' revivalist scepticism. The key point here is that this doubled position of 'internal sceptic' was a product of MacNamara's northern perspective; it is this that drives his particular parodic will to deconstruct. We can see this most clearly in the numerous temporal ellipses that the play performs and which add to the sense of historical confusion and translation. The Orange Order, for example, is presented as pre-dating William's arrival in Irish affairs; the Orange Order, in fact, seeks out William's aid because they see him as a 'staunch Orangeman'. Not only do these anachronisms allow for moments of brilliant comedic effect, they also establish a form of 'meta-nationalist' drama. This outstandingly funny 'pantomime', then, has left us with a remarkable record of Ulster's ideological tensions at the beginning of the twentieth century.

As well as a reworking of Gregory's play, *Suzanne and the Sovereigns,* with its parodic presentation of Ireland as a pretty young maiden, was also MacNamara's response to Yeats's *Cathleen Ní Houlihán* (1902), the play that he had found so inadequate when performed before a Belfast audience. *Cathleen Ní Houlihán* operates 'inside' *Suzanne* as another key site of intertextual meaning. The plot of *Suzanne* is in many ways a subversion of Yeats's piece and also a 'displaying' of the presumptions that inform Yeats's nationalist dramaturgy. In particular MacNamara reworks the idea of Yeats's iconic 'poor old woman' and her transformation into a beautiful young maid as young Irish men promise to make a sacrifice of themselves in 1798. In his most nationalist play Yeats proposed Cathleen, as Richard Kearney puts it, as a sacred symbol of 'unity and self-possession' in response to the profane 'reality' of 'division and dispossession'.[8] That idea of a sacred being ('Cathleen' as soul/spirit of Ireland) re-emerging in classic boundary moments (war, famine, etc.) is, of course, one of the central tropes of early revivalist drama. This mode is often read, as with Kearney above, as a primary example of cultural resistance as nationalism sought a cultural pathway that enabled both the retrospective construction of its own existence and a circumvention of that which it sought to resist. *Suzanne and the Sovereigns* writes back to, and in the process subversively appropriates, exactly this metaphorical operation (indeed, the play gets inside the metaphor machine). In MacNamara's vision the symbol of feminised Ireland is not allowed her stylised position as conceptual locus for ideas of unity and continuity. Rather, in *Suzanne* Ireland is seen as wayward and fickle, a young girl blowing random kisses to random kings. In the process of this exploration, not only are William and James made to look somewhat ridiculous, but more significantly the entire cult of personality surrounding such historical figures is made to look false, self-deluding and foolish.

The full decoding of this process only occurs, of course, when brought into contact with precisely the identity formations it seeks to parody. Given this reliance on reception, it is of note that following the play's first production the broadly nationalist paper the *Irish News and Belfast Morning News* was largely approving in its review, informing its readers that:

> The story runs through a mad and merry maze of grotesque happenings, with mock melodrama interspersed, the Siege of Derry and the Battle of the Boyne being 'worked in' as incidental items, and the whole proves a delightfully irresponsible, but none the less amusing, production. The Theatre may be congratulated on having made a decided success of this initial excursion into the realms of extravaganza, which in modern times has either been set apart and docketed as 'Gilbertian', or has degenerated into the inanities of pantomime – the simple application of satirical wit to presumably serious incidents and events, the possibilities of which form of dramatic art the authors of *Suzanne* have endeavoured, and not without success to indicate. (27 December 1907)

Disguised beautifully as harmless pantomime, the 'mad and merry' world of *Suzanne* actually allowed MacNamara the greatest licence to explore the historicity of history. The play's confused and elliptical timeframes provide MacNamara with the tools to demonstrate history as process.

Suzanne and the Sovereigns also, of course, draws on many of the techniques it aims to subvert. While it seeks to parody the manner in which history is (mis)-used to explain the present, *Suzanne,* equally, is a play that seeks to explore the nature of contemporary Ulster. This sense of 'doubleness' is reflected in the multiple timeframes and temporal manipulations that make up much of the play's plot line. It is a duality that also makes the parodic mode all the more useful for MacNamara's intentions; the occupation of multiple spaces simultaneously is, after all, one of the key functions of parodic translation. The seventeenth century thus becomes the place where MacNamara could most fully explore early twentieth-century northern Ireland. Thus MacNamara highlights the dangers of a newly empowered vision of William III, reinvigorated as it had been by the increasingly strong and organised Ulster anti-Home Rule campaign. Equally, though, MacNamara points to the dangers of counter-narratives connected with 'traditional' cultural nationalism. The most notable of these narratives include the mythologising personification of Ireland, as in Yeats's *Cathleen* vision, and the 'scapegoating' of certain historical figures, such as King James in Lady Gregory's play. Most notably, perhaps, the relevance of James and William to the problematic of Home Rule and Irish independence is questioned in *Suzanne.*

The programme for the play's first run, indeed, performs a comic explication on the historical facts to be found in the piece. Interestingly the only known protest against *Suzanne* concerned an illustration on this first run of programmes (Figure 1 shows the front page of this programme). The controversy surrounded the drawing (by John Campbell) which depicts King William astride a child's rocking-horse. This element of the programme was removed by the time the play moved into its second week. (Even before they had reached the theatre, the audience was forewarned of the historical irreverence contained within the play. Figure 2 is an advertising poster, also by John Campbell, showing William and James on roller-skates trying to capture the elusive Suzanne.) If the play's programme brilliantly performed its task as a humorous introduction to the plot, it also served as another early warning to the audience that its political sensibilities were about to be challenged:

> While disdaining any desire to be serious, we cannot overcome an ingrained tendency to instruct, as well as amuse, our audience. Let us amuse or not, instruct we will. Therefore many historical facts hitherto unsuspected may be confidently looked for. The play is not founded upon any recognised history, because, from exclusive information at the disposal of the authors, there is grave reason to suppose that the history of the Three Kingdoms is, in many points, not to be relied upon. If we can but correct some of the prevailing misconceptions our labours will not have been in vain. To give but one instance: the popular belief is that the object of the struggle between William and James was the possession of a crown. Nothing so ignoble! Derry was besieged for the same romantic reason that Troy was besieged: for the love of a beautiful maid.[9]

The introduction's suggestion that in the view of the writers 'the history of the Three Kingdoms is, in many points, not to be relied upon' references much of the meta-historical position taken up in the play. Through his elevation of 'historical fact' to grand parodic farce (and vice-versa), MacNamara inflates and disarms history and in the process displays its narratological base.

History is thus seen as a text that is unknowable in its totality. MacNamara's point throughout the play is that any political standpoint can only be informed by certain portions, or readings, of history. In a comic invocation of this notion that bears all the hallmarks of MacNamara, the programme for *Suzanne* extrapolates upon its earlier comments with a final warning 'Note' to the audience:

ULSTER LITERARY THEATRE.

SEASON 1908-9.

Week Commencing JANUARY 11th, in the EXHIBITION HALL,

SUZANNE AND THE SOVEREIGNS:

AN EXTRAVAGANZA BY

LEWIS PURCELL AND GERALD MACNAMARA.

BALLAD OF THE PLAY.

WILLIAM THREE. A hero-king.
Brave and kind and good look-ing.

JAMES THE SECOND. (For him see
Note above on William Three.)

SWEET SUZANNE. A maiden fair—
Pearly teeth and golden hair.

LUNDY. Traitor, villain, spy.
Bold and bad and very sly.

WILHELM JAN VAN TOOTIL. Great
Banner painter to the State.

First is, FRANCY J. M'CANN.
Second, WILLIAM KERNAHAN.
Third, SIR JOSEPH PENDERGAST:—
Deputation from Belfast.

PIETE ADOLPHUS VAN M'NALLY,

Figure. 1 Programme for early performance of *Suzanne and the Sovereigns*

Figure 2: Poster by John Campbell for the first production of *Suzanne and the Sovereigns.*

> The authors have attempted to write a play, not a textbook for students. But members of the audience who may be inclined to dismiss certain scenes and incidents as resting on no basis of historical fact are requested to suspend judgement until, in addition to the works of popular authors like Macaulay, Lecky, Froade [*sic*], and Leland, they have carefully studied and collated the undermentioned authorities.

The programme goes on to list an 'impossible' series of 'sources', a series which is extraordinary in its comic range and intent. The list begins by suggesting some fairly standard (if impossibly voluminous) reading that the reader/audience may like to consider, material such as *Journals of the House of Commons of Ireland, 1613–1800* (19 vols. Folio), *Journals of the Irish House of Lords* (18 vols.) and *Cane's History of Williamite and Jacobite Wars in Ireland.* Following this, however, the list is launched upon a tangent that can leave no doubt as to its intentions. As well as the above mammoth selection of records (the list in fact includes many more in the same vein), the reader is pointed in some fantastically curious directions. A greater understanding of the play's contentions, the audience is assured, will be gained by referring to, among others, the *Collectanea de rebus Hibernicus,* the *Memoires de Madame de la Fayette, Zeuss' Grammatica Celtica* and *Ceachta beaga Gaedhilge.* While, most extraordinary of all, the list concludes its suggested reading matter with the *Irish Auxiliary of the London Society for Promoting Christianity among the Jews: Third Annual Report* (Dublin, 1821).

This parody on the nature of historical narrative (here overtly represented as a series of textual sources) foreshadows the 'Cyclops' section of *Ulysses* with its numerous lists that conspire to raise the notion of history to the level of meaningless disconnected facts and figures. Famously in this section Joyce presents a 'heroic' figure seated at the bar of 'Barney Kiernan's pub', a figure covered with an impossible number of 'seastones' which were 'graven with rude yet striking art . . . tribal images of many Irish heroes and heroines of antiquity'.[10] Joyce follows this description of his mock-heroic figure with a list of names that steadily get more obscure, irrelevant, in some cases mythic and in others not Irish at all. The list conspires, in a similar manner to MacNamara's programme many years before, to parody the very nature of Irish historical narrative and its relevance to a contemporary construction of Irish identity; it also points to the textuality of historical process. Amongst the images of 'Irish heroes' engraved upon the seastones of this figure in Kiernan's pub are:

> Cuchulin, Conn of hundred battles, Niall of nine hostages, Henry Joy McCracken, Goliath, Charlemagne, Theobald Wolfe Tone, the Mother of the Maccabees, the last of the Mohicans, The Man in the Gap, The Woman who Didn't, Julius Caesar, Thomas Cook and Son, Herodotos, Jack the Giantkiller, Jeremiah O'Donovan Rossa.[11]

In the juxtaposition of these wildly disparate figures Joyce points to the 'constructedness' of an historical process that *creates* links and structures of meaning. The list parodies the 'invention of tradition' by creating its own mock tradition that stands outside the original. MacNamara's listing of historical sources in many ways predicts the more fully formed modernist mode seen in Joyce. The list of Irish heroes that colonises outwards into the truly mythic and the plainly non-Irish suggests the randomness of historical interpretation and selection. MacNamara some years previously had articulated a similar vision in the programme for his play of historic parody. At work in MacNamara's programme notes there is a constant question concerning the relevance of historical narrative/record in the formation of modernity's body politic, identities and loyalties. While the exposure of this problematic may be most clearly aimed at Ulster anti-Home Rule formations, it may also be read as a critique of some elements of the Abbey's representational strategies (Yeats's *Cathleen Ní Houlihán* and Lady Gregory's *White Cockade* for example).

The opening scene of *Suzanne and the Sovereigns* is set in William's 'Audience Chamber' in Amsterdam. On stage initially are Van Tootil (banner painter to William of Orange) and Piete (William's butler). The timeframe for this opening scene is a number of months before William's entrance onto the political stage in Ireland. From the first words spoken on stage it is clear, however, that the play negotiates a number of co-existent timeframes.

> PIETE: [*Dusting the furniture. Speaking with Jewish accent*] The Prince is expecting a deputation of Orangemen from Belfast today. [*Stops dusting and fools about balancing the feather duster*] I wonder what they want. [*More business*] I hope they don't want him to go to Belfast, for I hear it's an awful place. They are always having strikes and riots over there. If the Prince goes, I'll look for another job, for Belfast would be no place for me – I would rather be in dear old Amsterdam.[12]

Thus from the seventeenth century the butler on stage comments quite explicitly on contemporary Belfast, a place very accustomed to 'strikes and riots'. In the 1880s and 90s, as well as the early years of the twentieth century, Belfast had been the scene of many riots sparked off by general sectarian tension and the more invasive debates on the Home Rule question. In the early years of the twentieth century Belfast was also the location of trade union tensions.[13] Thus in the opening moments MacNamara establishes a kind of meta-narrative. Most striking of all, in terms of a playful temporality, is the indication that a delegation of the Orange Order is arriving in Amsterdam to request that William come to Ireland to aid their cause. It is a moment that plays with history as narrative (and narrative as 'history'), as the Orange Order is retrospectively presented in the act of inventing the sort of William that they will require to bring about the Orange Order.

This opening scene draws heavily on the intertextual potential of the parodic mode. What we have on stage is a kind of heterotopia – a space occupied by multiple co-existent frames of reference that are more normally mutually exclusive. The opening dialogue between Piete and Van Tootil, for example, contains other elements of paradox all designed to unsettle the audience's ability to fix time. Van Tootil is engaged at a canvas painting a portrait but takes time out to explain to Piete the reason behind his task. The explanation establishes the basic premise of the play, but it also further shakes the audience's sense of historical frame. Van Tootil, it turns out, is creating his portrait from a photograph:

> VAN TOOTIL: There is a great romance woven round this photo. Six months ago, the Prince of Orange was strolling along the banks of the Zuyden Zee when a wagonette chanced to pass him by. The occupants being foreign tourists, curiousity tempted him to turn his head to look at the receding vehicle, and his eyes fell on a beauteous maid – he smiled – she smiled and threw a kiss at him – he threw another – and she threw him a photograph – *this* photograph.

Van Tootil in this way sets up the romance between William and Suzanne; later in the play the audience discovers that Suzanne also threw kisses to James II, causing him also to fall immediately in love with her. The device of the photograph is particularly clever here, seventeenth-century Holland is of course a long way from the invention of such technology. The overlapping timeframe, and its connection to a banner painter for William of Orange, suggests a commentary on the representation of figures such as William and James. This representational fallacy, perhaps most directly applicable to the banner-based work of such organisations as the Orange Order and the Hibernians, is cleverly unpacked. Representations that claim the 'authenticity' of a photograph but which, in fact, contain all the discrepancies and conflations that are here played out in the move from impossible photograph to banner painter's art, are indexed as fallacies of historical manipulation. This motif is played out further when the delegation from the Orange Order arrives in the chamber and manages to mistake the butler for the Prince of Orange.

William finally makes it onto the stage and the Orange delegation (consisting of Sir Joseph Jackson, William John McAuley [referred to as 'Master'] and Francey McCann [known as 'Dem']) manage to confirm him as the man they seek. They immediately begin to beseech William to come to their aid. It is at this moment that the problematic of the North and its relationship to seventeenth and twentieth-century history is most clearly worked through. Or, perhaps more accurately, it is at this moment that the play begins to deal with the problematical relationship between twentieth-century Ulster and seventeenth-century Irish history. The Orange Order have in fact arrived in Holland not, as may have been assumed, to plead William's intervention on behalf of 'Ireland'; rather, these Orangemen are there simply to ask that William come to the rescue of 'Ulster'. As Sir Joseph proposes: 'Your Majesty, we wish respectively to draw your attention to the fact that our city (Belfast), and in fact most of Ulster, is at present in a state of unrest.' ('Master' McAuley pipes in at this point with 'Nothing but strikes', in an effort to back up Sir Joseph's point.) Sir Joseph tries further to explain the 'predicament' of Ulster by informing William that they had no reliable leader or royalty to guide them, to which William responds: 'Well – what's the matter with James?' While William's ignorance obviously frustrates the group they continue to explain their situation, telling the Prince that they like neither James's religion nor his politics. Sir Joseph concludes:

> SIR JOSEPH: [*Clearing his throat*] Your Majesty, at a meeting of the Ulster unionist Society we moved a resolution that henceforth we would pay no allegiance to King James, and that it was most desirable to have an Orange king as a reigning sovereign, and as we heard so much about you, and knowing you to be a staunch Orangeman, it was agreed that this deputation should approach you and give you the first offer of the throne of Ulster.[14]

The move that links William only to the political arena of Ulster nicely displays some of the play's key parodic intentions. While the plot in conventional terms revolves around the machinations of seventeenth-century European politics, the meta-performative intention clearly concerns twentieth-century Ulster unionism. The exchange that follows most clearly exposes the inner workings of the play as a response to that particular conflation of history and politics that was achieving hegemonic status in this period:

KING WILLIAM: [*Rising to his feet*]: Gentlemen, you do me a great honour. I am so overcome with emotion, that words fail me to properly acknowledge the great compliment you pay me. *But* tell me, where is Ulster? [*Sits down*] [*All look at each other in surprise and disgust*]

SIR JOSEPH: Your majesty, it is the most northern and most loyal portion of Ireland.

KING WILLIAM: [*Looking wearied*] Gentlemen, I am afraid we cannot come to terms. You must clearly understand my position. I am Prince of ALL Orange – not a piece of Orange. Is it reasonable to expect that I should give this country up for the chance of a part of Ireland?. . . .

SIR JOSEPH: But, Your Majesty, there is another matter. If you consent to our offer, you may succeed in becoming king of not only all Ireland, but England as well, if you defeat King James.

KING WILLIAM: Ah, that is not so bad. But what do you mean by defeating King James? We hope that our coming to Ireland would not lead to any unpleasantness. We couldn't care to be mixed up in any rowdyism.

William's unsureness and ignorance provides the audience, as the full decoders of the piece, with a figure who would not understand his standing in twentieth-century Ulster unionist politics. The future King William III here struggles to come to terms with the complex nexus of Ulster unionist needs and their wider European/British/Irish positioning.

William, despite the protestations of the Orange Order representatives, remains uninterested in the offer from Ulster. In a final effort at wooing the king, the group reveals their secret weapon as they tell him they have 'purchased, at enormous expense, a magnificent white horse for [William's] use exclusively on the battle field'. In the world of *Suzanne,* it is the Orange

Order that provides William with the horse on which he will be depicted on a myriad of Lodge banners. Even this offer is not enough (although in the end, of course, William does become involved and does accept that 'white horse') and William holds out against the delegation's advances. The Prince holds out, that is, until he discovers that by fortuitous coincidence his beloved Suzanne is in fact the daughter of one of the Orange delegation: 'Master' McAuley recognises his daughter in Van Tootil's portrait. This revelation changes everything as McAuley seizes the opportunity and, taking William's hand 'like a cattle dealer' (as the stage direction would have it), makes the final proposition: 'I'll tell you what we'll do – I'll let you have the girl, if you come with us and fight James. It's a bargain.' It is this moment of actual and symbolic exchange that most explicitly displays the play as a response to the Yeatsian vision of *Cathleen Ní Houlihán.* In MacNamara's vision of *Suzanne,* Ireland is transformed from Yeats's image of womanhood living in hope that her sons will make their sacrificial offering, into a young and foolish girl unaware of the monumental processes that accompany her progress/history. In the play the audience never sees Suzanne, rather it witnesses her 'construction' by the male protagonists on stage. Suzanne remains unknowable to the audience: while the play works through a series of effects the actual cause simply remains an imagined (unknown/unknowable) body (nexus of desire and meaning).

William, on hearing McAuley's offer, still remains unsure until McAuley plays his 'trump card'. William, hesitating, declares he will have to consider the matter, but McAuley swiftly intervenes telling him: 'But, there is no time to be lost, for King James is madly in love with her.' The news leaves William with no choice but to go to Ireland to save Suzanne from the clutches of James; he orders a boat be made ready for the journey and word to be sent ahead that Suzanne be placed inside Derry's walls to keep her safe. The action of the play now moves to inside Derry. The scenes that follow replay the Siege of Derry as a contest of cunning and military might, with Suzanne (not Derry or Ireland) as the 'prize' at stake. MacNamara's decision to situate the first of the play's Irish scenes in the context of the ongoing Siege of Derry is a powerful one; as discussed above, the historical vision of Derry under siege was a standard rallying cry in anti-Home Rule discourse throughout Ulster. Oliver MacDonagh, indeed, has described the Siege of Derry as the 'original and most powerful myth' of Ulster Loyalism.[15] Ian McBride also locates the idea of the siege as central to the emotional and political beliefs of Ulster Protestantism:

> Like other political myths, the story of the siege is invoked to legitimate present actions and attitudes, and while the narrative has retained its basic structure, each generation has found fresh meanings, emphasising or suppressing different components according to its own ideological needs.[16]

Throughout the anti-Home Rule campaign, the vision of the Siege of Derry had been superimposed onto the contemporary situation, with Ireland/Ulster represented as under the same threat of siege as had been the case at the end of the seventeenth century. In his representation of the siege at the level of romantic farce, MacNamara parodies exactly this process of history as reusable palimpsest.

In the course of these events the audience is introduced to one of MacNamara's most memorable characters in the figure of Lundy, the 'traitorous' Governor of Derry.[17] MacNamara himself, in the opening performance and for many years afterwards, took this role. In the course of the Derry action Lundy is seen to swap 'sides' innumerable times, depending on which king makes the most attractive proposition. Lundy at one moment protects Suzanne for William and at another plans to hand her over to James. In a brilliant exposition of 'history' as backward construct, Lundy is presented in life as literally having all the qualities assigned to him in infamy. Lundy not only possesses the traits but is also presented as self-reflexively aware of his own construction. James on first meeting him enquires of Lundy: 'I understand that you are a traitor by profession.' This normally ruinous allegation brings the candid response from Lundy of: 'Your Majesty flatters me, but it is nevertheless true – I am a traitaire and so was my father before me; that is why I am stuffed with straw and full of gunpowder.' The practice of stuffing an effigy of Lundy and throwing it on July bonfires is here retrospectively cast onto the real-life figure of the Governor of Derry. Indeed Lundy's self-reflexive awareness of future representations is played on throughout the course of *Suzanne*. The meeting of Van Tootil and Lundy, for example, is used to further play out this idea: Van Tootil is smoking a cigarette, which causes Lundy to scream for him to get away. On hearing Lundy's predicament (being stuffed with gunpowder) Van Tootil enquires how he arrived at such a situation: 'I am not quite clear about it myself', replies Lundy, 'Some horrible mistake. It all happened since I became an effigy. But do not question me. It is a sore point. 'Such moments occur within a plot structure of mix-ups, mistaken identities and strange military strategies. The 'Siege of Derry' ends with James whisking Suzanne away from Derry (towards the Boyne) and this news spurs William (just arrived by boat in Carrickfergus) to muster his forces. Suzanne's fate, he makes clear, will be decided at the Boyne.

The next and final act is set in 'the "White Horse Inn" near the Boyne' (as well as the Orange Order, it is revealed that 'White Horse Inns' dot the countryside well before William's actions). Just as in *The White Cockade,* the Battle of the Boyne is played off-stage and the audience learns of it through the conversations of various characters in the inn. Just as in *The White Cockade,* the White Horse Inn in *Suzanne and the Sovereigns* is populated by characters from different sides of the political/military divide. The scene opens with the innkeeper and some soldiers discussing the events of the day:

INNKEEPER:	There must have been a big crowd up in the field today.
SOLDIERS:	Terrible crowd – must have been thousands – a quare gran lock of banners – man, the flute bans war grate!
INNKEEPER:	I never saw so many ginger ale carts on the road before. I suppose all the value is over.
FIRST SOLDIER:	There might be a few skirmishes with the police, but that's all. The battle is practically over.
INNKEEPER:	And which side won?
FIRST SOLDIER:	I'm not exactly sure, Mister. We came away before the referee gave his decision.
INNKEEPER:	Did King William make a good speech?
FIRST SOLDIER:	Gran. He was in great form. You'd have thought he had lived in the North of Ireland all his life, if you'd heard him talking about our 'glorious constitution'.

In these closing exchanges the play's parodic intentions begin to inhabit ever more fully the words and actions on stage. While the Battle of the Boyne is discussed here, it is clear that the meta-discourse concerns the manner in which the events around the Boyne are represented within political and cultural discourses contemporary to the play's performance. The soldier's reference to the 'North of Ireland' also reveals a central concern of this (meta-) post-battle analysis. The link effectively transposes this seventeenth-century discussion, relocating it quite clearly in the context of early twentieth-century Ulster and its relationship to other nationalist/unionist discourses. In this scene the idea of history and its relationship to politics is recast in terms of 'play' and gaming. This process is given its most explicit form when all in the inn gather round to hear how the 'referee' came to his final decision (to award the battle to William): the result, it is announced, was '303 to 291 against James'. At this point all the characters in the piece are descending on the White Horse Inn, and it is left to one of the original Orange delegation (Dem) to explain the 'scoring' of the battle. Some of the crowd express surprise that the score is so close, as they had expected William to be the clear winner. The close result, it is explained, was due to the fact that William 'did not keep to the conditions'. Dem explains the nature of the problem further:

> DEM: Well, you see, he was to cross the river on a white horse and he didn't. It was a brown horse. He lost 15 points for that. The prayer brought him 27, and the fortunate escape 19, but then James was allowed 21 on that for being a good shot. Up till this James wasn't doing so bad at all, but the thing that killed him altogether was the running away. He lost 50 in the first place for running away at all, then 19 for exceeding the speed limit. But the road got that bad after a while that he couldn't go on. Then he lost 15 more for trying to run away and not being able. That settled *him.*

The Battle of the Boyne thus transformed into a point-scoring game is recontextualised as a narrative embedded within a series of modern-day point-scoring processes. The fate of James after the battle, raised to the level of a national tragedy of betrayal in Lady Gregory, is herein reduced (or raised further) to the level of personal farce by MacNamara.

MacNamara's final parodic unravelling of contemporary historical 'game playing' comes in the closing moments of the piece. In the confusion of the battle's aftermath it transpires that Van Tootil (the banner painter) has managed to elope with the forever unseen Suzanne. At the end of *Suzanne and the Sovereigns,* then, it is the banner painter(s) who finally win 'Ireland'. The implications are quite obvious concerning the iconic fetishism of both unionism and nationalism, whether this be centred on the actual banners of the Orange Order, the Hibernians, or the 'poor old woman' iconicity of Yeats's *Cathleen Ní Houlihán.* This final piece of meta-nationalist commentary is brought to a conclusion in the play's ultimate dénouement. William and James discover that they have both lost Suzanne to the banner painter and both unite together as friends sharing a common loss. William turns to James saying, 'In this hour of mutual sorrow, let us sink all party difference, and be truly brothers', an offer which brings the response from James, 'Till death, brothers'. The only problem remaining is deciding who should have Ireland's throne. 'Ireland' at this point becomes a kind of double presence and absence on stage. 'Suzanne', the target of both kings' desire, has escaped and what is left is a bare physical location that, it turns out, neither king has any real interest in retaining. William offers Ireland to James, proposing that he could rule England while James kept Ireland, but James has other plans:

> JAMES: I must refuse – really I – I don't want it.
> WILLIAM: You don't want to be king of Ireland?
> JAMES: God knows, I have enough trouble already.
> WILLIAM: [*Aside*] Hum – he is not so soft as I thought. [*Aloud*] Well, well we must think of something else I suppose.

William proceeds to offer the throne of Ireland to various people around him, but all refuse. In a final moment of desperation William threatens Lundy (who has previously been condemned to death for his traitorous actions): 'I will give you one chance for your life. The condition is that you accept the throne of Ireland.' It is an offer that draws one final brilliant last reply from Lundy: 'Burn me!' Lundy's glee is undisguised, and as he is hauled away to his death he shouts back to William: 'you are caught in your own toils. You have won Ireland and now you will never be able to get rid of it, never. It shall be always with you till you die. Revenge!'

By now hopefully it is clear that, while a fabulously comic burlesque, *Suzanne and the Sovereigns* may also be read as a rather remarkable deconstruction of nationalist practices (both 'Orange' and 'Green'). Most obviously this is a play that sought to unpack some of the processes of icon creation enacted by a nascent Ulster unionism and a re-empowered Orange Order. Its plot gets inside the 'myth machine' and in the place of history as some natural essential truth reveals a process of cultural translation and political need. But the emergence of this play in 1907 also marks an interesting intervention into the cultural-nationalist schema of the time. This play's parodic relocation of historical narrative to a 'third space' also writes back to the vision of such works as Gregory's *The White Cockade* and Yeats's *Cathleen Ní Houlihán.* The cultural-nationalist underpinnings of such works are subverted in MacNamara's piece as it demonstrates the narratological base of the politicised Irish historical process. As well as 'writing back', this piece may be seen as the beginning of MacNamara's process of 'writing forward', foreshadowing some of the parodic concerns of Irish modernism. MacNamara's vision of historicity is fuelled by the boundary situation occupying his northern hinterland. The play indexes the dangerous gaps of representation being opened up, as the Ulster Literary Theatre perceived them, not just by Ulster unionism but also by the Abbey in Dublin. MacNamara's piece seeks to be read as both a warning of representational gaps and as a location of possible unity. *Suzanne's* 'moments of danger' are neither Home Rule nor Ulster unionism; rather, *Suzanne's* northern moment of danger highlights the representational strategies that were increasingly being engaged in mapping various historical narratives onto a number of different Irelands.

Given the nature of the subject matter, audience reception was a definite worry. As Rutherford Mayne remembers: 'In December, 1907, at Christmas time, the Theatre made the most daring and audacious attempt in their history. To anyone who knows the city well, it might easily have had the same result as throwing a lit match into a barrel of gun-powder.'[18] In fact, it would seem that the play was received very well by both sides of the Belfast community. The broadly unionist *Nomad's Weekly and Belfast Critic* in its review of *Suzanne*'s first run, for example, approved of the play's inventive intervention on the Belfast theatre scene:

> What went we out to see? One may plead guilty to a certain amount of surprise at finding these serious students dipping so deeply into the well of satirical humour, but that the experiment met with the approval of the critical audience was proven by the endless torrent of laughter which greeted the efforts of the authors and performers alike . . . To Belfast people it may seem scarcely possible that the local dialect, the commonplaces of the crowd, could sound so absurdly ridiculous as they do in the mouths of the deputation of Orangemen, headed by Sir Joseph Jackson and backed by Francey McCann (the latter a 'type' as cleverly drawn as we are likely to see again in a month of Sundays), who wait upon William of Orange to beseech him to come over to Ulster . . . the production is another feather in the cap of the Ulster Literary Society [*sic*]. A delicious revival of historical humour. (6 January 1908)

The *Evening Telegraph* pointed out that: 'The whole entertainment, in fact, was of that unique sort that touches the heart, or risibility, of anyone, be he of whatever persuasion, and ought to offend none. The man who would be offended must indeed be devoid of the spirit of laughter' (27 December 1907). MacNamara's (and Purcell's) gamble paid off spectacularly; the play's exuberant good humour and 'openness' managed to quell any sectarian tensions that could well have arisen in a Belfast audience observing any number of their 'sacred cows' being slaughtered right before their eyes. *Suzanne* more fully than any of the group's plays beforehand announced the Ulster Literary Theatre as a significant counter-blast to the Abbey.

Suzanne and the Sovereigns also provided the Ulster Literary Theatre with a significant change in financial fortunes. As the week of its first production went on it became obvious that the group had a major success on their hands; the Exhibition Hall was now routinely full. The group's success did not go unnoticed. Edward Terry, the renowned English actor, was playing Belfast's Opera House in the same week as *Suzanne* opened. Terry could usually be relied upon to attract a large audience and the manager of the Opera House was therefore confused when the week progressed with very poor houses most nights. On hearing of *Suzanne's* success the manager sought out the Ulster Literary Theatre and offered the group a week-long run in the Opera House, an offer they took up straight after their Exhibition Hall run was completed that Christmas.[19] This marked the beginning of a long and close alliance between the Opera House and the Ulster Literary Theatre, an association that was to last until 1934. *Suzanne* would remain one of the group's best-loved productions. Indeed, only the fantastical adventures of an Orangeman named Thompson were to match the effortless popularity of 'Suzanne' and her suitors. Before the arrival of *Thompson,* however, MacNamara was to provide the Ulster Literary Theatre with a really most extraordinary response to the work of J.M. Synge.

Chapter Nine

A Fog in the Twilight

Gaels! he said, it delights my Gaelic heart to be here today speaking Gaelic with you at this Gaelic feis in the centre of the Gaeltacht. May I state that I am a Gael. I'm Gaelic from the crown of my head to the soles of my feet – Gaelic front and back, above and below. Likewise, you are all truly Gaelic. We are all Gaelic Gaels of Gaelic lineage. He who is truly Gaelic, will be Gaelic evermore. I myself have spoken not a word except Gaelic since the day I was born – just like you – and every sentence I've ever uttered has been on the subject of Gaelic . . . There is nothing in this life so nice and so Gaelic as truly true Gaelic Gaels who speak in true Gaelic Gaelic about the truly Gaelic language. I hereby declare this feis to be Gaelically open! Up the Gaels!

Flann O'Brien, *The Poor Mouth*

In the months following the success of *Suzanne and the Sovereigns,* Gerald MacNamara began to establish himself as a solo playwright with connections beyond the Belfast dramatic scene. In late March or early April of 1908, he sent the Abbey the script for a two-act play entitled *An August Day.* Joseph Holloway remembers borrowing the script (on 16 April) and thinking 'everything was truly mad in it'.[1] Holloway returned the script to W.A. Henderson, the secretary of the Abbey at the time, and he recalls that Henderson 'did not think the Directors would produce *An August Day.* Synge was dead against it. (The new dramatist treads on his corns too much for his taste, I suppose).'[2] *An August Day* was never produced and sadly the manuscript has subsequently been lost. However, Holloway's recollection that Synge did not approve of MacNamara's new work because it 'treads on his corns too much' has led a number of people to suggest that *An August Day,* after a serious rewrite, provided the base for MacNamara's next staged production,[3] *The Mist That Does Be on the Bog,* premièred at the Abbey on 26 November 1909, which was an instant hit with Dublin audiences.

The Mist That Does Be on the Bog is the story of one day in a small cottage in the West of Ireland as it is visited by various people seeking to experience the 'true West'. In an ironic inversion of Syngian dramaturgy, the cottage in this work is rented out by its actual inhabitants, a peasant couple named Quinn. The rest of the piece is subsequently played out in a stage cottage populated with characters in search of a true peasant abode, one just like they have seen at the theatre (such as the Abbey perhaps). *The Mist* was MacNamara's most direct parody of the work associated with the early Abbey. In particular *The Mist* parodies the Abbey's appropriation of the West and its peasants.[4] Once free of its original inhabitants, MacNamara's empty cottage becomes a usable 'other space', ready to be (re)filled with an ironically imitative act of representation. The redefinition of cultural space at work in *The Mist* seeks to unpack the revival's search for a 'sacred location' – a location that functioned as the keeper of Ireland's 'true self'. Crucially MacNamara's piece parodies not only the classic Syngian mode of drama but also the methodology out of which it arises. David Kennedy, for example, has argued that MacNamara not only parodies Synge's specific act of invention but also the more general 'Twilight' movement which provided its context. As Kennedy puts it: 'The shadowy darkness in which Yeats's imagination swathed this strange world owed more to . . . theosophical vapourings . . . than to the clear and precise images which are the authentic marks of Celtic literature. Ulster common sense instinctively rejected this charlatanism and guyed it in *The Mist*.'[5] Whatever we think of Kennedy's reading of Yeats's philosophical base, the location of resistance in 'Ulster common sense' is none the less interesting.[6] Kennedy here proposes the North as producing a distanced scepticism regarding the geo-politics of a Dublin-centric cultural movement and its fetishisation of a mythic West. While *The Mist* remains the MacNamara play least overtly concerned with the North, the North is nevertheless embedded within the work's commentary on the Abbey's politics of representation. Not only does the play parody the drama of identity focused on the West of Ireland; at work also is the problematic of how to locate the North within an aesthetic which appeared to leave no obvious pathway for its representation. By performing a kind of 'meta-West', with all its heightened sense of linguistic trickery, MacNamara manages to present that which is occluded as well as that which is 'over-represented'.

Synge's meeting with Yeats in Paris in 1896 led to the latter's famous advice that Synge should go to the Aran Islands in order to find there a life as yet unrepresented. Yeats's 'The Municipal Gallery Revisited' proposes that the early Abbey's course had been determined by the belief that, 'All that we did, all that we said or sang / Must come from contact with the soil'. It is this translation from soil to aesthetic, or rather the gaps in the process (*which* soil and *who* is to translate), that informs MacNamara's re-imagining of the West. Yeats's verse, furthermore, conjures a link between linguistic invention and the politics of identity mapping (Yeats's line seems embedded in a very precise physicality). MacNamara's use of language in *The Mist* brilliantly unpacks this process; in particular *The Mist* writes back to the 'language of imaginative life' that Synge so eloquently formed. In turn, MacNamara ratchets up the linguistic tensions to create a series of proto-Flann O'Brien moments wherein the language of the play becomes a form of meta-language; it is a process achieved through a Syngian style wound up to breaking point. The parodic 'meta' intent at work throughout the piece concerns not simply the creation of a rural language-scape by writers such as Synge and Gregory, but also the extracultural intentions that had deemed such a creation necessary.

Synge's relationship with the language that he sought to capture in his translation of Irish rhythms and patterns of speech is well documented and need not be rehearsed here. Some indication, however, of the methodology that informed Synge's work may prove useful, as *The Mist That Does Be on the Bog* is explicitly a critique of this element of Abbey dramaturgy. In his Preface to *The Playboy of the Western World* (written in January of 1907) Synge famously recalls that, while staying in a Wicklow cottage, he listened from his bedroom to the everyday conversations that went on in the kitchen below him. It is a seminal moment in Synge's development as a playwright, which he famously sets out in a much-quoted piece:

> When I was writing *The Shadow of the Glen,* some years ago, I got more aid than any learning could have given me from a chink in the floor of the old Wicklow house where I was staying, that let me hear what was being said by the servant girls in the kitchen.[7]

It is this communion with the language of the rural that Synge pinpoints as vital to his sense of the imaginative life of the 'real Ireland'. In the Preface he expands on this vision of his art: 'In a good play every speech should be as fully flavoured as a nut or apple, and such speeches cannot be written by any one who works among people who have shut their lips on poetry.'[8] Synge's vision of a people who have not 'shut their lips on poetry' seemed (to MacNamara at least) to leave little room for the industrial and political realities of the North. MacNamara's work was in many ways an attempt to write back against this formulation of 'Irishness'. Key to MacNamara's rereading of the Abbey's dramatic aesthetic and intention is just that sense of the North's occlusion from its methodology and performative expression. MacNamara set about the task of filling in some of these gaps as he attempted to write the North back into a vision from which it was explicitly missing. This was, of course, one of the fundamental tenets of the Ulster Literary Theatre's mission. The work of Rutherford Mayne and Lewis Purcell had already begun the task of opening up new performative areas of Irish identity. MacNamara, with *The Mist* and other works, developed this element of the Ulster Literary Theatre's project a stage further. While Mayne and Purcell sought to present a co-response to the various modes of identity proposed by the Abbey playwrights, MacNamara makes the construction of such a corresponding discourse the explicit subject of this play.

Just as importantly, *The Mist* is also an exploration of the problematics that had made this corresponding northern dialectic necessary. The political concerns of Home Rule and sectarian bigotry, for example, do not impinge on Synge's vision. As Maire Nic Shiubhlaigh would have it, Synge 'drew his inspiration from the hearths of the tiny whitewashed cabins and the harsh rocks of the Western seaboard, gathering tales and expressions from the old and the young of the most picturesque portion of Ireland'.[9] The implications of going to the 'tiny whitewashed cabins' and the 'Western seaboard' to *gather* folklore are exactly what MacNamara seeks to unravel in *The Mist*. MacNamara's play seeks to reveal the tensions and ambiguities that informed any such literary anthropological project. In this regard there is a telling moment in Lady Gregory's writings when she recalls her first 'sighting' of J.M. Synge on one of the Aran Islands:

> I first saw J.M. Synge in the North Island of Aran. I was staying there gathering folk-lore, talking to the people, and felt quite angry when I passed another outsider walking here and there, talking also to the people. I was jealous of not being alone on the island among the fishers and seaweed gathers. I did not speak to the stranger, nor was he inclined to speak to me; he also looked on me as an intruder, I only heard his name.[10]

Lady Gregory's memory perfectly exemplifies the notion of a space overly occupied with people seeking to interpret it. This remarkable demonstration (although Gregory would not have seen it as such) of Heisenberg's uncertainty principle (that one cannot observe without also changing that which is observed) goes to the heart of much of the parodic intent of *The Mist That Does Be on the Bog*. MacNamara plays out the problematic of contact and observation in the search for the 'real Ireland' in the 'stage cottage' of what soon becomes a play about how such plays are made.

MacNamara's Ulster voice was not the only one, of course, to locate Synge's work as raising problematic issues. In the same year that saw the first production of *In the Shadow of the Glen* (1903), Arthur Griffith published in the *United Irishman* a piece that directly responded to and satirised Synge's work. Griffith's short sketch, entitled *In a Real Wicklow Glen,* appropriated some of the motifs of Synge's work in order to reconfigure them into a more conservative (authentic in his terms) nationalist message. Griffith judged Synge's *Shadow of the Glen* to have provided an inappropriate and 'wrong' version of Irish women (the plot of Synge's work revolves around an unfaithful wife). In his sketch, Griffith provided his readers with a vision of saintly Irish womanhood. The action of his piece, like Synge's, is a cottage in a glen in the Wicklow mountains: a young lady calls to visit the old woman, Mrs Shaughnessy, who is a model of kindly generosity. Mrs Shaughnessy, on seeing the stranger, sends her young neighbour Norah to get some milk to give to the visitor. The whole scene is played out as a vision of Irish pastoral innocence and purity, as is nicely demonstrated in the following exchange:

MRS SHAUGHNESSY: Ah Norah, honey! won't you go to Patseen and get a fresh sup; I have me heart set on givin' this young lady a good drink of hot milk. She's terrible thin. I wisht I had you up here in the good mountain air and you'd soon be different *a leanbh.*[11]

Throughout the piece the old woman is called 'Mother' by everyone in the play; Griffith describes in this figure his perfect embodiment of Irish femininity, and of Ireland itself, which counters Synge's realist piece. The young neighbour Norah has married an older man, more out of financial need than love, but we are assured she has grown to love him. This situation is complicated by the arrival of John Kavanagh, Norah's childhood sweetheart. At first he proposes to woo Norah away, but Mrs Shaughnessy intervenes, telling him to mend his ways, give up drinking and return to a state of purity so that he may be worthy of Norah if ever she should be free to marry again. In the end Kavanagh bows before the old woman's wisdom, grateful for her words:

JOHN KAVANAGH: Mother (*kneels before her*) give me your blessing. So help me God, I will be a man worthy of your love.

MRS SHAUGHNESSY: May you get grace to keep your word. I will tell Norah (*She kisses his forehead*).[12]

And so, in response to Synge's vision, Griffith provides a vision of those more properly Irish ideals of loyalty, purity, temperance and understanding. Griffith's short sketch may be read in turn as a more fundamental nationalist rereading of the Syngian aesthetic. Synge was under constant suspicion by this wing of Irish nationalism that detected in his work a corruption of Irish/Ireland fundamentals. The technique of Griffith's sketch is a form of anti-pastiche, as it appropriates a Syngian style and attempts a kind of return to the disappearing source. The work of Gerald MacNamara takes a very different route and is more fully parodic in its description of a space different to that of Synge and Griffith.

The Mist That Does Be on the Bog opened on 26 November 1909 at the Abbey. This move to Dublin was part of the Ulster Literary Theatre's drive to widen the audience for their productions. The play was subtitled *A Fog in One Act,* which was obviously intended to shift the expectations of the audience while also performing a knowing glance towards revivalist aesthetics. The stage description establishes the work as set firmly in classic Syngian territory:

> A cottage in Connemara. Half door on back wall. Door right. A turf fire left. A stool, table, dresser, spinning wheel, fishing net, etc., on walls. Window close to half door back. An old woman seated at the fire mending a pair of socks.[13]

In the first of many intertextual *clin d'œil,* the audience discovers that the old woman and her husband are called Quinn (Bridget and Michael). Widow Quin is of course a significant character in Synge's *Playboy,* but Maire Quinn was also one of the actors who left the company after the controversy surrounding Synge's *In the Shadow of the Glen.* Bridget Quinn in *The Mist* will soon evacuate the stage, leaving it free for the 'performance' of a parody of the Abbey's work. MacNamara's appropriation of certain characteristics, phrases and plot devices from Synge operates as intertextual parodic signposts, signs that when decoded by the participating audience identify and articulate new sites of meaning and intention.

The first exchange on stage makes it clear that the piece is to be played out in a Syngian-styled linguistic register. Bridget has called to Michael telling him to get out of bed:

> MICHAEL: Woman, dear, can you not let me get a wink o' sleep?
> BRIDGET: Is it a wink of sleep you would be wantin' in the middle of the day and not a bit of turf in the house and the goat

> not milked, and not a hand put on the corn, and the hens out laying eggs the dear knows where and –?

As a straightforward imitation of Synge and his Abbey contemporaries this opening speech is, in fact, quite well accomplished, with its listing of chores concerned with farming and animal husbandry. However, MacNamara continues throughout the play to ratchet up the linguistic tension from the level of imitation to that of parody. The opening moments of the play establish the scenario that will allow the events of the piece to unfold. Bridget and Michael discuss the sign in their window advertising that they wish to rent out their cottage. Bridget reminds the dubious Michael of the reasoning behind the move: 'Didn't Father Doran tell us and him just come from Dublin that all the quality in the big world do be searchin' the country over for cottages just like this – and them in their motor cars?' It is clear that this peasant couple, and their community, is very aware of the nature of their cottage as 'commodity'. It is also evident that they are equally aware of the consumers they should target: the 'quality' of Dublin. In this brief exchange MacNamara establishes a crucial dialectic of Romantic vision versus modernity and consumerism. In so doing, he manages to make explicit a tension that is implicit in Synge; indeed, much of the intention of Synge's work is to circumvent this tension, proposing in his peasant folk a people removed from the pressures of modernity. *The Mist* counters this revivalist notion with a farming couple prepared to engage in 'lifestyle' consumerism, their rural location and 'folk ways' transformed into definable product.

The discussion that follows Bridget's reminder of Dublin and 'them in their motor cars' collapses these poles of Romantic ideal and modern reality. A 'motor horn toots' outside the cottage, causing Michael Quinn to exclaim with fright. Her husband's sense of fright much amuses Bridget and forces her to comment:

> BRIDGET: Well – is it scared you are Michael Quinn, scared of the sound of a motor and you never done talking about this 'scientific age' since you were made chairman of the new Technical School at Lisvarna?
>
> MICHAEL: It's one thing to hear a motor horn when the sun do be shinin' in the blue canopy of heaven and the young ewes do be dancin' in the corn – but it's another thing to hear the toot of a motor horn when the black clouds do be restin' on the top of the Slieve Girnin and the white mists do be comin' up from the bowels of the sea.

The exchange is centred around a tension between pseudo-Syngian romantic peasant language ('the young ewes do be dancin' in the corn'), the collision between superstition and modernity ('a motor horn when the black clouds do be restin' on the top of the Slieve Girnin') and the 'action' of establishing a 'Technical School' nearby. This insertion of a Technical School into a scene with all the hallmarks of Synge's West is performed, of course, by a playwright from a place more usually associated with modernity and industry. MacNamara in this way manages to signal an engagement with industrialised modernity within this scene of a classically romanticised West.

This tension between modernity, a romantic West and the act of representation is further highlighted by the arrival on-stage of the occupants of the motor car (the horn of which caused such consternation). Cissie and Gladys, two sisters, have been standing at the door listening to the above discussion for some moments before Gladys makes their presence known:

Gladys:	[*To Bridget*] Good evening, Ma'am.
Bridget:	Good evening, kindly lady, it's welcome you are, but it's a wild and stormy day, God bless us, to be out in the mountain side with the white mists driving up like shrouds from the rocky shores of Lough Corrib.
Cissie:	This is just the sort of place I have always pictured in imagination – we *must* stop here.
Gladys:	[*To Cissie*] Do be quiet, Cissie – if the old woman hears you, she is sure to put up the price.
Cissie:	But wasn't the old lady 'awfully folk'? Wasn't that grand about the 'white mists'?

In this moment of 'first contact' MacNamara exposes the tensions and ambivalences inherent in much of the contemporary representation of rural Ireland. Firstly, it is clear from Cissie's initial reaction that she has 'pre-read' exactly this sort of location, hence she is discovered in the act of mapping onto the 'real' place her pre-read expectations. This notion of pre-reading is reinforced by Cissie's description of Bridget as 'awfully folk'. The pair's romantically (revivalist) inspired search for the folk West is, however, countered by Gladys's more harsh introduction of the necessities of modernity, as she fears that Cissie's open enthusiasm will drive the rental price of the cottage upwards.

Through the different reactions of the sisters, MacNamara demonstrates the oppositional forces at work within any project to retrieve a romanticised past or place: almost inevitably it will end up couched within the very terms it seeks to disavow – modernity and consumerism. The sisters' search for a place beyond modernity's realities forces them to introduce some of these very ideas to that place. Countering this, the Quinns it would seem have long since acknowledged their putative premodern existence as a valuable product with which to negotiate the vicissitudes of modern life. After the exchange of pleasantries Gladys agrees to rent the cottage from the Quinns, who hurriedly ready themselves and leave the cottage to stay with Bridget's sister. The cottage on stage is now completely evacuated of its 'actual' peasant inhabitants, a situation that Cissie immediately seizes as advantageous:

> Cissie: Oh! Gladys – I'm so glad you have taken the cottage. [*Looking around*] Isn't it a picture? If we could only have our stage 'set' like this! Wouldn't it be a capital idea to rehearse our new play here?

The cottage on stage is now a meta-stage set as Cissie transforms it into a 'set' for a play they are preparing at home. Gladys, much enamoured with the idea, replies: 'Ideal. I'm glad we thought of bringing our costumes and "make up" box.' Thus the audience gets to watch as MacNamara transforms the action on stage into a meta-drama as a further play within *The Mist That Does Be on the Bog* unfolds (and the audience is thrown into an indeterminate space reminiscent of Pirandello). Following the initial sign of approval from her sister, Cissie suggests that they run through their parts in the play that very evening. Gladys goes further, proposing that they should 'do it in "costume"', for, as she puts it, 'They would be very poor actors who couldn't put a bit of local colour into their work with these surroundings.' The audience learns that the play they wish to rehearse is one written by Gladys. She, it turns out, has come to the West (on a driving holiday in a rented car – her husband Fred is still, at this stage, outside parking it) to seek inspiration for her dramatic creation. In the most blatant of MacNamara's nods to Synge, we discover that Gladys's new play is entitled, *What's All the Stir About?* – MacNamara's work, of course, appeared on stage not long after the protests against Synge's *Playboy*. The title of Gladys's play conjures up a number of possible readings: most obviously, it presents a sense of solidarity with Synge (suggesting the condemnation that Synge had experienced as misplaced), but it also nods towards a sense of confusion, suggesting Synge's work is not radical enough to deserve such energetic hostility. Typically with MacNamara, the rest of the play's action provides material to support both of these interpretations.

Interestingly Bulmer Hobson, while no fan of the play in question, had defended Synge from the sorts of attacks that had greeted the opening of his most famous work, and had drawn on the experiences of the Ulster Literary Theatre in the process:

> Whatever may be the demerits of Mr J.M. Synge's comedy, *The Playboy,* we may confess we are not greatly enamoured of the new fashion in criticism that last week turned the Abbey into a bear garden . . . If the Ulster Literary Theatre satirised Orangemen, Nationalists would be up in arms should the lodges wreck a performance; but apparently Mr Synge's burlesque of Irish peasant life can only be refuted by a strenuous application of a strong hand . . . the Abbey is purely the toy of a coterie. It has its own fashion with national material drawn from Irish life, to claim a fair hearing for them . . . We who believe in Sinn Féin demand liberty of speech and liberty of thought, not merely for ourselves, but for every man and every party in Ireland. (*Republic,* 7 February 1907)

The nature of this qualified defence is interesting in terms of MacNamara's slightly later theatrical response. In line with Sinn Féin's position at this time, Hobson reads the Abbey as simply the 'toy of a coterie' and places Synge's work firmly in this tainted context. But there is also a sense in which the Abbey playwright's problems are of a different order to those potentially facing the Ulster Literary Theatre's continuing project. As Ben Levitas puts it: 'Such liberality was partly borne out of the drastic sense of cultural conflict that was evident every day in Ulster, beside which the *Playboy* 'riots' were minor indeed.'[14]

Given this, it was all the more apt that MacNamara ensured that the realities of Ulster were never very far from this parodic revisioning of Synge's West. Just as the two sisters have agreed on their plan to rehearse their play, Gladys's husband Fred appears on stage. Fred's character represents on stage a sense of cosmopolitan scepticism, a note that he strikes with his first words on entering the cottage: 'This is a rum looking shanty. I say, girls, you look very much at home – have you really taken this pig-sty?' This scepticism is further highlighted by Gladys when she says aside to her sister: 'Isn't it a great pity that Fred has so little sympathy with the new movement in Ireland.' Fred thus provides a counter to the pseudo-revivalist musings displayed by the two sisters. At one point while the sisters are performing their play, Fred is seen at the back of the stage practising his golf swing, while at another crucial moment he attempts to discuss the sailing regatta at Bangor (Co. Down) with a visiting 'tramp'. By the time of his arrival, however, the sisters have changed into their costumes and cajole him into taking part in the dress rehearsal, for Fred is to play the crucial character of the tramp. The discussions that take place around Fred's involvement in the rehearsal provide an opportunity to discuss the conventions that had quickly developed around this form of drama. Cissie comments to Gladys that she has given Fred 'a big lot to say' in his role as the tramp, drawing the telling response from the young playwright: 'I did that purposely – you know the tramps in these folk plays always have more to say than anybody else on stage.'

With everyone now in costume the play within a play begins to take over the physical and spoken action on stage as the three players run through their lines from Gladys's piece. At this point the meta-action on stage becomes the central point of the play's construction, with Fred commenting: 'I think this is a bit cold-blooded – acting here in broad daylight without an audience, or even footlights.' All of this, of course, is pronounced on a stage lit by one and watched by the other. Cissie a short moment later is put off her opening dialogue with the thought that 'The fire is on the wrong side – it should be left', which forces Gladys to remind her that 'there's no audience. You can turn the other way.' To add to the uncanny effect of such playfulness, it soon becomes apparent from the opening lines of Gladys's work that her play is in fact a pastiche of Synge's *Riders to the Sea.* A brief comparison between the two works nicely demonstrates the ways in which MacNamara winds up the linguistic tension to a parodic register. The opening of Synge's *Riders to the Sea* is a famously foreboding scene of death and lamentation, with two young women examining a bundle of clothes to see if they are those of their missing brother, Michael. The two fear that if their brother is dead it will be the death of their mother also. Nora, one of the sisters, recalls the words of the local priest:

> NORA: 'If it's Michael's they are', says he, 'you can tell herself he's got a clean burial, by the grace of God; and if they're not his, let no one say a word about them, for she'll be getting her death', says he, 'with crying and lamenting'.[15]

When confirmation arrives that it is Michael who is lost, the final son (Bartley) dashes into the night, causing his mother Maurya to cry out: 'He's gone now, God spare us, and we'll not see him again. He's gone now, and when the black night is falling I'll have no son left me in the world.'[16]

This plot device is reworked in the opening of Gladys's play, which also concerns the fate of a missing son. On stage Gladys takes the part of the distraught mother:

> GLADYS: [*Starts in a whining tone*] Is Cornelius back yet?

CISSIE: He is not back yet, but the silver moon is only in its first quarter yet, and he might be delayed by the grace of the saints in O'Hanlon's pub.

Thus from the first moment the audience is confronted with a use of natural imagery and religious piety that falls well on the far side of Syngian imitation. The scene on stage is now openly an exercise in parodic intertextuality. Gladys's play articulates a 'serious' attempt to capture a Syngian style of language, a style that was also a form of translation. This series of interpretative levels are all embedded within MacNamara's play, *The Mist That Does Be on the Bog,* which now becomes not simply an imitative parody of revivalist aesthetics but also a parody of the process of imitation and translation. The language at work in Gladys's piece soon accelerates into an 'unintentional parody', while this is embedded further within MacNamara's intentional parody (of which Gladys's piece is also a function, of course). The two women continue to discuss the fate of the boy:

GLADYS: Do you think he will be comin' home by the long gap, and the wind risin' up from the north east and him burdened down by the weight of drink?

CISSIE: It's by the white rocks he would come, and him staggerin' the way he could steady himself against the south wind.

GLADYS: Cornelius asthore, it's this day and it will be this night that I will be lamentin' for you with the price of the heifer on you.

It is at this point that the final layer of intertextual referencing is added to the play's plot line, in a move that recalls Lady Gregory's memory of her first sighting of Synge. While still in dress rehearsal mode, Cissie's character moves over to the window of the cottage, just as she is supposed to do in Gladys's piece; looking out of the window, however, causes Cissie to break out of character as she exclaims: 'Oh! Gladys, come here quick – here's a tramp – a real tramp coming up the road.' Gladys running to the window immediately 'textualises' her vision of the tramp, telling her sister, 'isn't he just like the tramp in *The Wishing Bone?*'. Gladys's reaction obliquely articulates a pre-read West that simply needs to be translated into text to truly reveal its 'actual self'. The scene on stage is now layered with several levels of performative meaning, as Cissie makes the obvious suggestion: 'Wouldn't it be a good idea, now that we are in costume, to pretend to be cotter folk?' This meta-scene is further complicated by Gladys's suggestion that they continue on with the rehearsal of their play, for, as Cissie has pointed out, they are at the point in the play when they 'see the tramp coming up the path to break the news of the death of Cornelius'. Shortly thereafter the 'tramp' in *The Mist That Does Be on the Bog* arrives on stage to become an unwitting character in *What's All the Stir About?* The tramp (Clarence) enters the house pronouncing (with a nod perhaps to Christy's entrance in *Playboy*) 'God save all in this house', and the exchange that follows reveals the final brilliance of MacNamara's parodic imagination:

> CISSIE: Thank you kindly, stranger. Come and sit down by the fire and put a heat into your limbs, for it's myself that's thinkin' that your bones are aching and you travellin' on the hard roads this day.
>
> CLARENCE: [*Aside*] This is delightful. I could write a play here in one hour. [*To Cissie*] You speak kind words, lady, and true ones, for it's no joke crossing the hills when the fog is on them, and lying down under the heavens when the night is cold.

The 'tramp' (whose 'real name' is Clarence St John) is a playwright from Dublin who, like Gladys and Cissie, has come to the West of Ireland to seek inspiration for his work. Later in the piece St John will reveal that his plays are 'weak in what is called local colour', and his trip was designed to inject some such colour into them. For the moment, however, St John remains in character as a tramp playing along with the two sisters. The point here, of course, is that the women are also playing roles from a play and that the inspiration he sees before him ('I could write a play here in one hour') is in fact a cultural construct. What follows is some of MacNamara's most accomplished writing and stagecraft. St John is quickly convinced that he has struck inspirational gold, a place that will swiftly furnish him with a wealth of 'local colour' to add intellectual truth and validity to his work. Likewise the two women are certain that in the tramp they have found the perfect touchstone for their attempts to represent the West. The stage is thus occupied with a series of separate but intertwined language games, as each character sets out to improvise his/her perceived role.

Thus on stage the audience is confronted with a playwright in search of the real West, finding inspiration by observing the rehearsal of a play written by a woman who has also come to the West to seek inspiration for her work. Just as with Lady Gregory and J.M. Synge on Aran, the staged West has now become a space overly full of outsiders seeking to interpret it. More radically, MacNamara presents his audience with a playwright finding inspiration in a simulacrum of that which he had come to observe. The real

West of Ireland now becomes ever more distant as the number of interpretative lenses multiplies. The audience is confronted with a series of meta-dramaturgical exchanges, with the unintentional parodying produced by the characters on stage embedded further within the parodic will to deconstruct produced by MacNamara's play *The Mist That Does Be on the Bog*. The action on stage is now fully multivalent, allowing those in the auditorium to watch a number of different plays simultaneously. Cissie is convinced that she is managing to represent the West back to itself, while St John draws inspiration for future representations of the West from something that is itself a representation. The action on stage is now played out as a kind of cultural-nationalist 'false consciousness', a move, of course, that implicates those in the auditorium at the Abbey as well as those that have taken to its stage. In this moment of fake 'first contact' the characters are caught up in a mutually sustaining hermetic circle of interpretation, but one that is completely removed from the actual ontology of life in a small community in the West of Ireland.

The tramp's arrival is a brilliantly orchestrated move, one that offers MacNamara occasion for some brilliant humour as well as commentary upon his Abbey contemporaries. Gladys and Cissie continue to play their 'parts' but the strain of ad-libbing soon begins to show. Gladys has asked Cissie (referred to as Moira in this play within a play) to get some milk for the stranger:

> GLADYS: Moira, what is keeping you with the milk, and the stranger like to die with the thirst that's on him?
> CISSIE: Maybe it's yourself could find it, for I cannot.
> GLADYS: It's over there in the North-West corner.
> CISSIE: It's the poor shape I do be makin' at the findin' of it and without a compass . . .

Both women have, as the audience knows, just arrived in the cottage and therefore have no clue as to where anything actually is. Gladys's over-quaintness – 'in the North-West corner' – leads Cissie to introduce a touch of modernity in her ironic response that she cannot find it 'without a compass'. This tension between romantic presentation and the realities of day-to-day rural life is much of the point of MacNamara's parody within a parody. These revivalist enthusiasts are seen searching out a form of authenticity, but their performance only seems to push them further into an inauthentic position. The nature of this ambivalent desire is brought even more to the fore as it becomes clear that St John is much enamoured of Cissie. Finally, when Cissie is off-stage, St John makes his intentions clear:

> CLARENCE: I wish Moira [Cissie] would come back again, by Jove, such a fine girl! These Connemara girls have never been done full justice in any of the books ever I have read. There is no mistake about it – I'm head and ears in love with her already. I cannot carry on this deception any longer. I'll make a clean breast of it. I'll tell her who and what I am and make her an offer of marriage.

MacNamara once again contrives to expose the gap between text and reality as St John views the 'real' country girl as a kind of text, concluding that the real thing has never been done justice 'in any of the books' he has read. All the while, of course, the 'real' girl in question is very literally a textual invention acting out a role in a play. In a subsequent conversation with Cissie, St John reveals himself to be a Dublin playwright. The device of revelation turns out to be his false 'whiskers', which he pulls off to reveal his real self. In *The Mist* everyone is seen to be wearing a costume; even the Quinns are in the end seen as players who set out a certain scene for a play (or plays) to take place. The taking off and putting on of different costumes (the dapper Fred at one point moans about having to dress as a tramp for Gladys's play) in this way becomes a device for exploring the inescapably performative nature of any representation.

After his revelation, St John attempts to explain his motives to Cissie/Moira. His reasoning sheds a sceptical light on the sort of research trip carried out by revivalist figures like Synge and Gregory:

> CLARENCE: Moira, I have not come here disguised in order to deceive you – I had an object – I am writing a play. I could weave plots equal, if not superior, to any folk play I have ever seen – but – I am weak in what is called local colour – so I came here. I feared that had I been dressed as I usually am – in Dublin, I could not have gained your confidence, so I came disguised – as a tramp. Moira, this is my only fault, if fault it can be called.

St John's twin revelations, that he is a playwright and that he is in love, force Cissie to reveal her true identity (accomplished once again by taking off her costume). Cissie's revelation of her fashionable dress confuses the scene yet again: 'What does all this mean?' asks a much-perturbed St John:

CISSIE: It simply means that I have been in this cottage only an hour. I am staying with my sister who has rented the place for a week. I belong to Belfast.
CLARENCE: [*Turns away and hangs his head*] Belfast!
CISSIE: Yes, Belfast. [*Huffed*] You need not be so shocked – there is nothing the matter with Belfast.

And so even in the West, it would seem there is no escape from the North. In these final moments of the play, MacNamara brings the problematic relationship between the North and the rest of Ireland directly into the spiritual homeland of the revival – a small cottage in the West. The final stumbling-block to acceptance and understanding in these closing moments is Belfast. The playwright from Dublin thus finds himself in a cottage in the West with a playwright and her sister from the North, all of whom have come to make contact with the real 'soul' of Ireland. The ending marks a form of duality. Structurally there is a commonality between the intentions of the northerners and the southerner - all are in the West on similar missions. Yet there is no sense of personal reconciliation as Cissie continues to take offence at St John's reaction to Belfast:

CISSIE: Don't speak to me. You are disillusioned. You only loved the country girl – not me.
CLARENCE: Cissie – I assure you–
CISSIE: I won't listen to you. Disgust was on your face when I mentioned Belfast. You know it.

The problematic of the perceived North/South cultural schism, finally, cannot be resolved here in an invented West. MacNamara in response attempts to establish the need for other representational strategies if the problematic of Ulster and Home Rule are to be accommodated within a revivalist aesthetic seeking a pathway to national renewal. The revival strategy, for example, of reconfiguring the present via a romantic past is collapsed by MacNamara's play in a move that points to the impossibility of maintaining this dynamic. MacNamara inserts the supposed traits of the North, modernity and industrialism, into this classic Abbey landscape. Michael Quinn is chairman of a recently opened 'Technical School', while the first of the playwrights arrives at the cottage as part of a motoring tour in a rented car. Many of the play's key moments are thoroughly 'anti-Romantic'; the manner in which, for example, both playwrights and company have pre-read the place they are seeking and use disguise in order to gain entrance. The way, also, that their mission has its future representation built in (their present is haunted by the knowledge that they will represent their time in the cottage in a future play about being in a cottage). All of these traits are, in some senses, built around a schema that is proto-modernist. MacNamara's achievement seems all the more remarkable in these terms; here was a brilliantly funny parody of Synge, which also managed to reflect back to the Abbey a subverted version of its vision. In the guise of an outrageous comedy, MacNamara managed to deconstruct the early Abbey using some of its most treasured tools.

That said, the fact that the play was first produced at the Abbey could also be read as an interesting moment of *rapprochement,* with the performance occupying the same stage space as its parodic target. The visit of MacNamara's play to the Abbey, with its representation of classic Abbey material as a simulacrum of a simulacrum, also marks out the North as the location which could most fully comment upon the activities of the Dublin-centric literary élite. It is a key moment in the development of the North's inside/outside cultural-nationalist position. A number of years later, indeed, Joseph A. Power, a theatre critic writing in the *Dublin Evening Telegraph,* recalls the performance of *The Mist That Does Be on the Bog* as an opportunity for a rethink at the Abbey, an opportunity that was never taken up. Power was writing on the occasion of the arrival of a new manager at the Abbey (Fred O'Donovan) in 1917, and he takes the opportunity to survey the theatre's progress to that point:

> Many of the earlier plays of the Abbey school are wearing well, but I think the 'Kiltartan' goods are becoming somewhat frayed.
>
> It was in this style of things that my friend 'Gerald MacNamara' had in his mind when he wrote *The Mist That Does Be on the Bog,* a satiric effort which suffered from the fact the majority of Ulster audiences before whom it was presented had not had an opportunity of seeing the style of the play against which its banter was directed.
>
> It tickled the Dublin audiences, but it produced no visible effect in the Abbey, where things continued largely in the Kiltartan groove. (11 June 1917)

For Power, *The Mist* was a moment of lost potential, a signpost of possible other directions for the Abbey that was in the end ignored. Implicit in this commentary is the role of Ulster in conjuring these other possible pathways, an interpretation that further complicates the article's insistence that the Abbey hierarchy never fully engaged with these counter-visions. That the play was not as successful in Ulster because northern audiences lacked familiarity with the cultural intentions of the Dublin theatre also reinforces the sense of the audience's importance in decoding the full parodic potential of a play like *The Mist That Does Be on the Bog.*

Primarily Power expresses regret that the Abbey had not picked up on the parodic counter-codes provided by MacNamara's rereading of Synge. A short comic piece published in *Sinn Féin* seven months after the first performance of *The Mist* would suggest, however, that the dissenting voice expressed in Griffith's response to Synge (discussed above) had understood the power of MacNamara's parodic articulation. 'The Cross-Image: A National Drama' was published in *Sinn Féin* on 9 July 1910. The piece clearly demonstrates a tactical movement away from the anti-pastiche of Griffith's earlier piece to a more sophisticated stance using the power of parody to frame a counter-subject in the course of critiquing the original. As can be see from the extract below, the short sketch parodies the construction of 'Irish folk' and also questions the intentions behind such figures. The new subject posited by the piece interrogates the position of a literary élite appropriating rural images for their own purposes. The scene is set in a marvellously over-the-top stage-Irish village and involves some local characters discussing the nature of their stage-Irish subjectivity:

BURKE: (*After a silence*) 'Tis meself now that has just sold a sheep that died av faver to feed the polis.

POSTMISTRESS: An' I'm just after coming from lookin' into the letters an parcels that come into the office.

BURKE: (*After a silence*) We're a witty people.

POSTMISTRESS: 'Tis a pity the world knows nothing uv us.

BURKE: An' us artistic.

POSTMISTRESS: Sure, 'tis meself has a fine cravin' for the realistic dhrama.

(*Enter O'Slatterley, very drunk indeed*)

O'SLATTERLEY: The tap o' the mornin' to yez, bedad – I beg your pardon – God save all here.

(*Hiccups loudly and falls head foremost through his own door and remains prone, his feet alone showing*)

BURKE: He must be tired drunk.

POSTMISTRESS: 'Tis expected ov him. Sure, you wouldn't have him not amuse the gentry.[17]

Given the proximity of the publication of this sketch to the first performance of *The Mist* in Dublin, it seems highly probable that here, if nowhere else, the voice of MacNamara had been heard. The overuse of elaborate 'stage-

Irishisms', combined with the characters' self-reflexive articulation of themselves as constructs designed to 'amuse the gentry', all share a certain resonance with MacNamara's parodic vision.

The extra-mural intentions of this work (it fits neatly into *Sinn Féin*'s general hostility towards Synge and the Abbey), however, position this piece as more clearly a parodic 'counter-song'. MacNamara's work may be seen, in this regard, as a more complete parodic expression, at once a 'counter-song' but also a work of supplemental co-ordinated meaning. His aim was not to dismiss the Abbey but, rather, to highlight and supplement the gaps he discerned opening up in its productions. *The Mist* in the end is not simply a condemnation of the Abbey's 'return' to the West; rather, it points to this as just one of many possible moves. While the play's overt concern is the over-representation of the West, its covert concern is focused on the absence of the North. Given this deconstructive potential, then, it is all the more ironic that *The Mist That Does Be on the Bog* was the MacNamara play that impacted least on the North. His next piece, however, would prove to be his most popular and significant contribution to the Ulster Literary Theatre's project.

Chapter Ten

The Sacred and Profane Thompson

Caoilte, and Conán, and Finn were there,
When we followed a deer with our baying hounds,
With Bran, Sceolan, and Lomair,
And passing the Firbolg's burial-mounds,
Came to the cairn-heaped grassy hill
Where passionate Maeve is stoney-still;
W.B. Yeats, *The Wanderings of Oisin*

What constitutes the charm of our country, apart of course from its scant population, and this without the help of the meanest contraceptive, is that all is derelict, with the sole exception of history's ancient faeces. These are ardently sought after, stuffed and carried in procession. Wherever nauseated time has dropped a nice fat turd you will find our patriots, sniffing it up, on all fours, their faces on fire. Elysium of the roofless.
Samuel Beckett, *First Love*

In every era the attempt must be made anew to wrest tradition away from the conformism that is about to overpower it.
Walter Benjamin, 'Theses on the Philosophy of History'

Beckett's repudiation of Ireland's 'tradition' fetish, articulated here as waste product deposited in history's wake, identifies a modernist drive to do away with the myth-making pretensions of the revival period. Richard Kearney, discussing this element of the Beckettian worldview, suggests that he 'reveled in discontinuity and alienation', abhorring 'the mythic idioms of collective continuity and community', in their place positing an exploration of (what Beckett himself termed) the 'rupture of the lines of communication'.[1] It is exactly this rupture, captured in Beckett's insistence that 'There can be no communication . . . because there is nothing to communicate', that Kearney locates as central to Beckett's repudiation of, amongst other things, nationalism's cultural products.[2] Beckett's (post)modernist position aims to debunk the power of tradition over the secular existence of modern man. In reaction to identity as tradition, writers like Beckett responded with the need for a modernist authenticity: (as Kearney parses it) the drive to fashion, for one's self, one's own essence (while in the process, perhaps, unpacking the problematics of this notion also).

This Beckettian vision of rupture and discontinuity, which reads tradition as a falsely elevated waste product retained for perverse (expressed here as scatological) reasons, may be read as a sceptical response to the revival's articulation of continuity and tradition. A number of modern-day critics have isolated this obsession with tradition as one of the fundamental problems posed by the revival and its influence on what came after. Seamus Deane, for example, has argued that Yeats's lasting legacy is to have inscribed a Romantic philosophy into subsequent searches for a 'true' Irish identity. It is this that Deane reads as one of the more damaging inheritances of the revival period, locking many subsequent writers into a self-defeating and problematic search for a properly authentic sense of self.[3] Denis Donoghue, 'rereading' Deane's literary history in a more positive light, develops this idea in a different direction, linking the sense of a romantic search for 'Irishness' with the Romance formulation of the quest.[4] Thus Yeats, in Denis Donoghue's rendering, articulated an abstract quest, with a true identity, informed by tradition, as the goal. Rather than reductively binding, Donoghue contends, this is a quest that can be read as powerfully enabling in the ongoing project of Irish writing.

Beckett thus stands in for one side of this debate; in the wake of revival, and in response to it, Beckett presented the futility of such a quest. On one level the tension between the modernist and romantic-nationalist articulation of tradition concerns the nature of the profane and the sacred. At heart this is a conflict between a Yeatsian (revivalist) *piety* and Beckett's promotion of a modernist secular authenticity. Tradition stands at the centre of both these formulations. To one side is Yeats's insistence on tradition as the necessary basis for a reformulation of contemporary problematics, while, on the other, Beckett posits the impossibility (and illegitimacy) of this position. Where Yeats fostered links between historical moments, hence creating a discourse of tradition, Beckett believed that there 'can be no communication . . . because there is nothing to communicate'. Where Yeats attempts to make modern man at home in his past and to bring that past into proper dialogue with the present, Beckett presents a vision of alienation and an impossibility of finding home in the past or anywhere else. In essence this conflict may be read as the struggle to either establish or disavow a communicative link between the profane reality of everyday existence and that which we deem as somehow sacred or 'other' (beyond ourselves – whether this be history, tradition, belief). This kind of debate enacts a central dialectic in Irish literary history; namely, the relationship between the philosophy of the revival and those post-revival writers who responded to it. Beckett here stands in for a post-revival scepticism querying the viability of a project centred on (as he sees it) inauthentic versions of an invented authenticity.

The work of the Ulster Literary Theatre would suggest that such a post-revival scepticism had already been partially pre-coded into the performance of revival itself. The work of Gerald MacNamara certainly seems to provide signposts from within revival to possible routes towards a post-revival philosophy. Acting as one possible bridging point, for example, between this conflict of romantic-nationalist and (post)modern approaches to tradition and sacredness is Gerald MacNamara's 1912 production, *Thompson in Tír-na-nÓg*. In the course of this play MacNamara explodes the romantic-nationalist relationship between sacred and profane existence. *Thompson* concerns the impossibility of an identity quest informed by a mythic tradition and once again foreshadows the more thoroughgoing collapsing of this relationship apparent in the modernism of figures like Beckett, Joyce and Flann O'Brien. MacNamara's third and highly successful play, *Thompson in Tír-na-nÓg*, marks his most complete parodic unpacking of the various nationalist (Orange and Green) versions of identity at work in early twentieth-century Ireland. In the course of its fantastical progress *Thompson* lays bare the ideological translations inherent in the major political traditions informing the landscape of Ulster/Ireland in 1912. This extraordinary political burlesque asks the audience to look anew at the very idea of tradition. MacNamara manages this by reformulating the metaphorical or symbolic processes of tradition as actual plot devices. Richard Kearney, for example, in the course of discussing the continuing power held by certain narratives, highlights within the etymology of 'tradition' a form of temporal ellipse or collapse: 'tradition means – *tradere* – carrying or transferring the past into the present and the present into the past'.[5] It is this etymological root that MacNamara gives physical form on stage in *Thompson in Tír-na-nÓg*, as the main character negotiates his way through a different temporal dimension and attempts to bring the vision of sacredness that he finds there into correspondence with the profane reality of his own existence. In the course of this adventurous work, MacNamara simultaneously presents a

Yeatsian mythic recuperation as well as a proto-Beckettian impossibility of communication between the mythic and the profane.

Thompson in Tír-na-nÓg's opening night was on 9 December 1912. The play is the story of Orangeman 'Andy Thompson', who, by way of an unfortunate accident with some unstable gunpowder at a re-creation of the Battle of the Boyne, finds himself wandering in the land of Irish mythological heroes, 'Tír-na-nÓg'.[6] The play follows Thompson's adventures as he tries to communicate with a series of Irish mythological figures. As it develops, the piece explores concepts of mythic tradition, alienation and the (im)possibility of an authentic politics based on essentialist readings of myth, tradition and history. We should note at the outset that 1912 was a crucial year in Ireland's Home Rule 'quest'. On 11 April of that year the third Home Rule bill was introduced in the House of Commons. With the passing of the Parliament Act of 1911 it was considered inevitable that this third attempt at legislative action would pass through both Houses of Parliament – eventually. However, the most divisive element remained unresolved: the question of Ulster. For three days in June of 1912 (11th, 13th, 18th) the business time of the House of Commons was almost exclusively taken up debating the Thomas Agar-Roberts motion to exclude parts of the north-east of Ireland from the Home Rule bill (in other words, partition). The reaction to the bill in Ulster, in its political and paramilitary forms, gave added impetus and organisational drive to the powerful Ulster unionist grouping. The rhetoric calling for a defence of Ulster was given a powerful physical embodiment, for example, with the formation of the Ulster Volunteer Force (January 1913). As Joseph Connolly recalls: 'From the time that the Parliament Act of 1911 became law, the organisation of opposition to Home Rule was intensified. Ulster loyalty became loyalty to Ulster, unionism, and the Orange Order and threats to 'kick the crown into the Boyne' became a common feature of the Unionist meetings.'[7] This was the year (1912), in other words, that absolutely defined the Ulster unionist project.

Given the strains and tensions apparent in the North during this year of heightened political uncertainty, the decision by the Ulster Literary Theatre to stage *Thompson in Tír-na-nÓg* seems all the more remarkable. The story of an Orangeman appearing in Tír-na-nÓg and meeting such figures as Cúchulain, Conán, Queen Maev and Grania was certainly innovative; it was also somewhat perilous. Given that the mythic heroes and the Orangeman conspire to confuse, infuriate and completely misunderstand each other, the potential for angry reaction was (and is) all the more evident. Indeed even before the play had reached its final version the potential for negative reaction had already been highlighted. MacNamara's nephew, Gerald Morrow, recalls that the play had been drastically rewritten before its first performance. He remembers how the piece 'was originally written by request for the Gaelic League. It was then in three acts. But they rejected it because they said "it held up the Gaelic Heroes to ridicule". The author then made it into a one-act piece and gave it to the Ulster Theatre.'[8] Given the nature of MacNamara's project to unpack the inner workings of all forms of nationalism at work in Ulster/Ireland, it is interesting that *Thompson in Tír-na-nÓg* made not only the Gaelic League nervous. The multivalent power of MacNamara's parodic work is confirmed by Rutherford Mayne's memory of the play's early performances. Mayne records one night in the opening run of *Thompson* (when it was paired with Mayne's *The Drone*) which makes it clear that it was not only nationalists who were suspicious of MacNamara's intentions:

> when there was a full house for the two plays . . . with long queues for the 'gods', Mr. McCann, who was the manager of the Opera House, came round and asked us not to let off too strongly in *Thompson* because he had been informed that there were men up there who had been told that this play made fun of a certain Order, and that they were all lined up with rivets and bolts in their pockets. But we started off with *The Drone* and they got into really good humour with the result that when *Thompson* came on, instead of bolts and nuts and so forth landing on the stage, I never heard a play receive such acclamation at the end.[9]

These different recollections of *Thompson in Tír-na-nÓg*'s early reception confirm that Irish nationalism and Ulster unionism each detected a parodic decoding of their inner philosophies. What is equally clear is that organisations such as the Gaelic League and the Orange Order felt compelled to defend the legitimacy of certain narratives as sacrosanct. Tír-na-nÓg was, of course, a conceptual space amenable to romantic-nationalism's search for a form of sacred otherness. In opposition to this (but sharing some functional characteristics), the Orange Order's sense of its profane existence and duties can also be read as ordained by the sacredness of a specific ordering of post-seventeenth-century history. In the end, perhaps, it was the play's intervention into *both* of these narratives (historical and mythical) that allowed its audiences to accept its position as an 'other' interpretative space.

Tír-na-nÓg is usually thought of in terms of an after-life rendezvous for those mythic figures that have been called to Ireland's aid, and it was a space regularly called into the service of romantic-nationalism's martyrdom trope. It is this appropriation that is called into question in *Thompson in Tír-na-nÓg;* in response to Irish nationalism's inscription of a sacred Tír-na-nÓg as a space relevant to profane Ireland, MacNamara gives us Tír-na-nÓg as a *constructed* space explicitly dissociated with the political realities of Irish nationalism. Just as with William III in *Suzanne and the Sovereigns,* throughout this play the mythic inhabitants of Tír-na-nÓg remain baffled by the language and metaphorical allusions of nationalism: they consistently and profoundly fail to communicate with the ideas of profane Irish politics. It is the performance of this distance that we may locate as central to the success and the intentions of MacNamara's most ambitious work. The work of Mircea Eliade on the idea of after-life paradisal realms may, tangentially at least, help open up MacNamara's cultural philosophy, for the idea of a 'disconnected' space is posited by Eliade as one of the linking factors in various paradise myths. In effect Eliade locates two main categories of paradisal myths: those that allow for a process of communication (between profane and sacred realms) and those that describe sacred space as beyond communication. The former is occupied by sacred figures who retain an interest in and effect on the world they have left behind; the latter, to borrow Eliade's phrasing, is inhabited by *dii otiosi,* disconnected figures with no influence over or concern for the world they have left.[10] The force of MacNamara's parodic inversion in *Thompson* centres on the nature of Tír-na-nÓg's inhabitants as just such disconnected gods, or *dii otiosi.* Crucial, in these terms, to romantic-nationalism's appropriation of Tír-na-nÓg is the (implicit) transformation of its hero-inhabitants (such as Cúchulain) from *dii otiosi* into figures able to communicate with contemporary ideas of Irishness. *Thompson in Tír-na-nÓg* performs a critique of this very transformation; throughout the play, MacNamara explicitly transforms those in Tír-na-nÓg back into dissociated, disconnected *dii otiosi.* In response to the resolution in myth offered by other revivalist figures such as Yeats and Gregory (and also by the likes of Pádraic Pearse), MacNamara offers a vision of the incommensurable gap between profane reality and sacred vision. For MacNamara, like Beckett, no communication is possible here.

Thompson in Tír-na-nÓg, more than any other MacNamara play, openly explodes the 'artifice' of nationalism's search for sacred authentication. The ways in which this search is embedded within various modes of representation is highlighted, moreover, in more ways than the presentation of a disconnected space. The primary element of the communicative act – the language through which it is conducted – is continually presented as problematic. Throughout *Thompson* MacNamara indexes the act of translation as undermining and/or destabilising Irish nationalism's use of Tír-na-nÓg (in the sense that its inhabitants are made to speak a language that barely existed when their actions were recorded in medieval manuscripts). That said, the fact of translation is not the target of MacNamara's parody; after all, his work is also conducted in English. It is not the politics of language *per se* that MacNamara seeks to unpack in *Thompson;* rather, he highlights the *unacknowledged* nature of translation at work within contemporary cultural production and debate. For MacNamara this lack of acknowledgement functions to negate and make invisible the gap between the sacred subject and the translated representation (i.e. profane need). *Thompson in Tír-na-nÓg* makes it clear that MacNamara sees this as one of the more dubious elements of nationalism. In its place MacNamara begins to open up a performative space which points to the potential of treating myth openly as myth and thus acknowledging the act of translation. *Thompson*'s meta-mythic position further reveals MacNamara's potential as a post-nationalist voice from within revival.

Much of the point of *Thompson,* then, was to re-establish and affirm a very definite gap between sacred space and profane reality. As a result MacNamara overloads his *acknowledgement* of the translation process. In accordance with the drive to establish a gap between myth and profane need, MacNamara emphasises the fact of translation to the extent of making it the actual subject of large parts of the play. It is a strategy, moreover, that invokes much of Linda Hutcheon's comment that Brecht was a playwright 'who could use parody to make the entire issue of theatrical representation implode'.[11] In many ways MacNamara was such a writer too. Not only, then, is Andy Thompson seen as alienated from his surroundings, but (as with Brecht) MacNamara also manages to harry his audience out of their comfortable expectations by pointing to the artifice of what they are watching. And so the audience gets to observe as the characters on stage become meta-mythic characters, to the extent that they often speak about the nature of 'being mythic'. In so doing, MacNamara recuperates that dimension of myth lost within a romantic-nationalist world-view; namely, its ability to stand outside political reality.

If Tír-na-nÓg provides one nexus of nationalist meaning and counter-meaning, the figure of Andy Thompson introduces a further set of identity issues. MacNamara's decision to introduce an Orangeman specifically into the environs of one of cultural-nationalism's most sacred spaces is an interesting and daring one – particularly given the increasing power of the

Orange Order within Ulster unionism, as evidenced in the run-up to 1912. The Orange Order provided Ulster unionism with many of its sacred codes' frames of reference, and it was 1912 that provided both with one of their most powerful textual inscriptions of sacredness: the 'Ulster Covenant' was signed by thousands of Ulster Protestants on 'Ulster Day', 28 September 1912. Indeed, we do not have to look much beyond the title (Covenant) to pick up on some clear sacred demarcations. The biblical nuance functions to link the actions of the men of Ulster with their forefathers; it also obliquely placed the statement into the religious/political framework that stands at the centre of the Orange Order's sense of identity and mission. The influence of the Orange Order is also very apparent in the wording of the Covenant text that was to be signed by so many:

> Being convinced in our consciences that Home Rule would be disastrous to the material well-being of Ulster as well as the whole of Ireland, subversive of our civil and religious freedom, destructive of our citizenship, and perilous to the unity of the Empire, we, whose names are underwritten, men of Ulster, loyal subjects of His Gracious Majesty King George V, humbly relying on the God whom our fathers in days of stress and trial confidently trusted, do hereby pledge ourselves in solemn Covenant throughout this our time of threatened calamity to stand by one another in defending ourselves and our children our cherished position of equal citizenship in the United Kingdom, and in using all means which may be found necessary to defeat the present conspiracy to set up a Home Rule Parliament in Ireland. And in the event of such a Parliament being forced upon us we further solemnly and mutually pledge ourselves to refuse to recognise its authority. In sure confidence that God will defend the right we hereto subscribe our names. And further, we individually, declare that we have not already signed this Covenant. God save the King.[12]

The Covenant's text functions as a palimpsest, mapping itself onto ideals born out of the Orange Order's sacrosanct remembrance of the 'Glorious Revolution'. The profane reality of Ulster unionist politics is thus linked to the eternal founding fathers of the seventeenth-century. It is a text that demonstrates how the Orange Order and Ulster unionism also positioned themselves in terms of an always present historical duty. The signatories to the Covenant pledged to rely on the self-same 'God whom our fathers in days of stress and trial confidently trusted'. These moments of stress and trial may be listed as the classic historical points of crisis within unionist mythology: 1641, 1689 and 1690.[13] These instances of 'Irish betrayal' versus 'Protestant (unionist) loyalty' are thus recalled in the Covenant to provide a structure of continuity into which this latest battle can easily fit. Indeed this part of the Covenant foreshadows, from the opposite direction, the listing four years later of revolutionary continuity invoked by Pearse as he read the Proclamation from Dublin's GPO. The Ulster signatories not only identify themselves as defenders of the present in relation to a sacred past, they also position themselves as guardians of the future. Those who sign promise to defend not only themselves but 'our children also'. The text's sense of divine revelation provides a structure of stability and permanence wherein the battle against Home Rule can be read as the same battle that was fought at the Boyne.

This referencing of profane need to sacred revelation is essentially connected to that etymological conception of tradition as '*tradere* – carrying or transferring the past into the present and the present into the past'. In turn, this concept of tradition provides a very particular reading of the play's plot structure: *Thompson in Tír-na-nÓg* is thus essentially the story of a man who ends up in the 'wrong' part of sacred time. Thompson's Orangeman in arriving in Tír-na-nÓg is lost in a different version of sacredness to that which has helped define his profane existence. In the course of playing out the inevitable confusions of such a situation MacNamara indexes the arbitrariness of the sacred. Throughout the play 'the sacred' is demonstrated as a discourse and/or ideal that takes on a shape predetermined by the needs of those who articulate its very existence. *Thompson in Tír-na-nÓg* thus marks a brilliant moment of sceptical, while still hilarious, post-nationalist performance. In its performance we can see MacNamara unravelling many of the central tenets informing the main political groupings; groupings, we must remember, that were at this very moment contesting the meaning of 'Ulster'. It is in this play, more than any other perhaps, that we can most fully detect the singular positioning of a northern cultural nationalism that stood in direct and close dialogue with both the revival and Ulster unionism.

Thompson Takes to the Stage

Thompson in Tír-na-nÓg first appeared on stage less than three months after the signing of the Ulster Covenant, a fact that adds weight to Rutherford Mayne's memory of Orangemen with nuts and bolts in the audience. While the play's action follows the wanderings of Andy Thompson after he finds himself awakened in Tír-na-nÓg, much of its progress also involves the revelation of how he arrived at such a situation. The inhabitants of Tír-na-nÓg are at first welcoming but grow steadily suspicious of their new member, as he time and again demonstrates his lack of knowledge concerning 'Irish history'. Indeed at the end of the piece Thompson is put on trial for effectively 'breaking and entering' Tír-na-nÓg. Given the nature of MacNamara's third play for the Ulster Literary Theatre, the reaction in the Belfast of 1912 could easily have been somewhat mixed, and perhaps even largely hostile. The fact that the play so clearly parodied all sections of the audience would appear to have redeemed the piece, however, and *Thompson* went on to become the most often rehearsed piece in the Ulster Literary Theatre's repertoire. Rutherford Mayne remembers the context in which the play opened and the reaction that followed:

> The Home Rule controversy had begun to raise political temperature in Ulster in 1912, but that year again saw more of Morrow's [MacNamara's] daring when he staged for the first time his famous *Thompson in Tir-na-nOg*. In reality one of the most biting and sardonic comedies ever put on the Irish stage, it never fails to render the most outrageous and bigoted partisan in Irish politics, helpless with laughter even at his own side.[14]

Indeed reviews of the play's first performances suggest it was received as an unqualified success. The *Northern Whig*, for example, on the day after *Thompson*'s opening night, points to the Ulster Literary Theatre as a source for new experimental Irish drama:

> What the company can do with new and experimental stuff when they really put their backs into it is shown in *Thompson in Tir-na-nOg* . . . The idea on which the piece turns is a dramatic inspiration in itself; to shoot one of the King William's generals at the Scarva sham fight into 'Tir-na-nOg', the Irish land of perpetual youth, and confront him with the heroes of the ancient legends, Cuchulain, Finn, Angus, Maev, and the rest makes for inextinguishable laughter . . . [f]or three-quarters of an hour last night the audience rocked and roared as one has seldom heard theatre-goers in these degenerate days . . . [a]s a performance it stands out as the most finished thing the Ulster Players have given us. (10 December 1912)

Nevertheless, some reviewers were quick to pick up on the possibly troubling implications of the play's take on the relationship between myth and politics. One review in the *Belfast News-Letter*, for example, seems haunted by the potential for divisive reactions to the piece, but in the end it is MacNamara's even-handedness that appears to ensure cross-community endorsement:

> The play is a fantasy, and that will probably help to make its whimsical humour, satire, and topsy-turvy logic agreeable to all who witness it. Thompson is an ardent Orangeman, and he gives some solid and weighty

> reasons for the faith that is in him; whilst the inhabitants of Tir-na-nOg are Nationalists to a man, and they are equally cogent on the other side.
>
> But the author holds the scales pretty evenly, and his sole object being to secure the amusement of his audience he turns every incident and speech into a huge joke.
>
> So long as the audience accepts Mr. MacNamara's bona fides they will be kept in good humour, but one trembles to think what they might say if they imagined that beneath his levity there was some sinister motive.
>
> Which side would be the first to cry out one could not even venture to predict. But last night's audience decided that the honours were equal, and gave themselves up to uproarious laughter. (10 December 1912)

In the end, perhaps, the nature of the scales that MacNamara held was different to that indicated in the contemporary reviews. In the discussion that follows it will also become clear that the range and intent of this proto-modernist piece were far greater than was often acknowledged at the time of its performance.

The play opens with an exchange between the High King and Finn MacCumhal; their dialogue clearly locates the piece as outside the conventions of contemporary myth-based drama. The issues of language and translation noted above are made the explicit subject of the play's opening scene as the figures on stage are confused and bewildered by the strange sounds coming out of their mouths – they are speaking in English. The king's opening soliloquy establishes the play as simultaneously appropriating many of the conventions of revivalist drama (mythic figures discussing an Irish paradisal vision) while also performing at one remove from these conventions to provide a meta-nationalist dynamic.

> KING: [*Seated centre*] What has befallen our land this day, this land of eternal youth and happiness – beloved Tir-na-nOg. O sad is my heart, and my tongue is troubled with speaking in this new and curious language. Can it be that the knowledge of the Gaelic has utterly forsaken me, or is it but an evil spell which soon may pass away?[15]

Moments later Finn MacCumhal rushes onto the stage to reinforce the sense that everything is not as it should be in the Land of Youth; again his sense of an uncanny difference is the result of the distressing change in language that has occurred:

> FINN: O King, I am in dire distress; I have been stricken with a malady which troubles me to understand. I have lost all

> words of Gaelic and in their stead I speak this language which must sound most curious to thine ears. [*King shakes his head*] Ah! I see 'tis useless to address the King in such a barbarous language. [*Turns to go off left*]

While the King assures Finn that he too can understand this new and strange language that he speaks 'much against [his] will', the point is made that a Tír-na-nÓg 'in English' is a curiousity that needs some thought. The exchange between the two characters establishes the linguistic convention within which the action on stage will operate. It also highlights the fact that this move *is* a convention linked to the needs of cultural representation.

The scene of Tír-na-nÓg on stage is firmly established as a Brechtian constructed place; constructed, that is, to serve the needs of the audience for whom it is articulated. On stage MacNamara establishes a meta-mythic world that is allowed to express itself in exactly those terms. The performance of this post-revival Tír-na-nÓg as a meta-space is compounded by the fact that the characters themselves are semi-aware of their own status as textual characters. Throughout the play many of the figures on stage articulate their existence in terms of their own 'textuality'. When the figure of Cúchulain first appears on stage, for example, his initial exchange with the King contains an oblique reference to his own 'source'. Complaining of the strange sounds coming out of his mouth in place of his familiar Gaelic, Cúchulain makes it clear that he finds it troubling even if ' 'Twas not much Gaelic that *I* spoke; my sword spoke for me'. This reiteration of physical prowess draws from the king the assuring response: 'Well said, Cúchulain; thy words are like a saga'. The king's ironic turn of phrase highlights that Cúchulain's 'words' are indeed those of a character out of a mythic 'saga'.

This conceit is played out time and again. Later in the course of an argument where Cúchulain has suggested that Conán's deeds are not as great as Finn's, Conán replies to Cúchulain: 'What know you of Finn? You who belong to another cycle.' Conán's acerbic response articulates the characters that surround him on stage as textual products, the reference to 'another cycle' referring to the division of Irish myth into cycles or sets of narrative. This technique is reinforced moments later when Cúchulain draws on Queen Maev (who has entered, accompanied by Grania) to act as a witness in his defence, for Conán has countered Cúchulain's accusations with his own concerning Cúchulain's legendary deeds. In his counter-attack Conán calls into question the veracity of Cúchulain's defence of Ulster as retold in *The Táin*. In the narrative of Cúchulain's deeds, of course, it is

Queen Maev who is his enemy, yet here in MacNamara's Tír-na-nÓg it is Maev whom he calls on to defend his honour:

> CUCHULAIN: O Maev, Queen of Connacht, fairest of all women, bear me witness, did I not hold the Ford against Ferdia?
> QUEEN: O that thou surely didst, to my great sorrow, but who should say thee nay?
> CUCHULAIN: [*Pointing at Conan*] 'Twas he, the coward.
> QUEEN: Durst doubt the word of warriors of our cycle, thou low-born third cyclarian.

It is a moment of brilliantly executed parody, with MacNamara presenting a kind of intracommunal loyalty as enemies in life form in the after-life discreet groupings based on their textual positions within cycles of narrative.

Moments of linguistic play such as these are reminiscent of the later work of Flann O'Brien. Throughout *At Swim-Two-Birds,* for example, O'Brien takes this concept forward as he allows characters within the novel free range to discuss the nature of their own reality as character and as myth. Many years earlier MacNamara had sought to demonstrate the 'play' at work within the privileging of mythic narratives, and in particular in the manner in which different political realities remapped the mythic landscape to conform to their own vision. The sense that the play is an exploration of political discourse's mythic dimension is further enhanced by the final explanation of the linguistic transformation within Tír-na-nÓg. Angus, the figure in Tír-na-nÓg capable of conjuring spells and magic, confesses that it is he who has produced the change in language, obviously much to Finn's chagrin:

> FINN: But what language is it that you've put upon us?
> ANGUS: I ordered purest English.
> KING: English! What people are the English?
> ANGUS: They hail from the land beyond the Eastern Sea.
> KING: What! Those barbarians! A people who were wont to paint their bodies red and white and blue.
> FINN: And who, we're told, did eat their near relations.

It is an exchange that perfectly encapsulates the kind of play (in the sense of movement) at work in MacNamara's examination of the gap between the sacred and the profane. The parodic referencing of a communicative gap between the mythic dimension and the realm of real politic here only manages to demonstrate the ambiguity inherent to any such linkage. The characters' lack of knowledge concerning the world after their departure to

Tír-na-nÓg presents these mythic figures as explicitly *dii otiosi,* heroes/gods with no connection to the profane existence of the world they left behind. However, MacNamara, having presented the heroes as *dii otiosi* – a representation that performs a critique of nationalist mythic strategies – then proceeds to allow a certain form of play as he expands and contracts the gap between sacred and profane with temporal overlaps and superimposition. What we have here is a return to the staged heterotopia that MacNamara first experimented with in *Suzanne and the Sovereigns,* as various usually mutually exclusive frames of reference are allowed to co-exist in the same space. At one moment the figures are detached gods, yet this is undercut as the peoples to the east of ancient Erin are then recalled as painting their bodies red, white and blue. MacNamara's playfulness, superimposing contemporary icons and symbols onto this mythic landscape, serves to highlight that it is in the act of representation that a gap or lack of gap is maintained or denied.

This is an idea that is played out further as Angus informs the company that 'English now is spoken throughout our natal land'. The fact that those in MacNamara's Tír-na-nÓg find this idea incomprehensible throughout the play further serves to reinforce their remoteness and inability to deal with the contemporary timescape of Ireland. Angus's explanation of how he came to this knowledge introduces the figure of Thompson (who has as yet not appeared on-stage), as Angus tells how he came upon a stranger wandering in Tír-na-nÓg. The introduction of the wandering Orangeman opens up another interpretative space as Thompson discovers time and again an incommensurable difference between his version of sacred history (which has defined his political identity) and the version of the sacred surrounding him in Tír-na-nÓg. Angus relates how he came upon a figure that could not speak a word of Gaelic and so communication was impossible. The solution devised by Angus was to cast a spell to enable this unfortunate stranger to speak Gaelic, but he retells with amazement the reaction of this new figure in the Land of Youth: 'It was not that he *could not* speak the Gaelic. 'Twas that he *would not.*' From the moment of his first contact, then, Thompson stands as a kind of 'other' in Tír-na-nÓg; he may also be read as standing in for a Beckettian communication breakdown as he refuses to deal with the symbolic system of heroism that surrounds him. Crucially it is the introduction of, and contact with, this other form of profane/sacred dialectic (Thompson's Orangeman) that causes a radical shift in the very essence of communication in Tír-na-nÓg. Angus admits that in response to Thompson's refusal of Gaelic he has cast another spell to make everyone in Tír-na-nÓg speak English. The introduction of an English-speaking figure requires a complete rearticulation of Tír-na-nÓg; the political didactic is clear: Tír-na-nÓg as a 'pure Irish' space is mythic in more ways than one.

MacNamara's sense of an ambivalent relationship between politics and myth is further reflected in Angus's reasoning for shifting such an essential base element of Tír-na-nÓg's existence. Angus performs the mass act of translation so that all in Tír-na-nÓg 'might speak with [Thompson] and make him feel "at home"'. Much of the subsequent action on-stage revolves around the fact that Thompson cannot make himself 'at home' in this space. This incommensurable difference is highlighted by Thompson's reaction when Angus, now speaking English, relates to him the nature of the place in which he has found himself. Angus had explained to Thompson (off-stage) that he was standing in 'the land of youth and peace, and how [Angus] wished to bring him to [the] king and give him royal welcome'. On hearing this (Angus recalls) Thompson replied by promptly running away shouting 'Too safe, it's an asylum'. Thompson's reaction establishes a running joke whereby he doubts the word of everyone he meets, convinced that they are all inhabitants of a mental asylum (to use the phraseology of the day). This recurring comic invention also raises issues concerning the textual nature of the space in which Thompson finds himself. Essentially Thompson is unable to deal with the heroic figures he meets because they are not pre-read for him; they are not part of the historical/political schema that has informed his specific northern-Irish identity. Thus from his very first moments on stage it is clear that Thompson is very far from being 'at home' in this place; it is a text that he has never read. The figure of the bewildered Orangeman enters the stage (according to the stage direction) to the sound of 'great cheering and laughing' off-stage. Cúchulain goes forward to greet the obviously disturbed Thompson:

> THOMPSON: [*Looking off*] Away out o' that, you unmannerly young rapscallions. [*To Cúchulain*] Who the devil is them?
> CUCHULAIN: [*Looking off*] They are the Children of Lir. They give you welcome to the land of youth.
> THOMPSON: They have a quare way of doing it.
> KING: Did they say aught to give offence?
> THOMPSON: They were shoutin', 'Look at the ould lad'.

It soon becomes obvious that Thompson has no familiarity with this mythic narrative (the Children of Lir), an absence that stands in for his broader ignorance of a certain 'tradition' of mythic narrative. In the course of the introductions carried out by the king, Thompson is introduced to 'Finn the Great' and once again it is clear that Thompson cannot envisage any form of relationship between himself (his own profane authenticity) and this figure from Irish (and as he sees it, nationalist) myth:

> THOMPSON: [*Smiling*] Any friend of Finn McCool?
> FINN: I *am* Finn MacCumhal
> THOMPSON: [*Aside*] The sooner I get out of this place the better.

Indeed, much of the play is now taken up with the collision of exactly these twin discourses. Thompson becomes ever more sceptical of the veracity of everything around him; his actions articulate an Ulster identity that is unfamiliar with Tír-na-nÓg as a nexus of nationalist meaning. The inhabitants of Tír-na-nÓg, in their turn, become ever more wary of this new figure and how he came to be in their dwelling place (for it seems that no new heroes have come to Tír-na-nÓg for aeons). As a consequence the inhabitants of Tír-na-nÓg embark on a mission to discover the 'meaning' of this new arrival. Central to this process of discovery is the relationship between the Orangeman and his 'Ulster predecessor' Cúchulain. As this relationship develops Cúchulain's appropriation by nationalist discourse is investigated as a problematic locus of meaning. Cúchulain and Thompson find themselves referring to very different Ulsters, one ancient and one modern. Cúchulain, much concerned by Thompson's obvious lack of knowledge when it comes to the figures that surround him, enquires if Thompson has similarly not heard of him. The seeds of doubt had been sown when Cúchulain had introduced himself to Thompson, only to draw the reply 'Koo-who?':

> CUCHULAIN: But hast thou never heard of me in Erinn?
> THOMPSON: I'll tell you no lies, mister, I never did. What are ye, or what were ye?
> CUCHULAIN: I was of the Red Branch, foremost of the fighting men of Ulster.
> THOMPSON: Ulster! Put it there. [*Shakes hands*]. Why didn't ye tell me that before. [*Brings him down-stage to front and whispers*] Man, I took you for a luney like the rest. [*Points over his shoulder with his thumb*].
> CUCHULAIN: Were you ever in Ulster?
> THOMPSON: Was I ever in Ulster – was I ever in – was I ever out of it?

Once again MacNamara manages to combine a fine comic touch with a more radical subtext; it is clear that the historical narrative of place referenced by each of the characters is radically different. The Ulster of Thompson is the realm of anti-Home Rule sentiment, while Cúchulain is referencing something quite different indeed. Cúchulain's position is further complicated in that his mythic cycle is based around his defence of Ulster from the rest of Ireland – hence the discourse between these two 'Ulstermen' moves between numerous temporal slippages and acts of historical conflation. It is a scene of beautifully judged parody which subverts many of the fundamentals of contemporary political debate. Once Cúchulain and Thompson have established their common geographical lineage, for example, the 'historical' gap continues to open up between them:

CUCHULAIN: I hope that Ulster still holds sway in Erinn.
THOMPSON: I dunno about holdin' sway, but she can hold her own – and more.
CUCHULAIN: I am pleased to hear it, for I did love and still do love my Ulster. What part of Ulster have you come from?
THOMPSON: Scarva.
CUCHULAIN: Lies Scarva east or west?
THOMPSON: It's on the Great Northern.
CUCHULAIN: [*Reflectively*] Once I was the Great Northern.
THOMPSON: [*Looks at Cúchulain pityingly and says aside*] He's as bad as the rest, poor soul.

Cúchulain's hope that Ulster can still hold sway in Ireland engages with a quite different discursive moment to Thompson's response, a response that is tied to the twentieth-century position of Ulster in the fight to resist Home Rule. Thompson at first begins to find 'home' in Cúchulain's presence but soon the gap between romantic-nationalist mythology and the concerns of modernity becomes too large and communication collapses. Cúchulain describes himself in terms of his mythic (textual) persona – 'the Great Northern' – but this phrase invokes an altogether more modern image for Thompson, that of the 'Great Northern' railway line.

The performance of a gap between modern and mythic Ireland(s) is played out most explicitly in the scenes that follow Thompson's introduction to Cúchulain and the other inhabitants of Tír-na-nÓg. The king and his company have become increasingly uncertain of Thompson and doubt the validity of his status within the land of heroes, sensing ever more strongly that he is not of their kind. Angus suggests that Grania should work her 'woman's wit' on the stranger to discover his true origin and his purpose in coming to their home-place. After the stage has been evacuated, leaving only Grania and Thompson, Grania begins to talk sweetly to Thompson, asking him how he arrived in Tír-na-nÓg. In his turn, Thompson tries to explain the nature of the 'sham battle' in which he had been taking part, in the process revealing at last how he came to find himself in his current predicament:

> THOMPSON: I was takin' a short cut through the meadows, and while I was climbing a ditch, my ould gun burst in my hands, an' that's all I mind. I must a lay there all day, and then maybe in the night I wandered about, not knowin' where I was, and then I must have fell asleep, and when I wakened up in the mornin', I didn't know where I was, and I'm damned if I know now – excuse me.

Naturally enough Grania still does not understand the nature of the battle in which Thompson's 'ould gun' blew up in his hands. It becomes obvious that in this mythic realm there is no place for modernity's staged commemorations:

> GRANIA: And you know not if your army was victorious or not?
> THOMPSON: Sure I told you I was on King William's side. Of course we won the day.
> GRANIA: Why do you say 'of course'? The fortunes of war are so uncertain.
> THOMPSON: Sure it wasn't a real fight. It was a sham fight or a pageant fight.
> GRANIA: A make believe.

Grania is unable to deal with this concept of a battle with a pre-ordained outcome. Equally, and this idea will be played out further later in the play, it is obvious that Grania knows nothing of the deeds of King William. This is a key revelation in terms of the play's parodic intentions; it is a moment that clearly establishes another form of performative gap – in this case between the discourses of conflicting versions of sacredness (mythic, historiographical, political). The complexities of drawing on mythological sources to provide resolution to profane problems are highlighted once again when the two characters hit on the apparently straightforward issue of naming the people of 'Ireland':

> GRANIA: But you *have* been in a *real* fight?
> THOMPSON: O aye, I was in a scrap in Portadown last Sunday.

GRANIA:	And whom were you fighting in Portadown?
THOMPSON:	The Hibernians.
GRANIA:	[*Shocked*] The Hiberniana! But are not all the people in Erinn Hibernians?
THOMPSON:	In sowl they're not.
GRANIA:	Are all the people in Portadown Hiberniana?
THOMPSON:	Talk sense, woman dear.
GRANIA:	[*Looking towards audience*] Many changes must have come o'er Erinn since the days of Cuchulain and Oisin. Then we were all Hibernians. [*To Thompson*] I wish, dearest, that you were an Hibernian, too.
THOMPSON:	You'll never see the day. And what's more, I'll have nothing to do with you, for I'm no believer in mixed marriages.

The play's multivalent parodic intentions are here fully foregrounded as Grania turns to the audience to make her didactic point. Grania's commentary ('Many changes must have come o'er Erinn since the days of Cúchulain and Oisin') and its associated lament ('I wish, dearest, that you were an Hibernian, too') almost perfectly encapsulate the doubled nature of the parodic process. Taken in one way, there is a strong sense of parody as a supplemental (parallel) voice such as Grania looks out to the audience and launches what is effectively a revivalist rallying call. Her wish that everyone would simply think themselves Hibernian echoes a cultural-nationalist desire for culture to provide the common ground for a new sense of Irish unity. This is a desire, of course, that had been evidenced so powerfully throughout 1898 with its emphasis on Wolfe Tone and his 'common name of Irishman', a call that seems to haunt Grania's vision. Indeed, the nature of Grania's identity manifesto reminds us of the Ulster Literary Theatre's roots in the activities of 1898; it also reminds us that Gerald MacNamara thought of himself as providing a positive critique (rather than a rejection) of revivalist philosophy. Nevertheless, there is a reading of this crucial exchange that could also suggest it as a form of parodic 'counter-song'. The way in which Grania really cannot fathom the politics of Thompson's Ulster sets up a reading of the mythic (or the mythic past) as time/space completely incommensurate to the politics of modernity. It is a moment that once again seems to unpack the artifice of any narrative drawn from myth (or indeed from a particular reading of history) as a model or explanation for contemporary problematics. It is a moment, in other words, that has as much to say about the revival as it does about the Orange Order or Ulster unionism.

This is also an exchange that helps set up the play's dénouement. Thompson's final admission that he has fought against the Hibernians (the slippage of meaning between the two characters is much of the point) causes Grania to give a pre-arranged signal to the awaiting company. It had been decided that if Thompson was worthy of Tír-na-nÓg Grania was to have barked like a dog, if he was not she was to mew like a cat. Grania mews like a cat and the company off-stage rush on to 'arrest' the now thoroughly confused Thompson. The king confronts Thompson, informing him that: 'This land has always been reserved for warriors and patriots of Erinn. We consider you are neither one nor other, but by some mysterious hideous blunder, you have been thrust upon us.' Thompson is then put on trial. It is left to Finn to read the charge against him: 'Andrew Thompson, late of Scarva, Ireland, you are charged with trespass in Tír-na-nÓg, you have no right, title or authority to do the same, as you have never fought, died, or done anything in the cause of the Gael.' Cúchulain is placed in charge of conducting the prosecution in this trial, with Thompson taking charge of his own defence. The main charge brought before Thompson is that he is not a true Irishman. The reasoning behind this accusation mostly relates to Thompson's lack of knowledge of 'Irish history' as defined by the inhabitants of Tír-na-nÓg; of course, they themselves know nothing of the events that occurred after their putative existence. Thompson is confronted by Cúchulain demanding that he tell them something of the history of Ireland. Thompson in his turn attempts to mine his version of Irish history, locating as the nodal point William's victory at the Boyne. His explanation of this event and its commemoration places the central narrative of Orangeism in direct conflict with the framework of Irish nationalism's order of history:

CUCHULAIN: Let us hear something of the history of your country.
THOMPSON: Well, I know that King William won the Battle of the Boyne.
CUCHULAIN: When was this battle fought?
THOMPSON: On the 12th.
CUCHULAIN: Twelfth of what?
THOMPSON: Twelfth of July. Sixteen Hundred and Ninety.
CUCHULAIN: Were you present at this battle?
THOMPSON: Ach, you're all mad.

The actions of King William and his conflict with James are all, of course, unfamiliar to Cúchulain and his fellow inhabitants of Tír-na-nÓg. In Thompson's attempts to explain this period in Irish history and the commemorative processes that have been attached to it, the space between his Ulster and the Ulster of Cúchulain becomes ever more apparent. Cúchulain, for example, tries to figure out the nature of King James and his relationship to Ireland:

CUCHULAIN:	And did the Irish people welcome this English king?
THOMPSON:	Of coorse they did, for he was one of their own sort.
CUCHULAIN:	Do you mean he was Irish after all?
THOMPSON:	Not at all.
CUCHULAIN:	Then what do you mean by 'one of their own sort'?
THOMPSON:	Look here, Mr Cuckoo, I don't believe you're an Ulsterman at all.
CUCHULAIN:	Do you mean to say that the Irish people had no desire for an Irish king?
THOMPSON:	Ach, I couldn't tell you. It all happened a long while ago.
CUCHULAIN:	Do you Orangemen rejoice in the victory of a foreign prince over your own countrymen?
THOMPSON:	[*In a tired voice*] Aye.
CUCHULAIN:	And why?
THOMPSON:	[*Angry*] Because we don't want Home Rule.
CUCHULAIN:	Are you too lazy to rule yourselves?
THOMPSON:	Ach, it's not that, for there's heaps of them up in the South and the West that want Home Rule.
CUCHULAIN:	What kind of people are these?
THOMPSON:	They're no class – a lot of Gaelic Leaguers and Hibernians.
CUCHULAIN:	Are you not an Hibernian?
THOMPSON:	If you insult me like that, I'll strike you.
CUCHULAIN:	[*Turning to the Court*] On his own word the prisoner is not an Irishman.

This final confrontation brings the play's subtext to a climax. The problematic of Ulster and Home Rule is resolved, in Thompson's terms, in the historical narrative of seventeenth-century Ireland. The North is also clearly situated as an internal 'other' by Thompson, its political identity posited against 'them up in the South and the West'. The term 'Ireland' thus slips between multiple indicators of meaning in the discourse between Thompson and Cúchulain, until it is finally revealed as an abstract concept allowing no reciprocity between the mythic figure and the embodiment of modernity. Finally, Cúchulain can obviously not deal with the complexities of political discourse presented to him; he and the rest of the inhabitants are in the end returned to their pure status of *dii otiosi*.

While much of this final exchange obviously performs a nationalist comic critique of the Orange Order's worldview (a critique that had led to fears about protest in the theatre), there is also a more expansive parodic intention at work here. In the end MacNamara seems intent on parodying the more unsubtle uses of history, myth and culture by all forms of Nationalism. If the above dialogue seeks to unravel Ulster unionism's sense of divine mission as evidenced in the Ulster Day Covenant, it also unpacks some of the more extravagant claims of an Irish nationalism in search of historical authentication. As such, this powerful parody manages to locate a third space *from* which to speak; it also locates a third space *of* which to speak, namely the overarching notion of nationalism in its multiple Irish manifestations. The audience is finally confronted with a proto-Beckettian vision, one which points to the impossibility of the communicative act suggested by the mythic technique of contemporary revivalist writers and those that sought in the Orange Order a resolution and resistance of Home Rule. Thompson cannot find 'home' in this textual space; Cúchulain, also, cannot speak to the problematics of the contemporary situation. It is in *Thompson in Tír-na-nÓg* that Gerald MacNamara most fully collapses the gap between the Romantic revival and the rapidly emerging modern needs of the North of Ireland. It is in this sense the most complete fulfilment of the Ulster Literary Theatre's project to represent the specific problematics of the North not only *through* revival but also *to* the revival.

Conclusion
Out of Time?

Gerald MacNamara and the Ulster Literary Theatre after 1912

The years building up to the triumph of *Thompson* would later be described by Forrest Reid as the Ulster Literary Theatre's 'happiest period'.[1] These years had seen Ulster Literary Theatre productions continually increase in popularity, and the group had consolidated a series of impressive connections throughout Ireland and beyond. In 1907 the Ulster Literary Theatre had been invited to give performances at Belfast's Grand Opera House, a much larger venue than the small halls that had been home until then; the Grand Opera House would quickly become the Ulster Literary Theatre's base (certainly established as such by 1909), a relationship that would last until the 1930s. After 1910 the group also began to give regular performances at Dublin's Gaiety Theatre (rather than the Abbey) and would often draw large audiences in the capital. Recognition of their achievements around this time also came with a series of tours outside Ireland. In May 1911, for example, the company travelled under Whitford Kane's management to Kelly's Theatre, Liverpool, and the Gaiety, Manchester, and the following year (February 1912) the ULT gave a series of performances at the Royal Theatre, London. This exposure, and the positive reviews that went with it, resulted in a tour to the United States in December 1912, with performances at Washington, Baltimore and New York of Mayne's *The Drone.*[2]

As it turned out, however, these achievements and their wider recognition would turn out to be difficult to sustain in the years ahead. After 1912 life became more fraught for a nationalist theatre in Belfast and for those that sought to uphold its cultural and political tenets. The kinds of political playfulness and meta-revival parody performed by *Thompson in Tír-na-nÓg,* for example, were no longer so viable in Ulster. We have already seen the heightened tension that accompanied the signing of the Ulster Covenant in September 1912, and the ways in which this had caused fears of violence at the performance of MacNamara's play. These fears were never realised, but there is little doubt that the performances of *Thompson in Tír-na-nÓg* came at the end of an increasingly fraught period in Ulster, Irish and British politics. As noted in the discussion of *Thompson* above, these years were marked by escalating tensions surrounding the fraught negotiations on how Ireland was to be mapped in any proposed new constitutional arrangement. This was a search for a political dénouement that turned its attention in an ever more focused manner on Ulster. It is worth looking a little closer at the events of these years, as it is against this backdrop that the Ulster Literary Theatre's post-1912 history would be played out. Most obviously, and pertinently, the build-up to the third Home Rule bill of 1912 saw an increasingly open discussion about the possibility and/or viability of excluding at least some of the northern counties from whatever renegotiation of Union was finally agreed upon. Clearly this new form of political discourse increasingly impinged and impacted on the activities of a cultural group that had originated as an organ for the nationalist voice in Ulster.

We can trace the idea of a partitioning policy as something under serious consideration at least back to 1911; but it was on 11 June 1912 that Thomas Agar-Robartes, during the committee stage of the Home Rule bill's passage through parliament, suggested the exclusion of counties Antrim, Armagh, Londonderry and Down. Over the next two years this idea began to develop and a variety of permutations were considered at different moments along the way: the inclusion of counties Fermanagh and Tyrone, the inclusion or exclusion of Derry city, as well as, most radically of all, the exclusion of the entire Ulster province from Home Rule government. The final months of the bill's passage through both Houses of Parliament were particularly complex and fraught:

> 'In May 1914 the Home Rule bill was passed in the House of Commons for the third time, with the additional provision giving the Protestant counties the chance to opt out for six years. In the Lords this was amended to give the whole of Ulster – nine counties – a permanent opt-out. Between 21 and 24 July 1914 a constitutional conference at Buckingham Palace . . . failed to find a compromise. The main point at issue was the exact boundary of the 'Ulster' which was to be excluded from Home Rule. Certain areas, the city of Derry, South Down, South Armagh, Fermanagh and Tyrone, had Catholic majorities.[3]

The conference mentioned here took place on the very brink of Britain's declaration of war with Germany (4 August), an event that was to radically change the future of Ireland's bid for constitutional reform. The third Home

Rule bill was finally given royal assent the month following the onset of war, but its enactment was to be suspended until the war was over; the clause regarding Ulster's exclusion was also suspended from the bill, with the government agreeing to present some form of amending act to finally settle Ulster's position. Events during the course of the war would, of course, radically reshape Ireland's political destiny; the final passing of a Home Rule bill would turn out to be a stillbirth of sorts.

The political machinations at Westminster were matched by a quickening in the reshaping of Ireland's internal political landscape. On the one hand there was a growing impatience amongst advanced nationalists convinced that the parliamentary route to reform could not be fully trusted, weighted as it was, as they saw it, on the side of the British powers. In 1910 there had been a split within the ranks of Sinn Féin, with the Ulster Literary Theatre's co-founder Bulmer Hobson taking a leading role in the move towards more direct-action tactics. It was in this same year that the Unionist Party acquired its soon-to-be iconic new leader. The Dublin lawyer Sir Edward Carson would quickly emerge as one of the most powerful voices resisting the idea of Home Rule. Carson's presence and forceful arguments ratcheted up the stakes that would be played out in the coming years; as Michael Hughes puts it: 'From the outset he made it clear that he intended to combat Home Rule by constitutional means, but behind this there was always the threat of violence.'[4] In September 1911 the Unionist Party issued its 'Craigavon Declaration', which made it clear that they were prepared to establish a separate government for Ulster in Belfast if Home Rule were forced through. Following hard on the heels of the Ulster Covenant, the Ulster Volunteer Force was established in January 1913. This arming of the Ulster unionist cause provided the final catalyst for Irish nationalists, and in 1914 the Irish Volunteers was formed – a group that would have a major say in Irish nationalism's push for independence.

It was not just in London, then, that things came to a head regarding the 'Ulster question' in 1914. Preparations were made in this year to suppress any armed insurrection by Ulster unionist forces in reaction to the implementation of Home Rule. Indeed it was just these preparations that precipitated one of the key events during this period, when officers garrisoned at the Curragh threatened to 'resign their commissions rather than accept orders to march north to coerce Ulster'.[5] The Curragh Mutiny made it clear to the London government that it could not force Ulster into any arrangement it chose to reject. Moreover, the Ulster question only became more complex as the war progressed and thousands of Ulstermen lost their lives in the trenches of Europe. Most notably, the Ulster Volunteer Force raised enough volunteers to be granted a unique status within the British forces, with its men staying together to form the 36th (Ulster) Division. It was this group that would suffer horrendous losses at the Somme (July 1916) and provide Ulster unionism with its most iconic twentieth-century proof of loyalty. As well as one of the key battles of World War I, the experiences of the Ulster Division would forcefully impact on the resolution of the Irish question. unionist politicians, commentators and writers were quick to juxtapose the loyal actions of Ulstermen with the, as they read it, mutinous actions of those involved in the Easter Rising (which had taken place just months before the Somme). The ideological pull created in these years would shape the immediate future of Ireland; the final result would be the partition of the island and the creation of dual statehood in the early years of the next decade.

The results of this political settlement have of course been far-reaching in the subsequent histories of Ulster and Ireland. One such result, of particular interest to this study, has been a problematic schism in the various historiographies and lines of development – political, social and cultural – that have shaped the way we think about (Northern) Ireland. There is a very definite sense in which unionism becomes the dominant organising narrative in Ulster's historiography from this moment onwards, just as the move from cultural to direct-action nationalism becomes the hegemonic story in the pre-history of the Free State, and later Republic of Ireland. However, we are beginning to see that there are other often overlooked parts to this story; in particular, northern nationalism was still attempting to make space for itself in this new political landscape. While this is a much-needed corrective, there is little doubt that the task of northern nationalism rapidly became extremely difficult. Nevertheless, even if many of the key characters in the early history of the Ulster Literary Theatre had by now drifted away from the group and its aims, most notably Bulmer Hobson, who was at this stage a linchpin figure in the reborn IRB, there were still those who strove to keep the cultural-nationalist scene in Belfast alive and relevant. Naturally enough the fraught nature of life in Ulster during these years altered the horizon of possibility for cultural intervention and reinvention. We can now see just how difficult Gerald MacNamara's pantomimic sense of politics and history as parodic farce must have been to sustain. A new phase in history was unfolding, one that imposed itself ever more directly and violently on real bodies, and this was thus more difficult to immediately translate into textual and linguistic 'play'. In this regard Mary Burgess has noted that MacNamara's *Suzanne and the Sovereigns* 'had a less popular revival in Belfast during the winter of 1914. By then, as the implications of British involvement in the First World War and the arming of the Ulster Volunteer Force hardened loyalist attitudes, the myths of Derry and the Boyne were no longer a laughing matter'.[6] The fate of this revival points all too clearly to the ways in which the possibility and urgency of bringing 'revival' to the north was severely curtailed. Quite rapidly the project of revival as cultural agent of ideological change was overtaken in an Ulster occupied with momentous political forces and tensions. The revival's 'crease in time' was indeed a little shorter in Ulster.

Nevertheless, the Ulster Literary Theatre did keep going, and did produce some noteworthy work (see the Appendix for a full list of Ulster Literary Theatre productions after 1912). Indeed, despite the poor reaction to the revival of *Suzanne,* Gerald MacNamara would become the main driving force behind the Ulster Literary Theatre in the years after 1912. Looking back at the work produced in those years after the triumph of *Thompson in Tír-na-nÓg* it seems clear that a central strategy for survival involved the group moving away from its more overtly nationalist pronouncements. Ophelia Byrne has persuasively argued that in these years 'the nationalist component of the plays disappeared very rapidly' as the Ulster Literary Theatre sought a more depoliticised position in relation to the various emerging crises; this new position would result in plays less engaged with nationalist ideals and more concerned with the social realities of Ulster life.[7] Such a tendency had, of course, been a strong part of the group's work from the very beginning – indeed, as we've seen, it was much of the point of many successful early plays – but this newly focused concern for the vicissitudes of everyday life now began to move away from an overtly nationalist analysis of the action on stage. During this middle period in the group's history, from 1912 through to the early 1920s, those involved sought out a new kind of profile and position within Ulster's cultural life. This was not always easy and they were not always particularly successful in their efforts. While this is not to suggest that the group completely abandoned its revivalist motivating drive at this point, it is clear that the new circumstances required new strategies of performative negotiation.

The result was a rather mixed bag of new work produced by the group. However, given the circumstances in which they had to work there were still a number of impressive achievements during this period. Rutherford Mayne continued to produce reliably interesting works exploring the social-realist territory by now familiar to Irish audiences, including: *If* (November 1913), *Evening* (March 1914) and *Industry* (1917). Other notable writers would also contribute to the group's continued search for a relevant voice. Shan Bullock's *Snowdrop Jane,* a redemptive tale of northern farming life premièred at the Grand Opera House on 2 February 1915, while Bernard Duffy's well-received *The Old Lady* was first seen at the same venue on 11 December 1916. Another significant new voice was added at the end of the decade when George Shiels – who would be closely associated with the Abbey Theatre from the 1920s onwards with plays such as *Bedmates* (1921) and *First Aid* (1923) – premièred two plays with the Belfast group under the pen-name George S. Morshiel. *Away from the Moss* opened at the Grand Opera House on 25 November 1918, while *Felix Reid and Bob* was first staged on 12 November 1919, both plays revealing the incisive wit and ear for natural dialogue that would become such a recognisable part of the Abbey's repertoire in the years ahead. Other works now seem much less well judged. Helen Waddell (Rutherford Mayne's sister and a well-respected medieval scholar) contributed a strangely underworked play entitled *The Spoiled Buddha* in February 1915. The play centres on the comical musings of some vaguely 'eastern' religious statues which come to life to report on what they have observed from their position of unnoticed stony silence. The play was not overly successful in performance nor in the reviews it received; its retreat into a form of comical mysticism seems to reveal a broader lack of confidence in the company around this time. Unable to provide a proper nationalist analysis of the events that were determining Ulster's future or to fully engage with the national and international re-ordering of power, Waddell's play now appears representative of a difficult moment in the history of Belfast's first nationalist theatre.

Around this time (1915) the group also amended its name to simply the Ulster Theatre. While the dropping of the word 'Literary' from its name was probably a fairly sensible business decision, the move away from this Yeatsian anti-populist declaration also seems to mark another stage in the evolution of the company away from political engagement. In 1916 there was also something of a 'split in the camp' (as Forrest Reid put it), the nature of which is unclear, but it resulted in several of the leading actors leaving the company.[8] One consequence of this split was the confirmation of Gerald MacNamara as the creative leader of the company at this point and this would remain the case right up to the end of the Ulster Theatre in 1934. By the late period of the company, however (early 1920s to 1934), it was pretty obvious that it was in fatal decline. It is no real surprise that this turned out to be a difficult time. After partition those involved in the Ulster Theatre, as with the rest of the nationalist population in the North, found themselves on the 'wrong side' of the final solution to the Irish question. In some ways the Belfast group was in a good position to become a kind of 'National Theatre' for the newly created Northern Ireland, but this would hardly have been an attractive idea for such a group of nationalist thinkers.

This must have been a particularly frustrating time for those still remaining in Belfast who had originally gathered at Ardrigh in more hopeful times. F.J. Bigger's friends would later recall how the fact of partition would never cease to trouble the man who continued to live surrounded by United Irishmen memorabilia at Ardrigh:

> No one felt more than 'F.J.' the worry and trouble caused by 'the border'; he who had hitherto been free to roam at will all over Ireland, resented the petty inquisition there, and the obstacle placed in his way.[9]

So troubled by the new border was this one-time dedicated recorder of cultural life that Bigger apparently rarely crossed it for much of his later life. The general malaise which befell the understandably disillusioned Belfast nationalists is recorded by Gerald MacNamara's nephew, Gerard Morrow, who remembered the period with some sadness:

> The ten years from 1924 to 1934 were the most difficult of the Theatre's existence, and also the most uninteresting. Although fifteen new productions took place in the ten years there was none of outstanding merit and few, if any, could be revived at the Opera House.[10]

Indeed it was the ending of the company's relationship with the Grand Opera House that really signalled the end of its existence entirely. Dwindling audiences meant that the Ulster Theatre's 1934 season at the Opera House lost money and the management of the theatre made it clear that this could not continue. There is some suggestion that the group attempted to stick together for a few more years, but there is no real performance record to indicate any success in this regard, and certainly by the time of Gerald MacNamara's death in 1938 Ulster had seen the last of its first nationalist theatre group.[11]

Before it was all over, however, it was MacNamara who provided the group with most of its high points after 1912's *Thompson.* All the same, it was quite some time before the Ulster Literary Theatre felt it appropriate to return to the quirky parodic voice that was the hallmark of its leading light. Some five years elapsed before MacNamara returned to the stage with *The Throwbacks* in 1917, and then with the short piece *Sincerity* in 1918. *The Throwbacks* was a tale of time travel and the conflict that seems, in

MacNamara's world at least, inevitable. Unfortunately, brief plot summaries are all that remain of this play, as the manuscript has been lost, but these suggest that *The Throwbacks* was another of MacNamara's parodic metaphors on the nature of Irish identity and its very specific relationship to history. The vehicle for this politicised metaphor is a group of contemporary characters who take a drug which propels them back through time to become their own ancestors. The message clearly concerns the dangers of assuming an essential reciprocation between our own contemporary issues and those of our communal ancestors. The plot also, rather pessimistically, seems to suggest that Ireland was caught in a historical logic that was in some ways inevitable and which it was doomed to continually repeat. By 1917, of course, Ulster, like the rest of Ireland, was caught in a kind of political no man's land as the war still raged and the ramifications of the previous year's Easter rebellion were still being felt. It seems all the more courageous, then, that MacNamara should choose to re-create many of the problems of Home Rule Ulster within the environs of an ancient Irish tribal court (the place where our time-travellers find themselves).

A review by the *Northern Whig* of the play's first performance suggests that *The Throwbacks* was equally as inventive as MacNamara's earlier pieces:

> It has the same motif as his delicious *Thompson in Tir-na-nOg*, the plunging of present-day people – in this case by inhaling a magic powder – into the early ages of Irish history, all the characters becoming their own ancestors. Most of them are Kings and Chieftains, as of course the ancestors of all real, 'patriotic Irishmen' are always supposed to be; but amongst them we find unexpectedly a most aggressive and militant lady, strong on woman's rights and the inferiority of men.
>
> The four chiefs, from North, South, East and West, the former supported by a most amusing slave, are in revolt against the titular supreme monarch, but are equally quarrelsome amongst themselves, while the stiff Northerner is at odds with all the others. As can easily be imagined from these elements, the author extracts a great amount of fun and plants many shrewd hints amongst present-day Irish factions. The audience relished these hugely, and roared with laughter . . . Dublin, whose 'patriotic' audiences seem lacking in any sense of humour, might not enjoy the fun so much, for with strict and rather cruel adherence to historical truth, the author shows that in those alleged 'golden days' when Ireland is asserted to have been one harmonious nation, she was even more torn by internal dissension and less united into a nation than she is today. (4 December 1917)

The review nicely presents a series of tropes and conceits now recognisable as central to MacNamara's imaginative landscape: temporal and spatial conflation and confusion, 'history' over-determined by tradition, and northern nationalism's problematic relationship with the rest of the island. MacNamara's plot was also quite a brave move, given the context of its first performances at the Grand Opera House in 1917. The whole action of the play depends on the inability of the leaders of the four provinces to resolve a problem that was common to them all; the audience appears to have been left in no doubt, moreover, that their failure was the result of a geo-political schism born of a will to power that overruled more commonsensical shared solutions.

MacNamara's next piece, *Sincerity* had its first run at Dublin's Gaiety Theatre in May 1918. Judging by the reviews it was something of a failure in its opening run and was never revived in the years that followed. Given the tensions of an Ireland on the brink of an all-out war for independence, and all that this would entail for the nation's different communities, it was a particularly bold, if in the end not overly successful, move to put on a comedy which took religious harmony as its main theme. While much of MacNamara's previous work had obliquely investigated just this kind of territory, *Sincerity*'s structure would appear to have been strangely social realist compared to the other works from the same pen. *Sincerity* follows the story of a young boy who is raised by Protestant guardians and who grows up interested in Christianity and Confucianism; later in his life he is claimed by his Catholic father and in the end is married by the chief Rabbi. It is easy to see what MacNamara was up to here, with a play that explores the interconnectedness of all religious impulses but also privileges humanity over any specific confessional identity. In the end, perhaps the material could not quite cope with the weight of ambition. In 1923 MacNamara's next new play, *Fee Faw Fum,* was performed; very little information about this play remains beyond the fact that the company performed the piece in Derry, Liverpool and Dublin, and that the reviews it received were somewhat mixed.

The problems encountered by the group as a whole in the years immediately following appear to have impacted with particular severity on its most important creative figure. After the only partially successful *Fee Faw Fum* MacNamara would struggle for some time to re-create his earlier interventions onto the Irish cultural scene. Instead of full-blown staged productions, MacNamara's output over the next few years was restricted to comic sketches for impossible plays that were clearly never going to be staged. Between 1923 and 1924 he published in the *Dublin Magazine* a three-part series entitled 'Stage Directions for a Play called *William John Jamieson*' (the three parts were 'Characters', 'Scenery' and 'Production').[12] As befits the trickery of MacNamara, there was no play entitled *William John Jamieson,* nor did MacNamara intend that there ever would be. Rather, the articles lampooned much of the pretentiousness, as MacNamara saw it, of contemporary dramatic life and the egos that accompanied it. The years 1924 and 1925 saw MacNamara, again in the *Dublin Magazine,* publish a series of scripts for 'proposed' productions. As before, these works were certainly not intended for production but were in fact a series of satiric pieces based loosely around a number of 'Fairy Tales' (they were titled *The Babes in the Wood, Tcinderella* and *Little Devil Drought.*[13] This 'retreat' into the purely textual is in itself significant. The repeated return to outlines for plays that could never be staged was an apt metaphor for the larger cultural problematic being played out in the North in the years just after partition. Gerard Morrow's suggestion that these years 'were the most difficult of the Theatre's existence' is perhaps best illustrated by his uncle's absence from the theatre. In this case it is MacNamara's silence that acted as a metaphor and as a form of political comment. The arrival of a unionist-controlled government at Stormont and of a new state formation designed around a unionist ideology left very little, if any, room for the cultural expression of a northern nationalism. MacNamara's 'notes towards' a series of 'impossible' plays satirically expressed the impossibility of expression. As Mary Burgess writes in relation to the *William John Jamieson* series: 'A description by an established playwright of a play which both he and his readers are aware does not exist, will not be written, and will never be performed . . . was . . . a wry comment on the nature of drama in Belfast in the bleak 1920s. MacNamara was reduced to writing a kind of dramatic *samizdat* in the cultural closed shop of the north.'[14]

Fortunately this theatrical hiatus came to an end, and the dramatic voice of *Thompson in Tír-na-nÓg* was to be heard again in MacNamara's 1928 play *No Surrender!* In this work MacNamara reversed the course of his normal 'temporal play' – this time the piece is set in the future. *No Surrender!* presents its audience with an Ulster utopia that by the end begins its inevitable shift back towards a dystopian dénouement. Coming at the end of such a difficult decade for MacNamara and his Ulster Theatre colleagues, there is little surprise that this should be his most pessimistic (and Swiftian) creation. It is still very much a MacNamara play, however, and shows many flashes of his comic invention. *No Surrender!* is set in a peaceful Belfast in the mid-1990s, where all religious and historical 'quarrels' have been settled – Catholicism and Protestantism still exist but both have embraced the new

'Spiritualism' with equal vigour, thus ensuring a theological rapprochement – and the political power is divided between 'Vegetarians' and 'Beefeaters'. It is just the sort of place, in other words, that Gulliver could have visited. 'The Orange and Hibernian Museum of Antiquities' has been established to remind those in the North of their divisive past. The main exhibits had been the 'last Hibernian' and the 'last Orangeman', but the last Hibernian has just died as the play opens leaving only his Orange counterpart; soon after the play opens this final Orangeman also dies. This final representative of Orangeism is, of course, called Thompson and, we can presume, a relative of the Andy Thompson who found himself so unceremoniously dumped in Tír-na-nÓg.

The play's prologue reveals that a Belfast professor has discovered a mode of communicating with the dead and is now confident that he can return them from their realm to the present (the professor has in fact been appointed as 'Spirit medium-in-chief of Northern Ireland'). We discover this professor making contact with King William III and asking him to come to Belfast to witness the changes to Ulster and Ireland. The seeds of MacNamara's parodic intentions are sowed when the professor reveals that William has 'followed the movements of the Orange and Hibernian Orders since their inception – and he dislikes *both*'.[15] Throughout *No Surrender!* MacNamara returns to the idea that historical characters such as William of Orange would have absolutely no understanding of the uses to which their actions were put after their death, an idea that had provided so much of the humour in *Suzanne and the Sovereigns.* In this later play the Belfast professor finally persuades William to come back for 'a visit', but only on the understanding that all the Orangemen are gone (William's dislike of the Orange Order is, if anything, more pronounced than his dislike of the Hibernians). In fact William is only prepared to come because he learns that William Thompson, 'the last Orangeman', has, like his Hibernian counterpart, just died. Unfortunately for King William, it is soon discovered that the last Orangeman had a large family living outside of Ireland – they too are called Thompson and have remained Orangemen. This discovery shatters the peaceful assumptions of the northern political powers and also forces William to flee back to the realm from whence he came. It is a play of immense power and invention; it was also MacNamara's most bleak critique of the power of the past within northern Irish society. The past in this sense just will not stay dead and seems destined to haunt Ireland's present and future. This is in no way a partisan piece of writing. MacNamara if anything seems to have developed an even more pronounced post-nationalist imagination by this point; his sceptical eye is cast just as much on the sanctification of the past by the nationalist Hibernians as it is deployed to parodic effect on the entire edifice of Orangeism.

Nevertheless, it is also quite apparent that MacNamara's imagination had been deeply marked by the attitudes that shaped the years after partition. In particular, *No Surrender!* displays a pervasive dismay at the isolationist policies that had characterised the new unionist regime in the years after the creation of Northern Ireland. A conversation between an American visitor to the museum (Miss Smith) and the Prime Minister of Northern Ireland (Sir Thomas – there to greet King William on his arrival) perfectly encapsulates this parodic tone and its targets:

> Miss Smith: Why, you must be near 'perfection' in Ulster.
> Sir Thomas: Pretty near. We hope to be *completely* perfect next month.
> Miss Smith: Why next month?
> Sir Thomas: The Super-Grand Canal which runs from Derry round the boundary to Newry will *then* be complete – this will cut us off completely from the Irish Free State.
> Miss Smith: What a perfect *Ulster.*
> Sir Thomas: No, Miss Smith, we cannot call it 'Ulster'. That would be a terminological inexactitude. When the canal is *complete,* we will then call our country 'The Island of Saints'. . . [16]

The idea of turning the invisible political border into an actual physical break in the island's landscape obviously parodies the drive within a now dominant Ulster unionism to privilege narratives focused on autonomy and separatism. The symbolic distancing that such narratives were designed to invoke is here transformed into a process of physical fragmentation. It is a brilliant moment of Swiftian inventiveness, but it is also shadowed by a pessimism that seems to have begun to invade MacNamara's work in *The Throwbacks* and was only growing stronger by this point. With the idea that this imagined future Ulster is close to finishing a project of total geographical and political rupture, MacNamara seems to be signalling, if not the death-knell of a northern revival, at least the impossibility of its enactment under current conditions.

It was, therefore, all the more appropriate that MacNamara should call his next play *Who Fears to Speak?* This 1929 production completed a cyclical trajectory of sorts for the Belfast group, with a work that, as the title suggests, recalls the United Irishmen. In so doing MacNamara self-consciously revisited one of the narratives that had inspired the Ulster Literary Theatre's foundation. This was a play designed to highlight the very different status of the United Irishmen's narrative at the end of the 1920s in comparison to its role in Belfast's cultural life at the beginning of the century. There is perhaps something ironic in the very act of this returning gaze, given that by this point MacNamara was the only one of the Ulster Literary Theatre's founding figures to remain involved in Belfast's cultural scene; all the rest were by now either living 'across the border' or outside the country altogether. Clearly for MacNamara revisiting the United Irishmen in the years after political schism shed a certain irony on the context within which he now found himself working. The title, most obviously, points to the problem for nationalism and its associated agendas in the newly created Northern Ireland. In the case of that part of the island that remained within the Union, there is a sense in which a project of pseudo-nation-building had been thrust upon those who had sought to resist that very process when presented in the guise of Home Rule. The result was the institutionalisation of unionist power, with unionism embedded as the authorised narrative of the new state. One of the most direct consequences of this political hegemony was a squeezing out of nationalist discourse as a possible alternative voice. The title of MacNamara's new play indexed the problem of finding a space *from which* to speak and *of which* to speak, as much as it indexed the dangers of providing counter-narratives to those now seen as essential to the state's wellbeing. While *Who Fears to Speak?* is undoubtedly a slight piece, its interest lies in the parodic eye that MacNamara now casts upon the very idea of 'United Irishmen' in the wake of a partitioning policy. The audience is presented with a series of almost farcical scenes, and in the end the classic notions of union of purpose and united action are completely unravelled as we observe a group of United Irishmen's disorganisation and random action. There is humour here, but there is also a strong melancholic aura to MacNamara's final admission that the founding principles of the Ulster Literary Theatre were now never to be fulfilled. In this, one of the Belfast group's last new plays, we are left with a sense of the impossibility of 'united' action in the face of political fragmentation.

Another cycle was to be completed in 1934 with the appearance on stage of *Thompson on Terra Firma,* which tells the story of what happened to Andy Thompson after his return from his adventures in Tír-na-nÓg. When we pick up the story we discover that Thompson has returned home a committed 'Gaelic Leaguer' and is attempting to convert his family and friends from their involvement with the Orange Order. The piece is resolved, somewhat weakly, when Thompson receives a 'bang on the head' and is brought back to his normal ways and beliefs.[17] This resolution points to the now assured hegemony of the unionist worldview in Northern Ireland; the 'dream' of Gaelic culture as a unifying pan-Irish force is now revealed as such with Thompson's recovery – the play's dénouement ensures that normal service is resumed in 1934 Ulster. It is somehow fitting, then, that this tale of returning home was the last the world saw of Thompson and, indeed, of Gerald MacNamara. It was also almost certainly the last production of what remained of the Ulster (Literary) Theatre.

Looking back, the work of the Ulster Literary Theatre, and especially that of Gerald MacNamara, undoubtedly speaks with an incisive acuity to the contexts from which it emerged, but there is also a sense of a prescient aura around many of these performative and textual interventions. In particular, Gerald MacNamara continually appears to cast his parodic gaze forwards as much as backwards, a move that repeatedly results in a gesture of predictive historiography and/or mythography. In this regard it seems apt to end with a more playful MacNamara than that represented by his final two plays. This playful side to his parodying of northern politics is nicely captured in his 1918 short sketch 'Cúchulain II: A Belfast Idyll'.[18] It also captures MacNamara's ability to trace future cultural transformations, for in this story MacNamara returns to one of the revival's most empowered and empowering icons – Cúchulain. But this is a narrative centred on the appropriation of Ulster's hero by a Belfast Orangeman, a move that wonderfully predicts just such a process of appropriation by Ulster loyalism during the late twentieth-century northern Irish troubles. The story charts the progress of 'Billy Maquire', a 'quiet inoffensive' member of the Orange Order who goes about his daily life peaceably – except, that is, for the time round the 'twelve' of July, when Billy 'became a fighting man'.[19] It is on the eve of one such 'twelve', that Billy stands up to address his friends in 'a place of public refreshment':

> 'Boys, yous have all heard of "The Cock of the North"', they all answered in the affirmative, wondering what he was driving at. 'Well', he proceeded, 'but I don't suppose any of yous ever heard of the "*Hound* of the North"'. They all thought that his head was away with the drink, but didn't say so, for they saw by Billy's eye that the 'battle fury' was on him. 'Yous needn't be ashamed, boys, if you never heard of the "*Hound* of the North"', said Billy, 'for I only read about him in the *Fourth Edition.* "The *Hound*" was a man; a great Ulster fighting man – I read about him in a pome. He was a man of the name of Cuchulain. He bate, single-handed, all the men of the three other provinces – at least all the ones that faced him'.[20]

MacNamara's transference of some of Cúchulain's characteristics ('the battle fury') onto this Belfast Orangeman, as well as Billy's clear admiration for deeds that involve defeating 'all the men of the other three provinces', clearly signal the transformation ahead. After his opening pronouncements, Billy recites 'The Hound of Ulster', a poem he had learned the night before:

> When he had reached the last line, he hit the table a great blow with his huge fist and in a voice that made the advertisements rattle on the walls, he cried – 'I'm the new Cuchulain – the Hound of the North, and I'll hold the fort tonight.'[21]

The fort in question turns out to be the Sandy Row district of Belfast, for those in the pub have heard a rumour that some 'Volunteers' were planning a raid, in order to destroy the Orange Lodge arches built along Sandy Row in preparation for 'the twelve'. Billy, having heard of Cúchulain going into battle in a chariot, 'called for a taxi':

> Arrived at the 'Fort', he felt disappointed. The place was deserted. He stood at the corner and waited; no one approached. At last he called out at the top of his voice – 'Here I am, the Hound of the North! I defy yous all. Come out of yer "dug outs" and face Cuchulain II'.[22]

The story, while slight and almost certainly intended as nothing more than a piece of humourous entertainment for a Christmas magazine, does nevertheless provide more evidence that the 'sacred cows' that formed MacNamara's targets were in his future as well as his present. Once again MacNamara's return to an iconic revivalist narrative signals another complex irony; here we have a leading figure of the northern revival, a movement that had 'fought' to privilege the Ulster origins of Cúchulain, clearly indexing the transformative potential of just this process of geo-political mythologising. The 'boundary situations' encountered later in the century by Ulster's unionist and loyalist communities would also, of course, necessitate the now familiar return to putative mytho-poetic origins. MacNamara has been one of Ulster's more subtle, complex and funny recorders of just this process in all its contradictions, paradoxes and ambivalences.

The northern revival's strategies, and those deployed by MacNamara in particular, reveal this cultural moment as somehow 'beyond' the frames of reference normally aligned with this period. The revival and the post-revival managed to somehow co-exist in the midst of Ulster's frantic period of multivalent invention. Perhaps more than any other of its writers, Gerald MacNamara's parodic gaze now appears to find some resonance with Jean-

François Lyotard's conception of the postmodern writer as one whose work stands outside the rules of its time. Or, as Lyotard would have it: 'Those rules and categories are what the work of art itself is looking for. The artist and the writer, then are working without rules in order to formulate the rules of what *will have been done*.'[23] Hence, moreover, these rules 'always come too late for their author, or, what amounts to the same thing, their being put into work, their realization (*mise en oeuvre*) always begin too soon'.[24] In much of MacNamara's work there is a sense of having 'arrived too soon'. While claiming postmodern status for MacNamara is somewhat problematic (proto-postmodern perhaps?), it is clear that much of his writing appears to point to, and in some ways open up, ideas and positions that would be more fully occupied by writers such as Joyce, O'Brien, Beckett et al.

What is most important, in terms of this study at least, is that this prescient textual and performative space emerged out of the singular set of creative circumstances surrounding the search for revival in the North. There is clearly much more work to be done here; it is perhaps more urgent than ever that we fully reassess the ways in which 'northern writers' helped describe the imaginative structures that 'reinvented' Ireland(s). The self-reflexive spaces of Ulster's meta-revival are extraordinarily revealing about the gaps and silences informing Ireland's search for its postcolonial moment. The northern revival still seems somehow enabling, most especially in its performance of multivalent identity and its refusal of closure in the process of imagining community. This appears particularly true of the writers that gathered around Belfast's rejected sister company to the Abbey. Unfortunately, perhaps, while the Ulster Literary Theatre and its writers are indeed in need of greater study, this critical attention will now always be in the position of arriving 'too late'.

Appendix: First Productions of the Ulster Literary Theatre

(*Play*, writer, date, location)

The Reformers, Lewis Purcell (David Parkhill), 7th December 1904, Ulster Minor Hall, Belfast

Brian of Banba, Bulmer Hobson, 7th December 1904, Ulster Minor Hall, Belfast

Little Cowherd of Slainge, Joseph Campbell, 4th May 1905, Clarence Place Hall, Belfast

The Enthusiast, Lewis Purcell, 4th May 1905, Clarence Place Hall, Belfast

The Turn of the Road, Rutherford Mayne (Sam Waddell), 4th December 1906, Examination Hall, Queen's College Belfast

The Pagan, Lewis Purcell, 4th December 1906, Examination Hall, Queen's College Belfast

Suzanne and the Sovereigns, Gerald MacNamara (Harry Morrow) and Lewis Purcell, 26th December 1907, Exhibition Hall, Belfast

The Drone, Rutherford Mayne, 24th April 1908, Abbey Theatre, Dublin

Leaders of the People, Robert Harding (James Winder Good), 24th April 1908, Abbey Theatre, Dublin

The Mist That Does Be on the Bog, Gerald MacNamara, 26th November 1909, Abbey Theatre, Dublin

Captain of the Hosts, Rutherford Mayne, 8th March 1910, Grand Opera House, Belfast

Charity, Miss M.F. Scott, 4th December 1911, Grand Opera House

Red Turf, Rutherford Mayne, 5th December 1911, Grand Opera House

The Jerry Builders, William Paul, 5th December 1911, Grand Opera House

Thompson in Tír-na-nÓg, Gerald MacNamara, 9th December 1912, Grand Opera House

Family Rights, Miss M.F. Scott, 9th December 1912, Grand Opera House

Sweeping the Country, William Paul, 10th December 1912, Grand Opera House

Love and Land, Lynn Doyle, 24th November 1913, Grand Opera House

If, Rutherford Mayne, 25th November 1913, Grand Opera House

Evening, Rutherford Mayne, 2nd March 1914, Grand Opera House

Snowdrop Jane, Shan F. Bullock, 2nd February 1915, Grand Opera House

The Spoiled Buddha, Helen Waddell, 1st February 1915, Grand Opera House

The Old Lady, Bernard Duffy, 11th December 1916, Grand Opera House

The Tumelty Case, William Paul, 13th December 1916, Grand Opera House

The Throwbacks, Gerald MacNamara, 3rd December 1917, Grand Opera House
The Dark Hour, Robert Christie, 3rd December 1917, Grand Opera House
Industry, Rutherford Mayne, 6th December 1917, Grand Opera House
The Skipper's Submarines, Charles K. Ayre, 6th December 1917, Grand Opera House
The Summons, Lynn Doyle, 25th March 1918, Grand Opera House
Sincerity, Gerald MacNamara, 31st May 1918, Gaiety Theatre, Dublin
Away From the Moss, George S. Morshiel (George Shiels), 25th November 1918, Grand Opera House
The Lilac Ribbon, Lynn Doyle, 5th June 1919, Grand Opera House
Felix Reid and Bob, George S. Morshiel, 12th November 1919, Grand Opera House
The Lone Man, Charles K. Ayre, 14th November 1919, Grand Opera House
The Jew's Fiddle, H. Richard Hayward and Abram Rish, 18th December 1920, Gaiety Theatre, Dublin
Loaves and Fishes, Charles K. Ayre, 2nd November 1921, Grand Opera House
Turncoats, Lynn Doyle, 4th September 1922, Liverpool Play House
Fee-Faw-Fum, Gerald MacNamara, 2nd April 1923, Opera House, Derry
Phantoms, Rutherford Mayne, 28th November 1923, Gaiety Theatre, Dublin
The Land of the Stranger, Dorothea Donn-Byrne, 8th December 1924, Gaiety Theatre, Dublin
The Ship, St John Ervine, 10th December 1924, Gaiety Theatre, Dublin
Huge Love, Richard Hayward, 10th December 1924, Gaiety Theatre, Dublin
Missing Links, Charles K. Ayre, 15th December 1925, Gaiety Theatre, Dublin
No Surrender!, Gerald MacNamara, 23rd January 1928, Grand Opera House
Who Fears to Speak?, Gerald MacNamara, 24th January 1929, Grand Opera House
The Delph Dog, Larry Morrow, 21st September 1931, Grand Opera House
Cobbers Go Halves, Lewis Purcell, 24th September 1931, Grand Opera House
A Majority of One, William Liddell, 11th June 1934, Grand Opera House
The Ball Turns Once, Jack Loudan, 14th June 1934, Grand Opera House
Thompson on Terra Firma, Gerald MacNamara, n/d (most likely Christmas) 1934, Grand Opera House

List of ULT plays reproduced from www.irishplayography.com, *http://www.irishplayography.com/,* a comprehensive database of new Irish plays produced professionally since 1904. Original research Ophelia Byrne. Copyright Irish Theatre Institute.

Notes

Introduction

1. James and Margaret Cousins, *We Two Together,* p. 47.
2. Joseph Connolly, *The Memoirs of Senator Joseph Connolly: A Founder of Modern Ireland,* p. 59. Born in Belfast, Joseph Connolly would go on to become a major figure in nationalist circles; he was the co-founder of the first Freedom Club, which aimed to promote the ideas of Sinn Féin in 1911. He was a leader of the Irish Volunteers in Belfast in 1914–16 and was interned after the Easter Rising. In later years he was a member of the Seanad (1928–36), a director of the *Irish Press* (1931–2), Minister for Post and Telegraphs (1932), Minister for Lands and Forestry (1933–6) and Chairman of the Office of Public Works (1936–50).
3. St John Ervine, *The Theatre in My Time,* pp. 14–15.
4. Arthur Griffith, *United Irishman,* 31 Dec 1904.
5. Christopher Murray, *Twentieth-Century Irish Drama: Mirror Up to Nation,* p. 188.
6. Ophelia Byrne, *The Stage in Ulster from the Eighteenth Century,* p. 39.
7. Thankfully this project is part of a wider emerging interest in the Ulster Literary Theatre's work. Ben Levitas's recent study, *The Theatre of Nation: Irish Drama and Cultural Nationalism* (Oxford: Clarendon Press, 2002), for example, does draw on the work of the Ulster Literary Theatre, but the wide-ranging nature of Levitas's project means that the material included on the Belfast theatre is fairly limited. Mary Burgess and Laura E. Lyons have been amongst the first of a new group of scholars interested in the work of the Ulster Literary Theatre. See, for example, Burgess, 'Belfast Carnivalesque: The Satires of Gerald MacNamara', in Nicolas Allen and Aaron Kelly (eds.), *The Cities of Belfast* (Dublin: Four Courts Press, 2003), and Lyons, 'Of Orangemen and Green Theatres: The Ulster Literary Theatre's Regional Nationalism', in Watts et al. (eds.), *A Century of Irish Drama: Widening the Stage* (Indianapolis: Indiana University Press, 2000). At this stage still, however, for more specific and extended engagements with the northern company we have to look a little further back. Sam Hanna Bell's *The Theatre in Ulster: A Survey of the Dramatic Movement in Ulster from 1902 until the Present Day* (Dublin: Gill & Macmillan, 1972) is an excellent source of historical detail and narrative, but its critical or theoretical usefulness is necessarily limited. Haga Mengel's *Sam Thompson and Modern Drama in Ulster* (Frankfurt: Peter Lang, 1986) is more concerned to establish the Ulster Literary Theatre as a context for the later work of Thompson. Margaret McHenry's *The Ulster Theatre in Ireland* (unpublished PhD thesis, University of Philadelphia, 1931) remains one of the most valuable resources for any study of the Ulster Literary Theatre.
8. Mary Trotter, *Ireland's National Theatres,* p. 169.
9. David Gardiner, 'The Other Irish Renaissance: The Maunsel Poets', p. 54.
10. James and Margaret Cousins, *We Two Together,* p. 40.
11. Laura E. Lyons, 'Of Orangemen and Green Theatres', p. 35.

Chapter One – The North in Search of Revival

1. In this regard this study follows on from, and seeks to supplement (or contest where necessary), some excellent recent scholarship, all of which has sought to recover different perspectives on Irish theatre history and its various politics. See, for example, Lionel Pilkington, *Theatre and the State in Twentieth-Century Ireland* (2001); Mary Trotter, *Ireland's National Theatres* (2001); Ben Levitas, *The Theatre of Nation* (2002); P.J. Mathews, *Revival: The Abbey Theatre, Sinn Féin, the Gaelic League and the Co-operative Movement* (2003).
2. The quote is from Lionel Pilkington's *Theatre and the State in Twentieth-Century Ireland* (p. 1), and is reiterated as a driving impulse in the introduction to P.J. Mathews's *Revival* (p. 1).
3. ibid.
4. Karl Jaspers used the term '*grenzsituation*', which can be variously translated as 'boundary situation', 'borderline situation' and 'ultimate situation'. For more on this idea in its original context, see Karl Jaspers, *Philosophy, Vol. 2: Existential Elucidation* and Oswald O. Schrag, *Existence, Existenz, and Transcendence: An Introduction to the Philosophy of Karl Jaspers.*
5. Paul Ricoeur, 'Myth as the Bearer of Possible Worlds', pp. 261–2.
6. Joseph Campbell, *Northern Autobiography,* p. 75.
7. Campbell was imprisoned for his involvement on the anti-Treaty side of the war; see Eiléan Ní Chuilleanáin's, *'As I Was Among the Captives': Joseph Campbell's Prison Diary, 1922–1923.*
8. W.B. Yeats, *Autobiographies,* p. 559.
9. Declan Kiberd, *Inventing Ireland,* p. 25.
10. For a more extended political analysis of the position of northern nationalists during the Home Rule debate, see Eamon Phoenix's *Northern Nationalism: Nationalist Politics, Partition and the Catholic Minority in Northern Ireland 1890–1940.*
11. For more on these statistics, see Alan O'Day, *Irish Home Rule 1867–1921.*
12. Patrick Buckland, *Irish Unionism Two: Ulster Unionism and the Origins of Northern Ireland 1886–1922,* p. 1.
13. As quoted in ibid., p. 8. G.O.M stands for 'Grand Old Man', the name by which Gladstone was often known.
14. Paul Ricoeur, 'Myth as the Bearer of Possible Worlds', p. 262.
15. Ian McBride, *The Siege of Derry in Ulster Protestant Mythology,* p. 12.
16. Walker was the Governor of Derry, who held out against James's forces; his good example is compared in unionist historiography to Robert Lundy, who wanted to open the gates and let supplies into the city.
17. Ian McBride, *The Siege of Derry,* p. 68
18. John Wilson Foster, *Fictions of the Irish Literary Revival: A Changeling Art,* p. 176.
19. As quoted in Brighid Mhic Sherin, *Glimpses of Erin – Alice Milligan: Poet, Protestant, Patriot,* p. 3.
20. The other parts of the trilogy are *Oisín in Tír-nan-Óig* and *Oisín and Patrick.*
21. Ethna Carbery (the pen-name of Anna Johnston) was vice-president, working closely with Gonne as president.
22. A letter from Maud Gonne to Milligan (dated 30 December 1900) confirms Gonne's respect for Milligan's expertise in *tableaux vivants* – Milligan had perfected this form in many festivals around Ulster and the rest of Ireland. Gonne writes: 'Before leaving Ireland I write to ask if you will really help the *Inghinidhe na hÉireann* with the Gaelic tableaux we talked of when I and Miss Killeen were in Belfast. Without your help we

feel very much afraid of trying them as none of us have had much experience in *tableaux.*' (As cited in Robert Hogan and James Kilroy, *The Irish Literary Theatre 1899–1901*, p. 85.)

23. Susan L. Mitchell, 'A Contemporary Irishwoman', *The Shamrock and Irish Emerald*, 22 February 1919, pp. 10–11. Mitchell was a contemporary of Milligan's and a fellow poet; work by both women was included in AE's 1904 collection, *New Songs.* Indeed Mitchell's career was closely linked to that of George Russell; she collaborated with him on a number of projects, perhaps most notably acting as assistant editor on the *Irish Homestead.* Interestingly, AE in his Preface to *New Songs* singles out Milligan for special praise, making the case that: 'Miss Alice Milligan has indeed written memorable verses, I think the best patriotic poetry written in my time.'
24. Thomas MacDonagh, *Irish Review*, September–November 1914.
25. Milligan's creative output would of course continue in the early decades of the twentieth century: her most famous collection of poetry, *Hero Lays*, was published in 1908 and sold in large numbers. Amongst many other activities she would also be an early and energetic member of the Anti-Partition Committee.
26. For a more detailed biographical discussion see, Sheila Turner Johnston, *Alice: A Life of Alice Milligan.*
27. Eamon Phoenix, 'Francis Joseph Bigger: Historian, Gaelic Leaguer and Protestant Nationalist', p. 73.
28. See Jack Magee, 'Brothers in Arts: Joseph and John Campbell and the first Glens Feis', pp. 79–81.
29. Roger Casement used Ardrigh as his base during his frequent visits to Belfast after 1904; indeed Casement's final letter written in his cell before his execution is said to have been addressed to Brigid Matthews, F.J. Bigger's long-time housekeeper at Ardrigh.
30. The Belfast branch of the Gaelic League was founded in 1895. As Eamon Phoenix notes, the Gaelic League 'attracted significant Ulster Protestants in its early years'; the Belfast branch's first president was 'Dr. St. Clair Boyd, senior surgeon in the Samaritan Hospital and a firm Unionist who lamented the decline of "such a beautiful and noble language"'. However, this alignment of unionism with the Gaelic League would come under increasing pressure in the years after; the League's nationalist leanings would become increasingly incommensurate particularly to the new Ulster unionist formation. (See Phoenix's Introduction to *Feis na nGleann.*)
31. The title is a phonetic translation of the Irish for 'the poor old woman' – *'an t-sean bhean bhocht'*.
32. See Declan Kiberd, *Inventing Ireland*, pp. 9–25.
33. Ibid., p. 196.
34. The post-1969 reclamation of Cúchulain in the North by groups such as the UVF has specifically appropriated this dimension of the *Táin* story.
35. John Wilson Foster, *Fictions of the Irish Literary Revival*, p. 8.
36. Ibid., p. 9.
37. Alice Milligan (Iris Olkyrn), 'The Dark Rose of Rathmullan', first published in the October 1895 edition of the *Northern Patriot.*
38. Thomas MacDonagh, *Irish Review*, September–November 1914.
39. Alice Milligan, 'The Harper of the Only God', *Shan Van Vocht*, December 1896.
40. As quoted in Brighid Mhic Sherin, *Glimpses of Erin*, p. 7.

Chapter Two – Belfast in 1898: Echoes from the Tomb

1. Kevin Whelan, The Tree of Liberty: Radicalism, Catholicism and the Construction of Irish Identity 1760–1830, p. ix.
2. Edna Longley, *The Living Stream: Literature and Revisionism in Ireland,* pp. 69–70.
3. For more on this co-operation, see Marianne Elliot, *The Catholics of Ulster: A History,* p. 213 *passim.*
4. Ibid.
5. Joep Leerssen, '1798: The Recurrence of Violence and Two Conceptualisations of History', p. 41.
6. Elliot, *The Catholics of Ulster,* p. 213.
7. As quoted in Tom Dunne, '1798 and the United Irishmen', p. 55.
8. Peter Collins, *Who Fears To Speak of '98? Commemoration and the Continuing Impact of the United Irishmen,* p. 2.
9. Peter Collins's excellent recent study *Who Fears to Speak of '98?* is a much-needed corrective in this regard. Collins painstakingly traces the activities of Belfast nationalists in 1898 and demonstrates many of the tensions specific to Ulster at this time. There is still a sense, however, in which the impact of these events on the cultural imaginary of the time has not yet been fully decoded.
10. Selina Guinness, 'The Year of the Undead 1898', p. 19.
11. Ibid.
12. Leon O'Broin, *Revolutionary Underground: The Story of the Irish Republican Brotherhood 1858–1924,* p. 85.
13. Whelan, *The Tree of Liberty,* p. 172.
14. Collins, *Who Fears To Speak of '98?,* p. 30.
15. Gary Owens makes the point that the latter half of the nineteenth century marks a kind of high-water point in the production of public statuary. The 1898 monuments fit perfectly into this general strategy for demonstrating communal/national loyalties: 'Statues sprouted up on the public thoroughfares of London at a rate of one every four months during Victoria's reign. The streets and public squares of even modest-sized German towns bristled with patriotic sculpture: in a single decade some five hundred memorial towers were raised to Bismarck alone. Paris seemed so awash in statuary that at one point city officials considered imposing a moratorium on the building of new ones.' (Gary Owens, 'Nationalist Monuments in Ireland c. 1870–1914: Symbolism and Ritual', p. 103.)
16. Orlaith Mannion suggests that this part of the centenary process plays out the more symbolic control of space at the time: 'By the latter half of the nineteenth century, Ireland, like most of the British Empire, had many monuments dedicated to monarchs and generals. It was to combat this domination of public space by colonial symbols that nationalists erected statues of Irish patriots.' (Orlaith Mannion, 'Silent but eloquent reminders': the nationalist monuments in Cork and Skibbereen', p. 185.)
17. Owens, 'Nationalist Monuments in Ireland', p. 103.
18. In an effort to counter this male-dominated process Alice Milligan founded the Irish Women's Centenary Union in October 1897.
19. John Dillon did attempt to set up a rival Centenary Association but soon realised he would have to throw his lot in with the National Commemoration Committee headed by O'Leary, Connolly, Gonne et al. His rival, John Redmond, had in fact been interested in the legacy of 1798 for many years and published a pamphlet entitled *The Truth about '98* in 1886.

20. As quoted in Senia Paseta, '1798 in 1898: The Politics of Commemoration', p. 48.
21. Ibid., p. 50.
22. Alice Milligan, *Shan Van Vocht,* April 1897. For more on this see: Virginia Crossman, 'The *Shan Van Vocht:* Women, Republicanism, and the Commemoration of the 1798 Rebellion', pp. 128–139; Timothy J. O'Keefe, 'The 1898 Efforts to Celebrate the United Irishmen: The '98 Centennial', pp. 51–73.
23. Collins, *Who Fears to Speak of '98?,* p. 39.
24. Campbell, *Northern Autobiography,* p. 73.
25. Gillian McIntosh, *The Force of Culture: Unionist Identities in Twentieth-Century Ireland,* p. 24.
26. 'Wee Joe Devlin' (1871–1934), as he was known, worked as a journalist for the *Irish News* before winning the North Kilkenny Parliamentary seat in 1902. He would go on to win the West Belfast seat in 1906 and defeat Eamon de Valera for Belfast's Falls division in 1918, a seat he would retain until 1922. Devlin was also largely responsible for reinvigorating the Ancient Order of Hibernians in the early years of the twentieth century and would remain as the organisation's president until his death.
27. At one point, for example, Yeats had suggested that the Belfast nationalists postpone their commemorations until the following year to avoid drawing attention away from the Dublin events.
28. As quoted in *Shan Van Vocht,* 6 September 1897.
29. Ibid.
30. F.J. Bigger had long been obsessed with the United Irishmen's heritage. One entire room at Ardrigh was dedicated to mementoes and artefacts relating to their actions and he spent many long days searching churchyards throughout Ireland for the unmarked graves of their fallen number.
31. *Northern Patriot,* October 1895.
32. As Marcus Bourke writes: 'At a time when Irish history was rarely taught in the schools then controlled by the British, the '98 centenary movement took the place of a popular twelve-month course in this neglected subject for adults and young people alike.' (As quoted in Sophie Ollivier, 'Presence and Absence of Wolfe Tone during the Centenary Commemoration of 1798 Rebellion', p. 176.)
33. *Northern Patriot,* October 1895.
34. Collins, *Who Fears to Speak?,* p. 5.
35. Alice Milligan, 'The North is Up!', Christmas 1895.
36. Alice Milligan, *Life of Theobald Wolfe Tone,* p. 37.
37. Benedict Anderson, *Imagined Communities: Reflections on the Origins and Spread of Nationalism,* p. 9.
38. Alice Milligan, *Shan Van Vocht,* January 1898 (the typography has been retained from the original).
39. Milligan, *Life of Theobald Wolfe Tone,* p. 5.
40. Ibid., pp. 4–5.
41. As quoted in Crossman, 'The *Shan Van Vocht*', p. 137.

Chapter Three – 'Damn Yeats, We'll Write Our Own Plays!'

1. Maud Gonne had organised this treat for Dublin's children as a way of steering them clear of the jubilee celebrations.
2. Mathews, *Revival,* p. 17.
3. For a fuller history of this move, see Mary Trotter's *Ireland's National Theatres* and Lionel Pilkington's *Theatre and the State in Twentieth-Century Ireland.*

4. Lionel Pilkington's recent work, for example, explores the manner in which the early Abbey project may be read as embedded within a broad constructive unionist position.
5. Arthur Griffith, as quoted in Robert Hogan and James Kilroy, *Laying the Foundations 1902–1904*, p. 80.
6. Trotter, *Ireland's National Theatres*, p. xx.
7. See, for example, Nelson Ó Ceallaigh Ritschel, 'The Alternative Aesthetic: The Theatre of Ireland's Urban Plays'; Patrick Maume, *Life that Is Exile: Daniel Corkery and the Search for Irish Ireland.*
8. As quoted in Ó Ceallaigh Ritschel, 'The Alternative Aesthetic', p. 20.
9. Trotter, *Ireland's National Theatres*, p. xvi.
10. In his memoir, *Ireland: Yesterday and Tomorrow*, Hobson makes the case for his withdrawal of support. He suggests that he had sworn in new members of the IRB on the basis of its then Constitution, which stated that they would not be asked to partake in military action unless the idea for such action had received the unambiguous support of the majority of the Irish population. Hobson felt that this condition had not been met and could not therefore support an action that reneged on this principle; he spent the day of the Rising under IRB house arrest.
11. Trotter, *Ireland's National Theatres*, p. xvii.
12. Hobson, *Ireland: Yesterday and Tomorrow*, p. 1.
13. Ibid., pp. 1–2.
14. Ibid., p. 2.
15. Ibid., p. 2.
16. F.J. Bigger provided the financial backing for Hobson's newspaper; in the end, however, *Republic* was only to last six months, after which time it merged with the Dublin newspaper, *The Peasant.*
17. See Buckland, *Irish Unionism Two*. The Council, of course, remains the controlling body of the modern-day Ulster Unionist Party.
18. Hobson, *Ireland: Yesterday and Tomorrow*, p. 19.
19. William McDonald appears to have been a fairly significant figure in this group of Belfast nationalists, and he would be similarly involved in the very early days of the Ulster Literary Theatre. Joseph Campbell's *Northern Autobiography* records, however, that he died at a very young age from tuberculosis (probably sometime around 1905).
20. Hobson, as quoted in Sam Hanna Bell, *The Theatre in Ulster*, p. 2–3.
21. Ibid.
22. Hobson, *Ireland: Yesterday and Tomorrow*, p. 4.
23. Hobson's use of the phrase 'political and social conditions in the North of Ireland' may thus be speaking to late 1960s Northern Ireland as much as to the early years of the century and the beginnings of the Ulster Literary Theatre.
24. Murray, *Twentieth-Century Irish Drama*, p. 188.
25. Hanna Bell, *The Theatre in Ulster*, p. 2.
26. Ibid.
27. Ibid., p. 1.
28. See Campbell's *Northern Autobiography*, pp. 85–86.
29. As quoted in the Introduction to John Killen (ed.), *Rutherford Mayne: Selected Plays*, p. 3.
30. Campbell, *Northern Autobiography*, p. 94.
31. Ibid., pp. 94–95.
32. Interestingly the collection also contained work by the Belfast man George Roberts, who was to have a direct effect on the future direction of the company in 1904.

33. Campbell, *Northern Autobiography*, p. 94.
34. As Eamon Phoenix explains, the Antrim Glens had remained largely unchanged due to their isolation: 'Until the opening of the Antrim Coast Road in the 1850s, Irish was universally spoken in the Glens and on Rathlin [island]'. For more on this, see Phoenix's Introduction to Phoenix et al.'s *Feis na nGleann*, p. xii.
35. Ibid.
36. Páraic O Cléireacháin, 'Feis Na nGleann 1904–2004', in Phoenix et al., *Feis na nGleann*, p. 3.
37. Jack Magee, 'Brothers in Arts: Joseph and John Campbell and the First Glens Feis', p. 79.
38. See Campbell's *Northern Autobiography*, p. 89.
39. George Roberts would appear to have had something of a knack for getting involved in controversial exchanges and debates. Most famously he would fall out with James Joyce over his refusal, despite a previous agreement, to publish *Dubliners* with Maunsel press (founded by Roberts in 1905). For more on this, see David Gardiner, 'The Other Irish Renaissance'.
40. Hanna Bell, *The Theatre in Ulster*, p. 4.
41. 'The Five Brothers', *Belfast Telegraph*, 20 September 1954.
42. Hanna Bell here uses another variation on the spelling of 'Ulad'. Both these variations were widely used but the journal was actually entitled *Ulad*.
43. Sam Hanna Bell as quoted in Kathleen Danaher (ed.), *Journal of Irish Literature*, vol. xvii, nos. 2 and 3, May–September 1988, p. 9.
44. W.B. Yeats, *Cathleen Ní Houlihán* in Richard Allan Cave (ed.), in *Selected Plays*, p. 20.
45. Richard Kearney, 'Myth and Motherland', p. 70.
46. The same may be said of the decision to stage the little-known piece by James Cousins, *The Racing Lug*. This piece was in many ways a northern forerunner of Synge's *Riders to the Sea*. Cousins was a Belfast man (a fact that may have increased the play's appeal for the ULT) and his story of death at sea is played out in 'A North of Ireland fishing village' (as the play's notes describe it). It is, in fact, a slight and not overly successful piece that was first performed by the Irish National Theatre Society on 31 October 1902 (at the Antient Concert Rooms, Dublin). The script for the play can be found in Robert Hogan and James Kilroy's *Lost Plays of the Irish Renaissance*.
47. As quoted in Hanna Bell, *The Theatre in Ulster*, pp. 3–4.
48. As quoted in the Introduction to John Killen (ed.), *Rutherford Mayne: Selected Plays*, p. 2.
49. Harry Morrow (Gerald MacNamara), essay entitled 'The Rise of the Ulster Players'. It would appear that this essay was intended for publication, possibly in *The Crystal*. It can be found in the Rutherford Mayne archive at the Linen Hall Library, Belfast.

Chapter Four – 'Draw It Not Too Rigidly'

1. This advertisement for new members and subscribers is found on the back cover of the programme for the Ulster Literary Theatre's 1904/5 season.
2. See Hanna Bell, *The Theatre in Ulster*, p. 4.
3. Stephen Gwynn MP (1864–1950), was born in Dublin but spent his formative years in Donegal. A nationalist Member of Parliament for Galway (1906–1918), Gwynn also vigorously contributed to various cultural debates and organisations, as outlined in his autobiography, *Experiences of a Literary Man* (1926).
4. Parkhill's articles contain advice such as: 'The furniture should be of a simple character, and well made, having no carving, which is generally a blind for bad

workmanship. The carpet should not be of a plain colour, but of small design and multicoloured, to hide the clippings and pieces of thread that inevitably fall to the ground when sewing' *Ulad,* no. 2, February 1905, p. 31.

5. James Power, 'The Ulster Literary Theatre', *Ulad,* no. 4, September 1905, p. 5.
6. Power does temper his stark argument somewhat by conceding that: 'It is not merely the admixture of foreign blood that gives a marked personality to this corner of Eirinn; the people of the North differ from those of the South in every country the world over, and the truth of this as it applies to our own land is forced upon every Southerner who, like myself, has spent several years in the country of Cuchullin' *Ulad,* no. 4, September 1905, p. 5.
7. Power illustrates his point by suggesting that: 'Ulster *has* "its own way of things"; Belfast differs as widely from Dublin as Madrid from Seville; and for it to ape the South, East or West were every whit as reprehensible as that the people of those districts should continue in slavish imitation of things English' *Ulad,* no. 4, September 1905, p. 5.
8. The identity of this writer, 'Connla', has caused some confusion and controversy. It was originally thought to be a pen-name used by James Connolly (who of course spent quite a bit of time in Belfast around these years), but it now seems reasonably clear that it was a pen-name used by James Cousins.
9. Burgess, Mary, 'Belfast Carnivalesque', p. 75.
10. *Ulad,* no. 1, November 1904, p. 8: Good backs up this rationale by pointing out that 'Several fine actors have arrived in Dublin'.
11. W.B. Yeats, *Samhain,* no. 4, December 1904, p. 17.

Chapter Five – The Ulster Literary Theatre's Early Myths

1. Frantz Fanon, *The Wretched of the Earth,* p. 168.
2. In this regard the analysis undertaken by these chapters finds a certain resonance with Marilynn J. Richtarik's recent study of the Field Day Theatre Company. In the introduction to that study, Richtarik makes the point that: 'The time is now ripe for an empirical study that takes into account those aspects of the Field Day project that make it unique–the interplay between local circumstances, political compromises, financial restraints, and personalities that finally make it possible to talk about 'a Field Day play' rather than simply 'a play Field Day has done' (Marilynn J. Richtarik, *Acting Between the Lines: The Field Day Theatre Company and Irish Cultural Politics 1980–1984,* p. 3). These final chapters propose that the time is now ripe for just such a study of 'Ulster Literary Theatre plays'.
3. *Nomad's Weekly and Belfast Critic,* 24 December, 1904.
4. *The Enthusiast* appeared in the third number (May 1905), while *The Little Cowherd of Slainge* had been published in the first number (November 1904).
5. Article found in the Rutherford Mayne Archives, Linen Hall Library, Belfast. The text is unclear in parts; words in brackets are my best guess based on context.
6. Campbell, *Northern Autobiography,* p. 93.
7. As quoted in Norah Saunders and A.A Kelly, *Joseph Campbell: Poet and Nationalist 1879–1944,* p. 32.
8. Ibid., p. 37.
9. Campbell, *Northern Autobiography,* p. 62.
10. As quoted in Saunders and Kelly, p. 49.
11. See Eiléan Ní Chuilleanáin (ed.), *'As I Was Among the Captives': Joseph Campbell's Prison Diary, 1922–1923.*

12. Campbell, *Northern Autobiography,* p. 93.
13. Carlingford Lough is at the very south-east of Ulster; it was used by Reynolds as one of the nodal points in describing the territory of Ulster/Ulad. The border of modern-day Northern Ireland also runs down the middle of the Lough.
14. Campbell, *Northern Autobiography,* p. 65.
15. Ibid., p. 66.
16. The mythic space as 'non-place' was, of course, exactly what made it such an amenable mode for Yeats, Gregory, et al. as they sought (but perhaps failed to find) cultural refuge from the machinations of Irish real politic and the rapidly evolving paradoxes of their own class's position within that politics.
17. See Mengel, *Sam Thompson and Modern Drama in Ulster,* p. 69.
18. James and Margaret Cousins, *We Two Together,* p. 30.
19. James Cousins, Introduction to *Ben Madighan and Other Poems,* p. 16.
20. James Cousins, Preface to *Ben Madighan and Other Poems,* p. 7.
21. James and Margaret Cousins, *We Two Together,* p. 32.
22. Lewis Purcell, *The Pagan,* Scene I, no page numbers: all further quotation from this source.
23. Sam Hanna Bell, as quoted in Mengel, *Sam Thompson and Modern Drama in Ulster,* pp. 65–6.
24. Article found in the Rutherford Mayne Archives, Linen Hall Library, Belfast. The original typography has been retained.
25. W.J. Lawrence's review of the ULT visit to the Abbey. As found in the Rutherford Mayne Archive, Linen Hall Library, Belfast.

Chapter Six – Dramatic Federalism:Representing the Not So Mythic North?

1. As quoted in Burgess, 'Belfast Carnivalesque', p. 78.
2. Seamus Heaney, *The Redress of Poetry: Oxford Lectures,* pp. 194–5.
3. Seamus Deane, *Celtic Revivals,* p. 146.
4. As quoted in the Editor's Introduction to *Rutherford Mayne: Selected Plays* (ed. John Killen), p. 2.
5. Campbell, *Northern Autobiography,* p. 93.
6. Interview with Cathal O'Shannon as found on tape entitled 'Compilation of Archive Material: The ULT 1904–1934' in BBC Community Archives (Cultra, Co. Antrim).
7. As quoted in Trotter, *Ireland's National Theatres,* p. 134.
8. From the version of *The Drone* found in *The Drone and Other Plays* (Dublin: Maunsel & Co. Ltd, 1912); all subsequent quotations from this source.
9. Ulster Literary Theatre poster found in Rutherford Mayne Archive, Linenhall Library, Belfast.
10. From the version of *The Turn of the Road* found in *The Drone and Other Plays* (Dublin: Maunsel & Co. Ltd, 1912), p. 76. All further quotes from this short play are taken from this source.
11. As quoted in the Editor's Introduction to *Rutherford Mayne: Selected Plays,* p. 7.
12. Lewis Purcell, 'The Enthusiast', *Ulad,* no. 3, May 1905, p. 29. All further quotations are from this source.
13. Mathews, *Revival,* p. 29.

Chapter Seven – Gerald MacNamara's Other Space:Myth Writes Back

1. As quoted in Murray, *Twentieth-Century Irish Drama,* p. 3.
2. Thankfully in recent years there has been a reawakening of interest in this remarkable

playwright: see Lyons, 'Of Orangemen and Green Theatres' and Burgess, 'Belfast Carnivalesque'.

3. Burgess, 'Belfast Carnivalesque', p. 78.
4. Ibid., p. 77.
5. Longley, *The Living Stream,* p. 104.
6. D.E.S. Maxwell, 'Irish Drama 1899–1929: The Abbey Theatre', in Seamus Deane (ed.), *Field Day Anthology of Irish Writing* (Derry: Field Day Publications, 1991), vol. II, p. 564.
7. Gérard Genette, *Palimpsests: Literature in the Second Degree,* p. 10.
8. Linda Hutcheon, *A Theory of Parody: The Teachings of Twentieth-Century Art Forms,* p. 5.
9. Simon Dentith, *Parody,* p. 6.
10. Ibid., p. 5.
11. See Ibid., p. 5 *passim.*
12. Hutcheon, *A Theory of Parody,* pp. 33–34.
13. Ibid., p. 8.
14. Rutherford Mayne, 'Gerald MacNamara (1866–1938)', *Dublin Magazine,* NS vol. XIII, no. 2, April–June 1938, p. 55.
15. The result of this work was the edition of the *Journal of Irish Literature,* edited Kathleen Danaher (vol. XVII, nos. 2 and 3, May–September 1988); this journal contains transcripts of all known extant works.
16. Hanna Bell, *The Theatre in Ulster,* p. 47.

Chapter Eight – Cathleen Who? Suzanne and Her Dangerous Moments

1. For more on Joyce and parody, see David Kiremidjian's *A Study of Modern Parody: James Joyce's* Ulysses *and Thomas Mann's* Doctor Faustus.
2. Rutherford Mayne is not alone in recalling how the play's evolution was tied up with Morrow's home life: 'It [*Suzanne*] had been originally produced by him at a private performance some time previously, at his home at Hanover House.' As will be seen, Mayne was also not alone in concluding that 'to put it on the public stage in Belfast was a daring venture'. Rutherford Mayne, 'Gerald MacNamara', p. 53.
3. For more on this see, Hanna Bell's *The Theatre in Ulster.*
4. Laura E. Lyons makes the point that Van Tootil is based on the actual painter Jan Wyck. It was, as Lyons reminds us, Wyck's 1692 painting of William III that was the first to 'depict the king in heroic manner: sword out and riding a white horse whose front legs are slightly raised' (see Lyons, 'Of Orangemen and Green Theatres', p. 42). John Campbell's sketch of William on a rocking-horse is clearly a parodic reworking of this iconic imagery (see Fig. 1, p. 153).
5. Lady Gregory, *The White Cockade,* as found in *The Collected Plays II: The Tragedies and Tragic-Comedies,* pp. 228 and 229.
6. Ibid., p. 230.
7. Ibid., p. 242.
8. Kearney, 'Myth and Motherland', p. 70.
9. Programme cover for *Suzanne and the Sovereigns* as found in Kathleen Danaher Parks's unpublished PhD thesis, 'Gerald MacNamara, Ulster Playwright' (University of Delaware, 1984). A copy of this thesis is held at the Linen Hall Library, Belfast.
10. James Joyce, *Ulysses,* p. 285.
11. Ibid.
12. *Suzanne and the Sovereigns, The Journal of Irish Literature* (ed. Kathleen Danaher), vol.

XVII, nos. 2 and 3, May–September 1988, p. 24. All further quotations are taken from this source.

13. James Connolly and Jim Larkin were both active in Belfast in the years before the play's first production. Indeed the consequences of their activities may go some way to explaining the sympathetic response that greeted the performance of *Suzanne* in 1907. Joseph Connolly, for example, recalls this as a time of trade-union-inspired working-class solidarity: 'The unique feature of the 1907 riots was that for the first time in modern Belfast history the contending parties were not orange and green, nor Catholics against Protestants, but the combined forces of Catholics, Protestants and non-conformists, all united together as labour, against the hard-boiled and unyielding Belfast employers. It was an incredible position to witness in our city and some of us wondered what the outcome would be. The big industrialists, the shipping magnates, the linen lords and the big bosses generally were definitely alarmed at the hitherto unknown menace, a union of workers, orange and green, which was simply concentrated on fighting for an increase in wages and more tolerable conditions in their working lives and forgetting all about William of Orange, the battle of the Boyne and the supposed special interest that the pope took in their city' (*Memoirs of Senator Joseph Connolly,* ed. J. Anthony Gaughan, p. 67.)
14. The Ulster Unionist Council (1905) had been established a short while before *Suzanne's* appearance on stage. Sir Joseph's description of the reasoning behind their trip to Amsterdam clearly parodies the recently established Ulster Unionist Council's motivations and mission.
15. As quoted in McBride, *The Siege of Derry in Ulster Protestant Mythology,* p. 10.
16. Ibid., p. 11.
17. Lundy had been the governor at the start of the siege and is vilified for reputedly ordering the opening of the gates in a bid to end the siege.
18. Rutherford Mayne, 'The Ulster Literary Theatre', *The Dublin Magazine,* NS vol. XXXI, no. 2, April–June 1955, p. 18.
19. For more on this stroke of good fortune, see Hanna Bell's *The Theatre in Ulster.*

Chapter Nine – A Fog in the Twilight

1. As quoted in Robert Hogan and James Kilroy, *The Abbey Theatre: The years of Synge 1905–1909,* p. 246.
2. Ibid., p. 246. The history of MacNamara's second play shares a number of similarities with G.B. Shaw's *John Bull's Other Island* (1904). In his case Shaw had written the play at the request of Yeats but the Abbey subsequently shied away from performing it. The reasons for refusing Shaw's piece may also find a certain resonance in the Abbey's refusal of MacNamara's *An August Day.* In Shaw's play, as with MacNamara's, Irish 'folk' are seen to 'play up' to their stage-Irish representations. Tim Haffigan, for example, arrives on stage in the first scene pronouncing: 'Tim Haffigan, sir at your sevice. The top o' the mornin to you, Misther Broadbent'. In his Preface for the piece Shaw made the point that his play 'was uncongenial to the whole spirit of the neo-Gaelic movement, which is bent on creating a new Ireland after its own ideal, whereas my play is a very uncompromising presentment of the real old Ireland' (Bernard Shaw, Preface for *John Bull's Other Island* (London: Archibald Constable & Co., 1907), p. v.). Synge's reported reaction to *An August Day* would suggest that he felt here was another piece that takes too close an aim at his own version of 'real old Ireland'.
3. See, for example, Kathleen Danaher, *The Journal of Irish Literature,* vol. XVII, nos. 2 and 3, May–September 1988, and Hanna Bell, *The Theatre in Ulster.*

4. The *Irish Independent*'s theatre critic, 'Jacques', commented at the time of the play's first performance at the Abbey: 'The author calls his work "A fog in one act". A most apt title. The little play is most obviously a skit on the kind of dialogue put into the mouths of Irish peasants by dramatists and novelists who deal with Irish peasant themes' (*Irish Independent,* 27 November 1909.)
5. David Kennedy, 'The Drama in Ulster', in Sam Hanna Bell, *The Arts in Ulster: A Symposium,* p. 55.
6. His conflation of this obvious Synge parody and the work of Yeats is also somewhat problematic; nevertheless, his concept of an Ulster difference remains interesting regardless of the accuracy of his analysis of the different functions of revivalist writing.
7. J.M. Synge, Preface to *The Playboy of the Western World,* as found in T.R. Henn (ed.), *The Complete Plays,* p. 174.
8. Ibid., p. 175.
9. Nic Shiubhlaigh, 'An Un-Irish Play', p. 23.
10. Lady Gregory, 'Synge', as found in E.H. Mikhail (ed.), *J.M. Synge: Interviews and Recollections,* p. 86.
11. Arthur Griffith (published under pen-name 'Conn'), 'In a Real Wicklow Glen', *United Irishman,* 24 October 1903.
12. Ibid.
13. *The Mist That Does Be on the Bog,* in *The Journal of Irish Literature,* vol. XVII, nos. 2 and 3, May–September 1988, pp. 58–69, p. 58. All further quotations from this short play are taken from this source.
14. Ben Levitas, *The Theatre of Nation,* p. 132.
15. J.M. Synge, *Riders to the Sea,* as found in T.R. Henn (ed.), *The Complete Plays,* p. 96.
16. Ibid., p. 99.
17. 'The Cross-Image: A National Drama', *Sinn Féin,* 9 July 1910.

Chapter Ten – The Sacred and Profane Thompson

1. Kearney, 'Myth and Motherland', p. 72.
2. Samuel Beckett, as quoted in Kearney, 'Myth and Motherland', p. 72.
3. It is this perceived problem that leads Deane to conclude his essay with the well-known remark that: 'Everything, including our politics and our literature, has to be rewritten–i.e. re-read. That will enable new writing, new politics, unblemished by Irishness, but securely Irish' (Seamus Deane, 'Heroic Styles: The Tradition of an Idea', p. 58.)
4. See Donoghue's Afterword, in *Ireland's Field Day,* p. 117.
5. Kearney, 'Myth and Motherland', p. 63.
6. Every 13th July the 'Sham Battle' occurs at Scarva, Co. Down. During the event the Battle of the Boyne is replayed in full period costume.
7. *Memoirs of Senator Joseph Connolly (1885–1961),* p. 73.
8. Interview as recorded in Hanna Bell, *The Theatre in Ulster,* p. 43.
9. Rutherford Mayne, as quoted in Hanna Bell, *The Theatre in Ulster,* p. 44.
10. As an example of this type of paradisal myth Eliade offers a key idea in the religious practices of the Aranda tribe of central Australia, one which involves a narrative of 'Eternal Youth' who are thought to live in the sky. It is an idea that has much in common with Tír-na-nÓg; but crucially for Eliade those who inhabit this realm are *deus otiosus* - gods with no relevance or connection to the profane existence of those below them. For more on this mythological system, see Mircea Eliade, 'Cosmogonic Myth and "Sacred History"', in Alan Dundes (ed.), *Sacred Narrative: Readings in the Theory of Myth,* pp. 137–51.

11. Hutcheon, *A Theory of Parody*, p. 104.
12. Text taken from A.T.Q. Stewart's *The Ulster Crisis: Resistance to Home Rule 1912–1914*, p. 62.
13. The dates, of course, refer in turn to the 1641 rebellion, the Siege of Derry and the Battle of the Boyne.
14. Mayne, 'Gerald MacNamara (1866–1938)', p. 54.
15. *Thompson in Tír-na-nÓg*, as found in the *Journal of Irish Literature*, Vol. XVII, nos. 2 and 3, May–September 1988, pp. 74–88, p. 74. All further quotations are taken from this source.

Conclusion

1. As quoted in Byrne, *The Stage in Ulster*, p. 40.
2. For more on this touring history, see ibid.
3. Michael Hughes, *Ireland Divided: The Roots of the Modern Irish Problem*, p. 36.
4. Ibid., p. 31.
5. Ibid., p. 35.
6. Burgess, 'Belfast Carnivalesque', pp. 82–3.
7. See Byrne, *The Stage in Ulster*, p. 39.
8. For more on this split, see ibid.
9. John S. Crone, 'F.J. Bigger', as found in John S. Crone and F.C. Bigger (eds.), *In Remembrance: Articles and Sketches*, p. xxxv.
10. As quoted in Byrne, *The Stage in Ulster*, p. 41.
11. For this suggestion I am indebted to Hugh Odling-Smee of the Linen Hall Library, who put forward a persuasive argument for dating the end of the Ulster (Literary) Theatre to the death of 'Gerald MacNamara' in 1938. However, while the group may well have tried to stay together as a coherent company, the records suggest that they did not succeed in getting any new work, or indeed a revival of an old work, to the stage during these years.
12. All published in the *Dublin Magazine:* 'Characters', vol. I, no. 3, 1923, pp. 212–18; 'Scenery', vol. I, no. 4, 1923, pp. 263–71; 'Production', vol. I, no. 7, 1924, pp. 598–605.
13. All published in the *Dublin Magazine: The Babes in the Wood,* vol. I, no. 8, 1924, pp. 684–98; *Tcinderella,* vol. II, no. 2, 1924, pp. 118–28; *Little Devil Drought,* part one: vol. II, no. 5, 1924, pp. 312–21, part two: vol. II, no. 6, 1925, pp. 376–85.
14. Burgess, 'Belfast Carnivalesque', p. 87.
15. Gerald MacNamara, *No Surrender!*, the *Journal of Irish Literature* (ed. Kathleen Danaher), vol. XVII, nos. 2 and 3, May–September 1988, p. 93.
16. MacNamara, *No Surrender!*, p. 99.
17. Rutherford Mayne's memory of *Thompson on Terra Firma* reflects much of the critical reception to MacNamara's final play: 'though it contained some of his flashes of wit, the humour was too intermittent and some of the incidents too long drawn out. As the title would at once suggest, the play deals with Thompson back on earth after his visit to Tír-na-nÓg, but to the astonishment of his wife and neighbours, he has become an ardent Gaelic Leaguer and scholar, and an extreme nationalist. The problem of how to obtain his return to sanity is eventually solved by an accidental "clout on the head" and everybody lives happily ever afterwards' (Rutherford Mayne, 'Gerald MacNamara (1866–1938)', p. 55).
18. Gerald MacNamara, 'Cúchulain II: A Belfast Idyll', *Christmas Lady of the House,* pp. 17–18.
19. Ibid., p. 17.

20. Ibid.
21. Ibid.
22. Ibid., p. 18.
23. Jean-François Lyotard, *The Postmodern Condition: A Report on Knowledge*, p. 81.
24. Ibid.

Bibliography

Archives and Special Collections

F.J. Bigger Collection, Belfast Central Library

Rutherford Mayne Archive, Linen Hall Library, Belfast

Theatre and Performing Arts Archive, Linen Hall Library, Belfast

British Newspaper Library, Colindale

BBC Community Archive, Cultra, Co. Antrim

Newspapers and Magazines Cited

Belfast Telegraph

Evening Telegraph

Freeman's Journal

Irish Daily Independent

Irish News and Belfast Morning News

Irish Times

Lagan

Nomad's Weekly and Belfast Critic

Northern Patriot

Northern Whig

Samhain

Shan Van Vocht

Sinn Féin

The Dublin Magazine

The Magpie

The Peasant

The Republic

The Shamrock and Irish Emerald

The Studio

Ulster Guardian

United Irishman

Weekly Independent

Books

Adamson, Ian, *The Identity of Ulster* (Belfast: Nosmada Press, 1982)

—, *The Ulster People* (Belfast: Nosmada Press, 1991)

AE, *New Songs* (Dublin: O'Donoghue & Co., 1904)

Agamben, Giorgio, *Homo Sacer: Sovereign Power and Bare Life* (Stanford CA: Stanford University Press, 1998)

Akenson, Donald Harman, *Small Differences: Irish Catholics and Irish Protestants 1815–1922* (Dublin: Gill & Macmillan, 1988)

Allen, Nicholas and Aaron Kelly (eds.), *The Cities of Belfast* (Dublin: Four Courts Press, 2003)

Almqvist, Bo, *The Heroic Process: Form, Function and Fantasy in Folk Epic* (Dublin: Glendale Press, 1987)

Anderson, Benedict, *Imagined Communities: Reflections on the Origins and Spread of Nationalism* (London: Verso, 1991)

Anderson, Clare, 'The Political Uses of History in Mid Nineteenth-Century England', *Past and Present* (no. 36, April 1967)

Anderson, Malcolm, *The Irish Border: History, Politics, Culture* (Liverpool: Liverpool University Press, 1999)

Anonymous, *Commercial Ulster and the Home Rule Movement* (Belfast: Olley & Co. Ltd, 1893)

Anonymous, *Mr Gladstone's Speech to the Belfast Chamber of Commerce and the Chamber's Reply* (Belfast: 1893)

Anonymous, *Proceedings of the Ulster Unionist Convention, Under the Presidency of Duke of Abercorn* (Belfast: Olley & Co. Ltd, 1892)

Anonymous, *The Case for the Union*, Liberal Unionist Association (London: Cassell & Co., *circa* 1886)

Attridge, Derek (ed.), *Semicolonial Joyce* (Cambridge: Cambridge University Press, 2000)

Atwood, Margaret, *Strange Things: The Malevolent North in Canadian Literature* (Oxford: Clarendon Press, 1995)

Bardon, Jonathan, *A History of Ulster* (Belfast: Blackstaff Press, 1992)

Barry, Kevin (ed.), *James Joyce: Occasional, Critical and Political Writing* (Oxford: Oxford World's Classics, 2000)

Barthes, Roland, *Image, Music, Text* (London: Fontana Press, 1977)

—, *Mythologies* (London: Vintage, 1993)

Beckett, Samuel, *First Love* (London: Calder & Boyars, 1973)

Bell, Geoffrey, *The Protestants of Ulster* (London: Pluto Press, 1976)

Benjamin, Walter, 'Theses on the Philosophy of History', in *Illuminations* (London: Fontana Press, 1992)

Bhabha, Homi, *The Location of Culture* (London: Routledge, 1994)

Blumenberg, Hans, *Work on Myth* (Cambridge MA: MIT Press, 1985)

Brady, Ciaran (ed.), *Interpreting Irish History: The Debate on Historical Revisionism* (Dublin: Irish Academic Press, 1994)

Brater, Enoch, and Rudy Cohn, *Around the Absurd: Essays on Modern and Postmodern Drama* (University of Michigan Press, 1990)

Brett, David, *The Construction of Heritage* (Cork: Cork University Press, 1996)

Buckland, Patrick, *Irish Unionism One: The Anglo-Irish and the New Ireland 1885–1922* (Dublin: Gill & Macmillan, 1972)

—, *Irish Unionism Two: Ulster Unionism and the Origins of Northern Ireland 1886–1922* (Dublin: Gill & Macmillan, 1973)

Burgess, Mary, 'Belfast Carnivalesque: The Satires of Gerald MacNamara', in Nicolas Allen and Aaron Kelly (eds.), *The Cities of Belfast* (Dublin: Four Courts Press, 2003)

Byrne, Ophelia, *The Stage in Ulster from the Eighteenth Century* (Belfast: Linen Hall Library, 1997)

Cameron, Keith, *The Nation: Myth or Reality?* (London: Intellect Books, 1994)

Campbell, Joseph, *The Little Cowherd of Slainge, Ulad* (no. 1, November 1904)

—, *The Garden of the Bees and Other Poems* (Belfast: W. Erskine Mayne, 1905)

—, *Northern Autobiography,* as found in Sr Assumpta Saunders, (Guest Editor), *Journal of Irish Literature: Special Joseph Campbell Issue* (vol. VIII, No. 3, September 1979)

Clayton, Pamela, *Enemies and Passing Friends: Settler Ideologies in Twentieth Century Ulster* (London: Pluto Press, 1996)

Clune, Anne (ed.), *Conjuring Complexities: Essays on Flann O'Brien* (Belfast: Institute of Irish Studies, 1997)

Collins, Peter, *Nationalism and Unionism: Conflict in Ireland 1885–1921* (Belfast: Institute for Irish Studies, 1994)

—, *Who Fears to Speak of '98? Commemoration and the Continuing Impact of the United Irishmen* (Belfast: Ulster Historical Foundation, 2004)

Connolly, James, *Selected Writings* (London: Pluto Press, 1997)

Connolly, Joseph, *The Memoirs of Senator Joseph Connolly (1885–1961): A Founder of Modern Ireland,* ed. J. Anthony Gaughan (Blackrock, Dublin: Irish Academic Press, 1996)

Coupe, Laurence, *Myth* (London: Routledge, 1997)

Cousins, James, *Ben Madighan and Other Poems* (Belfast: Marcus Ward & Co. Ltd, 1895)

Cousins, James and Margaret Cousins, *We Two Together* (Madras: Ganesh, 1950)

Crawford, Robert G., *Loyal to King Billy: A Portrait of the Ulster Protestants* (London: C. Hurst & Co., 1987)

Crone, John S., and F.C. Bigger (eds.), *In Remembrance: Articles and Sketches* (Dublin: Talbot Press Ltd, 1927)

Crossman, Virginia, 'The *Shan Van Vocht:* Women, Republicanism, and the Commemoration of the 1798 Rebellion', *Eighteenth-Century Life* (vol. 22, no. 3, 1998, pp.128–39)

Cupitt, Don, *The World to Come* (London: SCM Press, 1982)

Danaher Parks, Kathleen, 'Gerald MacNamara, Ulster Playwright' (unpublished thesis, University of Delaware, 1984)

Davies, Douglas, 'Raising the Issues', in Jean Holm and John Bowker (eds.), (London: Pinter Publishing, 1994)

Dawson, R.A., 'An Illustrator of Celtic Romance: John P. Campbell', *The Studio* (15th October 1909)

De Paor, Liam, *Divided Ulster* (Harmondsworth: Penguin Books, 1970)

Deane, Seamus, *Celtic Revivals* (North Carolina: Wake Forest University Press, 1987)

—, *Field Day Anthology of Irish Writing* (Derry: Field Day Publications, 1991), vol. II

—, 'Heroic Styles: the Tradition of an Idea', *Ireland's Field Day* (Derry: Field Day Theatre Company, 1985)

—, 'The Literary Myths of the Revival: A Case for Their Abandonment', in Joseph Ronsley (ed.), *Myth and Reality in Irish Literature*

Dentith, Simon, *Parody* (London: Routledge, 2000)

Derrida, Jacques, *Of Grammatology,* trans by Gayatri Chakravorty Spivak (Baltimore: John Hopkins University Press, 1976)

Dudley Edwards, Owen (ed.), *Conor Cruise O'Brien Introduces Ireland* (London: Andre Deutsch Ltd, 1969)

Dundes, Alan (ed.), *Sacred Narrative: Readings in the Theory of Myth* (Berkley: University of California Press, 1984)

Dunne, Tom, '1798 and the United Irishmen', *Irish Review* (vol. 22)

Eliade, Mircea, 'Cosmogonic Myth and "Sacred History"', in Alan Dundes (ed.), *Sacred Narrative: Readings in the Theory of Myth* (Berkeley: University of California Press, 1984)

—, *Myths, Dreams and Mysteries* (London: Harvill Press, 1968)

Elliott, Marianne, *The Catholics of Ulster: A History* (London: Allen Lane, 2000)

Ervine, St John, *The Theatre in My Time* (London: Rich & Cowan Ltd, 1933)

Falls, Cyril, *The Birth of Ulster* (London: Constable & Co., 1996)

Fanon, Frantz, *The Wretched of the Earth* (Harmondsworth: Penguin Books, 1990)

Fitzpatrick, David, *The Two Irelands 1912–1939* (Oxford: Oxford University Press, 1998)

Flannery, James W., *W.B. Yeats and the Idea of a Theatre: the Early Abbey* (New Haven: Yale University Press, 1976)

Foley, Imelda, *The Girls in the Big Picture: Gender in Contemporary Ulster Theatre* (Belfast: Blackstaff Press, 2003)

Friel, Brian, *Selected Plays* (London: Faber & Faber, 1984)

Gardiner, David, 'The Other Irish Renaissance: The Maunsel Poets', *New Hibernia Review* (vol. 8, no. 1, Spring 2004, pp. 54–79)

Genette, Gérard, *Palimpsests: Literature in the Second Degree* (Lincoln: University of Nebraska Press, 1997)

Gilbert, Helen, and Joanne Tompkins, *Post-Colonial Drama: Theory, Practice, Politics* (London: Routledge, 1996)

Gilbert, Paul, *The Philosophy of Nationalism* (Oxford: Westview Press, 1998)

Girard, René, *Violence and the Sacred* (London: Athlone Press, 1988)

Gladstone, W.E., 'The Irish Question' (1886), in *Special Aspects of the Irish Question: A Series of Reflections in and Since 1886* (London: John Murray, 1892)

—, 'Lessons of Irish History in the Eighteenth Century' (1887), in *Special Aspects of the Irish Question: A Series of Reflections in and Since 1886* (London: John Murray, 1892)

Good, James Winder, *Irish Unionism* (Dublin: Talbot Press, 1920)

Graham, Colin, *Deconstructing Ireland* (Edinburgh: Edinburgh University Press, 2001)

Green, Alice Stopford, *Ourselves Alone in Ulster* (Dublin: Maunsel & Co. Ltd, 1918)

Gregory, Augusta Lady, *The Collected Plays II: The Tragedies and Tragic-Comedies* (Coole Press, 1970)

—, *Selected Writings* (Harmondsworth: Penguin Books, 1995)

—, 'Synge', in E.H. Mikhail (ed.), *J.M. Synge: Interviews and Recollections* (London: Macmillan, 1977)

Grene, Nicholas, *The Politics of Irish Drama: Plays in Context from Boucicault to Friel* (Cambridge: Cambridge University Press, 1999)

Griffith, Arthur (under pen-name 'Conn'), 'In a Real Wicklow Glen', *United Irishman* (24 October 1903)

Guinness, Selina, 'The Year of the Undead 1898', in *New Voices in Irish Criticism* (Dublin: Four Courts Press, 2000)

Gwynn, Stephen, *Experiences of a Literary Man* (London, 1926)

Hanna Bell, Sam, et al. (eds.), *The Arts in Ulster: A Symposium* (London: George G. Harrap & Co. Ltd, 1951)

—, *The Theatre in Ulster: A Survey of the Dramatic Movement in Ulster from 1902 Until the Present Day* (Dublin: Gill & Macmillan, 1972)

Harrington, John P., 'The Founding Years and the Irish National Theatre That Was Not', in Watt et al. (eds.), *A Century of Irish Drama: Widening the Stage.*

Heaney, Seamus, *The Redress of Poetry: Oxford Lectures* (London: Faber & Faber, 1995)

Hepburn, A.C., *A Past Apart: Studies in the History of Catholic Belfast 1850–1950* (Belfast: Ulster Historical Foundation, 1996)

Herr, Cheryl (ed.), *For the Land They Loved: Irish Political Melodrama, 1890–1925* (Syracuse NY: Syracuse University Press, 1991)

Hobson, Bulmer, *Brian of Banba, United Irishman* (April 1902)

—, *Ireland: Yesterday and Tomorrow* (Tralee: Anvil Books Ltd, 1968)

Hogan, Robert, and Richard Burnham, *The Rise of the Realists 1910–1915* (Dublin: Dolmen Press, 1979)

Hogan, Robert, and James Kilroy, *The Abbey Theatre: The Years of Synge 1905–1909* (Dublin: Dolmen Press, 1978)

—, *The Irish Literary Theatre 1899–1901* (Dublin: Dolmen Press, 1975)

—, *Laying the Foundations 1902–1904* (Dublin: Dolmen Press, 1976)

—, *Lost Plays of the Irish Renaissance* (Proscenium Press, 1970)

Hosking, Geoffrey, and George Schöpflin (ed.), *Myths and Nationhood* (London: Hurst & Company, 1997)

Hughes, Michael, *Ireland Divided: The Roots of the Modern Irish Problem* (Cardiff: University of Wales Press, 1994)

Hutcheon, Linda, *A Poetics of Postmodernism: History, Theory, Fiction* (London: Routledge, 1988)

—, *A Theory of Parody: The Teachings of Twentieth-Century Art Forms* (New York: Methuen, 1985)

Innes, C.L., *Woman and Nation in Irish Literature 1880–1935* (London: Harvester Wheatsheaf, 1993)

Innes, C.L., 'Naked Truth, Fine Clothes and Fine Phrases in Synge's *Playboy of the Western World*', in Joseph Ronsley (ed.), *Myth and Reality in Irish Literature.*

Jaspers, Karl, *Philosophy, Vol. 2: Existential Elucidation* (University of Chicago Press, 1970)

Joyce, James, *Ulysses* (Oxford: Oxford University Press, 1993 – the 1922 text)

Kavanagh, Peter, *The Irish Theatre* (Tralee: The Kerryman Ltd, 1946)

Kearney, Richard, 'Myth and Motherland', *Ireland's Field Day* (London: Hutchinson, 1985)

Kearney, Richard, *Postnationalist Ireland: Politics, Culture, Philosophy* (London: Routledge, 1997)

Kelly, James, *Prelude to Union: Anglo-Irish Politics in the 1780s* (Cork: Cork University Press, 1992)

Kennedy, David, 'The Drama in Ulster', in Sam Hanna Bell (ed.), *The Arts in Ulster: A Symposium* (London: George G. Harrap & Co. Ltd, 1951)

Kiberd, Declan, *Inventing Ireland: The Literature of the Modern Nation* (London: Vintage, 1996)

Kiremidjian, David, *A Study of Modern Parody: James Joyce's* Ulysses *and Thomas Mann's* Doctor Faustus (London: Garland, 1985)

Kirkland, Richard, 'Dialogue of Despair: Nationalist Cultural Discourse and the Revival in the North of Ireland, 1900–1920', *Irish University Review* (vol. 33, no. 1, Spring/Summer 2003), pp. 63–78

Laffan, Michael, *The Partition of Ireland 1911–1925* (Dundalk: Dundalgan Press, 1983)

Leerssen, Joep, '1798: The Recurrence of Violence and Two Conceptualisations of History', *Irish Review* (no. 22, 1998)

Levi-Strauss, Claude, *Myth and Meaning* (London: Routledge, 1978)

Levitas, Ben, *The Theatre of Nation: Irish Drama and Cultural Nationalism 1890–1916* (Oxford: Clarendon Press, 2002)

Lloyd, David, *Anomalous States: Irish Writing and the Post-Colonial Moment* (Dublin: Lilliput Press, 1993)

Lloyd, David, *Nationalism and Minor Literature: James Clarence Mangan and the Emergence of Irish Cultural Nationalism* (Berkeley: University of California Press, 1987)

Longley, Edna, *From Cathleen to Anorexia: The Breakdown of Irelands* (Dublin: Attic Press, 1990)

—, *The Living Stream: Literature and Revisionism in Ireland* (Newcastle-upon-Tyne: Bloodaxe Books Ltd, 1994)

Loughlin, James, 'The Irish Protestant Home Rule Association and Nationalist Politics', *Irish Historical Studies* (vol. XXIV, May 1985)

Loughlin, James, *Gladstone, Home Rule and the Ulster Question* (Dublin: Gill & Macmillan, 1986)

Lyons, F.S.L., 'Dillon, Redmond, and the Irish Home Rulers', in Martin (ed.), *Leaders and Men of the Easter Rising: Dublin 1916* (London: Methuen & Co. Ltd, 1967)

Lyons, Laura E., 'Of Orangemen and Green Theatres: The Ulster Literary Theatre's Regional Nationalism', in Watts et al. (ed.), *A Century of Irish Drama: Widening the Stage* (Indianapolis: Indiana University Press, 1984)

Lyotard, Jean-François, *The Postmodern Condition: A Report on Knowledge* (Manchester: Manchester University Press, 1984)

MacDonagh, Oliver, *States of Mind* (London: George Allen & Unwin, 1983)

MacManus, Anna (Ethna Carbery), *The Four Winds of Eirinn* (Dublin: M.H. Gill & Son, 1902)

—, *In the Celtic Past* (Dublin: M.H. Gill & Son, 1904)

MacNamara, Gerald, 'Cúchulain II: A Belfast Idyll, *Christmas Lady of the House,* 1918.

MacNamara, Gerald, plays as found in *Journal of Irish Literature,* ed. Kathleen Danaher (vol. XVII, nos. 2 and 3, May-September 1988) *Suzanne and the Sovereigns; The Mist That Does Be on the Bog; Thompson in Tír-na-nÓg; No Surrender!; Who Fears To Speak?*

Magee, Jack, 'Brothers in Arts: Joseph and John Campbell and the first Glens Feis', in Phoenix et al. 9eds.), Feis *na nGleann: A Century of Gaelic Culture in the Antrim Glens* (Belfast: Stair Uladh, 2005)

Mahon, Derek, *Selected Poems* (London: Viking, 1991)

Mallory, J.P., *Aspects of* The Táin (Belfast: December Publications, 1992)

Mannion, Orlaith, '"Silent but Eloquent Reminders": the Nationalist Monuments in Cork and Skibbereen', in Lawrence M. Geary (ed.), *Rebellion and Remembrance in Modern Ireland* (Dublin: Four Courts Press, 2001)

Mansergh, Nicholas, *Nationalism and Independence: Selected Irish Papers* (Cork: Cork University Press, 1997)

Martin, F.X. (ed.), *Leaders and Men of the Easter Rising: Dublin 1916* (London: Methuen & Co. Ltd, 1967)

Marx, Karl, *The Eighteenth Brumaire of Louis Bonaparte* (Peking: Foreign Language Press, 1978)

Mathews, P.J., *Revival: The Abbey Theatre, Sinn Féin, the Gaelic League and the Co-operative Movement* (Cork: Cork University Press, 2003)

Maume, Patrick, *Life that Is Exile: Daniel Corkery and the Search for Irish Ireland* (Belfast: Institute for Irish Studies, 1993)

—, *The Long Gestation: Irish Nationalist Life 1891–1918* (Dublin: Gill & Macmillan, 1999)

Mayne, Rutherford, *The Drone and Other Plays* (Dublin: Maunsel & Co. Ltd, 1912)

—, 'Gerald MacNamara (1866–1938)', *Dublin Magazine* (NS vol. XIII, no. 2, April–June 1938), pp. 53–6

—, 'The Ulster Literary Theatre', *Dublin Magazine* (NS vol. XXXI, no. 2, April–June 1955), pp. 15–21

—, *Rutherford Mayne: Selected Plays*, ed. John Killen (Belfast: Institute of Irish Studies, 1997)

McAuley, James W., 'Cúchulain and an RPG-7: The Ideology and Politics of the Ulster Defence Association', in Eamonn Hughes (ed.), *Culture and Politics in Northern Ireland 1960–1990* (Milton Keynes: Open University Press, 1991)

McBride, Ian, *The Siege of Derry in Ulster Protestant Mythology* (Dublin: Four Courts Press, 1997)

McBride, Lawrence W. (ed.), *Images, Icons and the Irish Nationalist Imagination* (Dublin: Four Courts Press, 1999)

McCormack, W.J. (ed.), *The Blackwell Companion to Modern Irish Culture* (Oxford: Blackwell Publishers Ltd, 2001)

McHenry, Margaret, *The Ulster Theatre in Ireland* (unpublished PhD thesis, University of Philadelphia, 1931)

McIntosh, Gillian, *The Force of Culture: Unionist Identities in Twentieth-Century Ireland* (Cork: Cork University Press, 1999)

McNulty, Eugene, 'From *The Wild Irish Girl* to *The Shan Van Vocht:* Remembering the Future in the 1890s', *Canadian Journal of Irish Studies* (vol. 30, no. 1, Spring 2004)

—, 'Revival's Limit, or a Post-Revival Space? Gerald MacNamara's "Christmas Laughter", *Irish Studies Review* (forthcoming)

Mengel, Haga, *Sam Thompson and Modern Drama in Ulster* (Frankfurt: Peter Lang, 1986)

Mercier, Vivian, *The Irish Comic Tradition* (London: Souvenir Press Ltd, 1991)

Mhic Sherin, Brighid, *Glimpses of Erin – Alice Milligan: Poet, Protestant, Patriot* (Belfast: Fortnight Supplement)

Mikhail, E.H. (ed.), *J.M. Synge: Interviews and Recollections* (London: Macmillan Press Ltd, 1977)

Milligan, Alice, *Hero Lays* (Dublin: Maunsel & Co., 1908)

—, *The Last Feast of the Fianna* (London: David Nutt, 1900)

—, *Life of Theobald Wolfe Tone* (Belfast: J.W. Boyd, 1898)

—, 'The North is Up!', *Weekly Independent* (Christmas 1895)

—, *Oisin and Padraic, Daily Express* (4 and 11 November 1899)

—, *Oisin in Tir-nan- Oig, Daily Express* (7 and 14 October 1899)

—, *Poems* (Dublin: M.H. Gill & Son, 1954)

—, *A Royal Democrat* (Dublin: M.H. Gill & Son, 1892)

—, *Two Poems* (Dublin: no publisher, 1943)

Milligan, Charles F., *My Bangor from the 1890s* (Bangor: Bangor Council Booklet, 1975)

Mitchell, Susan L., 'A Contemporary Irishwoman', *The Shamrock and Irish Emerald* (22 February 1919)

Moody, T.W., and J.C. Beckett (eds.), *Ulster Since 1800: A Social Survey* (London: British Broadcasting Corporation, 1957)

Moody, T.W., *The Ulster Question 1603–1973* (Dublin: Mercier Press, 1974)

Moran, James, *Staging the Easter Rising: 1916 as Theatre* (Cork: Cork University Press, 2005)

Morash, Christopher, *A History of Irish Theatre 1601–2000* (Cambridge: Cambridge University Press, 2002)

Morris, Catherine, 'Becoming Irish? Alice Milligan and the Revival', *Irish University Review* vol. 33, no. 1, Spring/Summer 2003

Morton, Grenfell, *Home Rule and the Irish Question* (Harlow: Longman, 1980)

Murray, Christopher, *Twentieth-Century Irish Drama: Mirror Up to Nation* (Manchester: Manchester University Press, 1997)

Newmann, Kate (ed.), *Dictionary of Ulster Biography* (Belfast: Institute of Irish Studies, 1993)

Nic Shiubhlaigh, Maire, 'An Un-Irish Play', in E.H. Mikhail (ed.), *J.M. Synge: Interviews and Recollections* (London: Macmillan, 1977)

Ní Chuilleanáin, Eiléan, *'As I Was Among the Captives': Joseph Campbell's Prison Diary, 1922–1923* (Cork: Cork University Press, 2001)

Ó Dochartaigh, Niall, *From Civil Rights to Armalites: Derry and the Birth of the Irish Troubles* (Cork: Cork University Press, 1997)

O'Brien, Flann, *The Poor Mouth* (London: Flamingo, 1993)

O'Broin, Art, *A Short History of Ulster* (Dublin: Mercier Press, 1995)

O'Broin, Leon, *Revolutionary Underground: The Story of the Irish Republican Brotherhood 1858–1924* (Dublin: Gill & Macmillan, 1976)

O'Byrne, Cathal, *As I Roved Out: A Book of the North* (Belfast, 1946)

Ó Ceallaigh Ritschel, Nelson, 'The Alternative Aesthetic: The Theatre of Ireland's Urban Plays', in Watt et al. (ed.), *A Century of Irish Drama: Widening the Stage*

O'Day, Alan, *Irish Home Rule 1867–1921* (Manchester: Manchester University Press, 1998)

O'Driscoll, Dennis, 'Remembering the Past', in *The Crane Bag of Irish Studies* (Dublin: Blackwater Press, 1982)

O'Driscoll, Robert, *Theatre and Nationalism in Twentieth-Century Ireland* (Oxford: Oxford University Press, 1971)

O'Grady, Standish, *History of Ireland, Vol. II: Cúchulain and his Contemporaries* (London: Sampson, Low, Searle, Marston & Rivington, 1880)

O'Halloran, Clare, *Partition and the Limits of Irish Nationalism* (Dublin: Gill & Macmillan, 1987)

O'Keefe, Timothy J., 'The 1898 Efforts to Celebrate the United Irishmen: The '98 Centennial', *Eire-Ireland* (no. 23, Summer 1988)

O'Sullivan, Seumas, *Essays and Recollections* (Dublin: Talbot Press, 1944)

Odling-Smee, Hugh, *'Its Own Way of Things': A Celebration of the Ulster Literary Theatre* (Belfast: Lagan Press, 2004)

Ollivier, Sophie, 'Presence and Absence of Wolfe Tone During the Centenary Commemoration of 1798 Rebellion', in Laurence M. Geary (ed.), *Rebellion and Remembrance in Modern Ireland* (Dublin: Four Courts Press, 2001)

Ormsby, Frank (ed.), *Poets from the North of Ireland* (Belfast: Blackstaff Press, 1979)

Overing, Joanna, 'The Role Of Myth: An Anthropological Perspective or: The Reality Of The Really Made-Up', in Geoffrey Hosking and George Schopflin (eds.), *Myths and Nationhood* (London: Hurst & Co., 1997)

Owens, Gary, 'Nationalist Monuments in Ireland *c.* 1870–1914: Symbolism and Ritual', in Brian P. Kennedy and Raymond Gillespie, *Ireland: Art into History* (Dublin: Town House, 1994)

Paseta, Senia, '1798 in 1898: The Politics of Commemoration', *Irish Review* (No. 22)

Paterson, John L., *David Harvey's Geography* (London: Croom Helm, 1984)

Phoenix, Eamon, *A Century of Northern Life: The Irish News and 100 Years of Ulster History 1890s-1990s* (Belfast: Ulster Historical Foundation, 1995)

— et al. (eds.), *Feis na nGleann: A Century of Gaelic Culture in the Antrim Glens* (Belfast: Stair Uladh, 2005)

—, *Northern Nationalism: Nationalist Politics, Partition and the Catholic Minority in Northern Ireland 1890–1940* (Belfast: Ulster Historical Foundation, 1994)

Pilkington, Lionel, *Theatre and the State in Twentieth Century Ireland* (London: Routledge, 2001)

Purcell, Lewis, *The Enthusiast, Ulad* (no. 3, May 1905)

—, *The Pagan* (Dublin: Maunsel & Co. Ltd, 1907)

Quinn, Peter A., 'Yeats and Revolutionary Nationalism: The Centenary of '98', *Eire/Ireland* (vol. 15, no. 3, 1980), pp. 47–64

Richtarik, Marilynn J., *Acting Between the Lines: The Field Day Theatre Company and Irish Cultural Politics 1980–1984* (Oxford: Clarendon Press, 1994)

Ricoeur, Paul, 'Myth and History' in Mircea Eliade (ed.), *The Encyclopedia of Religion* (London: Macmillan, 1987), vol. 10

—, 'Myth as the Bearer of Possible Worlds', Hederman and Kearney (eds.), *Crane Bag Book of Irish Studies* (Dublin: Blackwater Press, 1982)

—, *The Symbolism of Evil* (Boston: Beacon Press, 1969)

Ronsley, Joseph (ed.), *Myth and Reality in Irish Literature* (Ontario: Wilfrid Laurier Press, 1977)

Rose, Margaret A., *Parody: Ancient, Modern, and Post-modern* (Cambridge: Cambridge University Press, 1993)

—, *Parody/Meta-Fiction: An Analysis of Parody as a Critical Mirror to the Writing and Reception of Fiction* (London: Croom Helm, 1979)

Saunders, Sr. Assumpta (Guest Editor), *The Journal of Irish Literature: Special Joseph Campbell Issue* (vol. VIII, no. 3, September 1979)

Saunders, Norah, and A.A. Kelly, *Joseph Campbell: Poet and Nationalist 1879–1944* (Dublin: Wolfhound Press, 1988)

Savage, D.C., 'The Origins of the Ulster Unionist Party', *Irish Historical Studies* (vol. XII, no. 47, May 1961)

Schrag, Oswald O., *Existence, Existenz, and Transcendence: An Introduction to the Philosophy of Karl Jaspers* (Pittsburgh: Duquesne University Press, 1971)

Shaw, Bernard, *John Bull's Other Island* (London: Archibald Constable & Co., 1907)

Spivak, Gayatri Chakravorty, *The Post-Colonial Critic: Interviews, Strategies, Dialogues*, ed. Sarah Harasym (London: Routledge, 1990)

Stewart, A.T.Q., *The Narrow Ground: Aspects of Ulster 1609–1969* (Belfast: Blackstaff Press, 1992)

—, *The Ulster Crisis: Resistance to Home Rule 1912–1914* (Belfast: Blackstaff Press, 1997)

Stewart, Bruce, 'Anthologising Ireland: *Irish Literature* (1904) and Its Contexts', *Irish Review* (vol. 23, Winter 1998), pp. 105–26

Synge, J.M., *The Complete Plays*, ed. T.R. Henn (London: Methuen Drama, 1981)

Trotter, Mary, *Ireland's National Theatres: Political Performance and the Origins of the Irish Dramatic Movement* (Syracuse NY: Syracuse University Press, 2001)

Turner Johnston, Sheila, *Alice: A Life of Alice Milligan* (Omagh: Colourpoint Press, 1994)

Ulster Young Unionist Council, *Cúchulain: The Lost Legend* (Belfast: UYUC, 1986)

Vandervelde, Karen, 'An Open National Identity: Rutherford Mayne, Gerald MacNamara, and the plays of the Ulster Literary Theatre', *Éire/Ireland* (vol. 39, nos. 1 and 2, Spring/Summer 2004), pp. 36–58

Walker, Brian, *Dancing to History's Tune: History, Myth and Politics in Ireland* (Belfast: Institute of Irish Studies, 1996)

—, *Past and Present: History, Identity and Politics in Ireland* (Belfast: Institute of Irish Studies, 2000)

—, *Ulster Politics: The Formative Years 1868–86* (Belfast: Institute of Irish Studies, 1989)

Ward, Margaret (ed.), *In Their Own Voices: Women and Irish Nationalism* (Dublin: Attic Press, 1995)

Ward, Margaret, *Unmanageable Revolutionaries: Women and Irish Nationalism* (London: Pluto Press, 1989)

Watt, Stephen, Eileen Morgan and Shakir Mustafa (eds.), *A Century of Irish Drama: Widening the Stage* (Indianapolis: Indiana University Press, 2000)

Welch, Robert, *The Abbey Theatre 1899–1999: Form and Pressure* (Oxford: Oxford University Press, 1999)

Whelan, Kevin, *The Tree of Liberty: Radicalism, Catholicism and the Construction of Irish Identity 1760–1830* (Cork: Cork University Press, 1996)

Wileman, William, *Rome Rule in Ireland: The Facts of the Case Plainly Stated* (London: William Wileman, 1886)

Williams, Raymond, *Drama from Ibsen to Eliot* (Harmondsworth: Penguin Books, 1964)

Wills, Garry, *Saint Augustine* (London: Orion Books, 2000)

Wilson Foster, John, *Colonial Consequences: Essays in Irish Literature and Culture* (Dublin: Lilliput Press, 1991)

—, *Fictions of the Irish Literary Revival: A Changeling Art* (Syracuse NY: Syracuse University Press, 1993)

Witoszek, Nina, *The Theatre of Recollection: A Cultural Study of the Modern Dramatic Tradition in Ireland and Poland* (Stockholm: Stockholm Studies in English, 1988)

Yeats, W.B., *Autobiographies* (Dublin: Gill & Macmillan, 1955)

—, *W.B. Yeats: Selected Plays,* ed. Richard Allen Cave (Harmondsworth: Penguin Books, 1997)

—, *Yeats's Poems,* ed. A. Norman Jeffares (Dublin: Gill & Macmillan, 1989)

Index

Titles of plays, books and newspapers are in italics. References to illustrations are indicated by page numbers in italics.